Beyond the Bottom Line

Integrating Sustainability into Business and Management Practice

Beyond the
Bottom
Line

**Integrating
Sustainability
into Business and
Management Practice**

Edited by Milenko Gudić, Tay Keong Tan and **Patricia M. Flynn**

Greenleaf
PUBLISHING

Principles for Responsible Management Education

**Greenleaf Publishing/PRME Book Series –
For Responsibility in Management Education**

© 2017 Greenleaf Publishing Limited

Published by Greenleaf Publishing Limited
Salts Mill, Victoria Road, Saltaire, BD18 3LA, UK
www.greenleaf-publishing.com

Cover by Sadie Gornall-Jones.

MIX
Paper from
responsible sources
FSC® C004959

Printed and bound by Printondemand-worldwide.com, UK.

British Library Cataloguing in Publication Data:
  A catalogue record for this book is available from the British Library.

ISBN-13: 978-1-78353-327-5 [hardback]
ISBN-13: 978-1-78353-560-6 [PDF ebook]
ISBN-13: 978-1-78353-561-3 [ePub ebook]

Contents

Introduction
Beyond the Bottom Line: Integrating Sustainability into Business Practices

Milenko Gudić
Refoment Consulting and Coaching, Serbia

Tay Keong Tan
Radford University, USA

Patricia M. Flynn
Bentley University, USA

Introduction

The time when businesses single-mindedly pursue the financial bottom line is waning. More and more of today's business leaders are pursuing growth, improving practices, and creating value for their organizations by leading in economically sound, environmentally friendly, and socially responsible ways. In the age of growing consumer activism, environmental consciousness, and rapidly-advancing technology, businesses should be actively integrating sustainability principles into their strategies and practices to satisfy the concerns of a wide circle of stakeholders, secure customer loyalty and internal employee motivation, and foster their reputation. Worldwide, business leaders and managers are increasingly regarding sustainability programs as a contributor to both their companies' short-term financial interests and long-term shareholder value.

In 2000, under the auspices of the UN Secretary-General Kofi Annan, the United Nations Global Compact (UNGC) was created to give impetus to this significant paradigm shift toward business sustainability and social responsibility. It is the largest corporate sustainability initiative in the world today, with more than 8,000 participating organizations. The UNGC includes ten principles on human rights, labor, environment and anticorruption to guide businesses in incorporating sustainability practices throughout their organizations. The UNGC principles are:

Human Rights
Principle 1: Businesses should support and respect the protection of internationally proclaimed human rights; and
Principle 2: make sure that they are not complicit in human-rights abuses.

Labor
Principle 3: Businesses should uphold the freedom of association and the effective recognition of the right to collective bargaining;
Principle 4: the elimination of all forms of forced and compulsory labor;
Principle 5: the effective abolition of child labor; and
Principle 6: the elimination of discrimination in respect of employment and occupation.

Environment
Principle 7: Businesses should support a precautionary approach to environmental challenges;
Principle 8: undertake initiatives to promote greater environmental responsibility;
Principle 9: encourage the development and diffusion of environmentally friendly technologies.

Anticorruption
Principle 10: Businesses should work against all forms of corruption, including extortion and bribery. Businesses should support and respect the protection of internationally proclaimed human rights and make sure that they are not complicit in human-rights abuses.

Closely aligned with the UNGC principles are the Principles for Responsible Management Education (PRME), an initiative launched in 2007 under the auspices of the UN Secretary General Ban Ki-moon. The PRME community, which brings together more than 650 business schools and universities in 83 countries around the world, advances the global goals and sustainability agenda through multidisciplinary research collaboration and curricular reform to incorporate cross-cutting social, environmental, and humanitarian issues into management teaching and business education.

The PRME are:

Principle 1 | Purpose: We will develop the capabilities of students to be future generators of sustainable value for business and society at large and to work for an inclusive and sustainable global economy.

Principle 2 | Values: We will incorporate into our academic activities and curricula the values of global social responsibility as portrayed in international initiatives such as the United Nations Global Compact.

Principle 3 | Method: We will create educational frameworks, materials, processes, and environments that enable effective learning experiences for responsible leadership.

Principle 4 | Research: We will engage in conceptual and empirical research that advances our understanding about the role, dynamics, and impact of corporations in the creation of sustainable social, environmental, and economic value.

Principle 5 | Partnership: We will interact with managers of business corporations to extend our knowledge of their challenges in meeting social and environmental responsibilities and to explore jointly effective approaches to meeting these challenges.

Principle 6 | Dialogue: We will facilitate and support dialog and debate among educators, students, business, government, consumers, media, civil society organizations, and other interested groups and stakeholders on critical issues related to global social responsibility and sustainability.

The call for contributions to this book was made globally to entrepreneurs, business leaders, scholars, educators, journalists, and public leaders; anyone interested in championing sustainability within businesses. The topic clearly resonated with individuals across the globe. The unexpectedly strong response from potential contributors and collaborating authors from around the world resulted in the development of two books instead of one. This first book, *Beyond the Bottom Line: Integrating Sustainability into Management Practices,* looks at how the ten UNGC principles and the sustainability agenda embodied in the PRME can inform our business practices. The second volume, *Redefining Success: Integrating Sustainability into Management Education,* identifies problems, presents evidence, and offers solutions that will further assist academics in bringing global sustainability issues into their classrooms and scholarship. Both books also touch upon the post-2015 development agenda for the nations of the world and the related 17 Sustainable Development Goals (SDGs) that were approved in a high-level plenary meeting of the UN General Assembly in September 2015.

Beyond the Bottom Line explores the conceptual and practical issues relating to how responsible management practice can help address the social, environmental, and humanitarian impacts of business organizations. It was written for practitioners, policy-makers, academics, businesses, institutions, and organizations. In addition to conceptual materials, this volume provides best practices and innovations on how to overcome practical challenges in communities, workplaces, and other organizational settings.

The authors of the chapters in this book are managers and leaders working in businesses, activists from civil society, public leaders in government service, and academics from a wide range of disciplines – all change-makers who share a common concern for sustainability performance in business organizations. These 27 authors and editors come from 13 countries: Canada, Denmark, France, Germany,

Greece, India, Italy, the Netherlands, Nigeria, Serbia, Singapore, the United Kingdom, and the United States. It has been an honor and pleasure to work with them. This book reflects their research, purposive writing, and creative expression, and each chapter is written to speak to a diverse, global audience. It is hoped that this publication will in some small way give voice to each of these passionate writers, and at the same time offer hard-earned lessons to business leaders and managers in the trenches of practice.

Organization of the Book

This book is an edited collection that explores the conceptual and practical issues related to how responsible management practices can help address the social, environmental and humanitarian impacts of business. The chapters identify problems, present evidence, and offer solutions that will assist organizations in successfully implementing the Ten Principles of the UNGC and the six PRME principles and thus foster organizational viability and success but not at the expense of the larger community and future generations. Several of the authors also provide guidance and examples of how to effectively bring issues of sustainability and corporate social responsibility (CSR) into the classroom and faculty research.

The book is organized in four sections. Section 1 introduces conceptual and empirical rationales for including the Ten Principles of the UNGC and the six PRME in management practice and education. Section 2 provides company case studies to demonstrate specific organizational challenges, strategies and examples of best practices and innovations in going beyond the bottom line. Section 3 focuses on countries facing further challenges and roadblocks to integrating the principles of the UNGC due to significant levels of poverty or long-standing traditions of human-rights abuse. Section 4 looks to the future with authors proposing ways to improve and accelerate the integration of the UNGC principles into business practice.

Section 1

In Chapter 1 Ewest demonstrates that leaders are a critical factor in how organizations practice responsible global management and address the UNGC principles. Prosocial leadership is shown to provide a vital perspective that helps leaders balance profits and sustainability, and ultimately act as global stewards who take responsibility for the world's economic and social issues. The chapter concludes with possible approaches and alternative strategies for developing prosocial leadership, both within and outside the classroom. Bachini and Vradelis (Chapter 2) then follow a leader from his position at a successful for-profit company in Silicon Valley to one at a mission-driven nonprofit social services organization. The chapter documents the learning process the leader goes through as he finds it necessary to alter his traditional leadership style to bring about meaningful change. In order to succeed in his new environment, the leader must listen to and engage everyone in the organization. The authors include experiential role-play exercises for leaders seeking to implement the UNGC goals into their organizations. Puaschunder (Chapter 3) explores the value of public-private partnerships in fostering sustainability and economic development. The Global Alliance for Information and Communication Technologies (ICT) for Sustainable Development (GAID), established by the UN in 2006 to facilitate dissemination of technological solutions generated by businesses to the larger community, is used to demonstrate the potential benefits of partnerships between nonprofit and for-profit organizations. The author identifies challenges and missed opportunities for GAID, as well as ways to create and improve such partnerships to foster long-term economic growth. Scott (Chapter 4) focuses on off-grid solar lighting as an environmentally beneficial technology and tool for promoting sustainable development. Using theory-based research and case studies, the chapter offers concrete recommendations and insights into best practices and business models for firms to profitably engage in the UN Global Compact. It also provides powerful lessons for business schools and a concrete platform for engaging students in PRME as future generators of sustainable value for business and society.

Section 2

In Chapter 5, Jensen focuses on CSR in the global world, highlighting the innovative and collaborative approaches of two Danish companies, Maersk and Novo Nordisk. These companies are members of the Leadership Development Program (LEAD), which are organizations identified for their willingness to go above and beyond the Global Compact to implement advanced sustainability measures and the SDGs. Case studies of organizations operating in a country that requires large companies to report to the public on their social, environmental and humanitarian actions and impacts provide valuable insights into the innovative and collaborative approaches taken that result from partnerships with governments, civil society and other companies. Bhaskaran and Sharma (Chapter 6) explore the implementation of the UNGC principles in a company committed to going beyond compliance and seeking opportunities to create a lasting footprint of social value. Their case study of Tata Steel India offers numerous examples of policies and best practices that were instrumental in fulfilling the corporation's commitment to human rights in the workplace. Bevelander and Page (Chapter 7) then focus on socially responsible decision-making when raising investment capital. The case study of Karmijn Kapitaal explicitly connects business decision-making with ethical and other value-based considerations, and demonstrates how the six PRMEs can be integrated into a key pedagogy used by business schools to educate future business leaders. In Chapter 8, Naschberger and Ravikumar address the issues of gender diversity and corporate sustainability. Based on survey responses and interviews, this case study of a German multinational company, a signatory of the UNGC since 2002, provides insights, examples and best practices of an organization committed to the advancement of women, not only as a fundamental human right but also to enhance the company's long-term sustainable value.

Section 3

Nwagwu (Chapter 9) analyzes the challenges of incorporating the UNGC principles at the workplace in countries with a significant share of the population at the "bottom of the pyramid" (BoP). Using a local bank and a global food retailer in Africa as examples, the author demonstrates that profitable, inclusive businesses can exist and generate significant benefits for addressing the multidimensional limitations of poverty, creating value for the business community as well as to the poor who live in these areas. Addressing the fact that more than a third of the world's population does not have access to safe sanitation, Kellogg's case study (Chapter 10) is also based on the African continent. Following up on SDG 6 ("ensure access to water and sanitation for all,") the author asks "How can business and management education address the need for household toilets for the urban poor?" Kellogg provides insights on potentially successful business opportunities in this area, and with respect to PRME how the topic of sanitation can be integrated into a wide range of business and liberal-arts courses. Ajao, Bozionelos and Quental's chapter (11) addresses issues of human rights, gender equality, governance and leadership in Nigeria. Presenting the kidnapping of the Chibok Girls as a case study, the analysis demonstrates the interrelationships among these issues in a society in which there is pervasive discrimination against girls and women. With specific reference to the UNGC principles, the chapter highlights the role that leadership and education, more generally, can play in crisis situations such as this. Kakkar and Fox (Chapter 12) use an ecological restoration program in limestone mines in India to demonstrate how the principles of the UNGC and PRME can provide an engagement framework for embedding corporate sustainability in education, research and campus practices. The restoration program not only serves as a model for successful reclamation, but also as an example of how engagement with local stakeholders can be the turning point for long-term success and the critical role academia-business partnerships can play.

Section 4

Williamson and Lynch-Wood (Chapter 13) consider how the UNGC functions as an instrument of regulation and governance of firms, and raises the question of why so few firms have become signatories and then "complied" with the UNGC in its 15 years of existence. The authors explore the reasons more firms are not engaging with the UNGC and offer suggestions on how to facilitate a reduction of the hurdles that knowledge, agreement and resource conditions now create. Chymis, D'Anselmi and Triantopoulos (Chapter 14) make the case for explicitly including public institutions in discussions and implementation of the UNGC, the SDGs and PRME. They argue for a new generation of leaders to help reshape public institutions that will not only result in improved transparency, accountability, effectiveness and efficiency of these organizations, but also foster an environment that will enhance ethical and sustainable business practices in the private sector.

The book concludes with a summary of the lessons learned from the chapters, and identification of a wide range of opportunities for organizations to further integrate sustainability principles into their strategies and practices. This is supplemented with analyses on the role that management education can play in advancing sustainability and social responsibility. As noted earlier on in this chapter, an upcoming volume with a parallel focus to this book, *Redefining Success: Integrating Sustainability into Business and Management Education*, will specifically address the problems, opportunities, and solutions on how to incorporate sustainability issues into management education around the globe.

Section 1
Conceptual and Practical Rationales

1

Prosocially Centered Leadership Creates Global Stewards

Timothy Ewest
Houston Baptist University, USA

The increasing concerns over social, environmental, and economic problems are most often met with limited action by global communities and national businesses. Consumption of the planet's resources and increasing social problems continue to outpace progress against them (Monfreda *et al.*, 2004; International Forum for Human Development, 2006). National and global communities are generally slow in taking responsibility for the world's social, environmental, and economic problems, partly due to their significant investment in existing global trade systems. And, with many or most of these systems based in whole or in part on profit-focused free-market principles, many people see free markets as the initiating cause of social and environmental problems worldwide. The present state of ambivalence by numerous organizations and communities around the globe has led many to ask, "Who will take responsibility for a world that is facing social, environmental and economic issues, which lead to community and ecosystem breakdown?" (Palazzo and Scherer, 2008, p. 734).

Yet, economic growth, driven and framed by free-market principles, has been vital to increasing the living standards of millions of individuals around the world. For example, the employment of free-market principles in China, absent any aid, brought 280 million people out of poverty (Appleton *et al.*, 2010), although this growth has simultaneously resulted in severe environmental and societal degradation (Tilt, 2013; Xu, 2014). Alternatively, well-designed programs such as The Millennium Development Goals, which endeavored to use charitable contributions from developed countries to help support growth in developing and underdeveloped countries, has been considered by many to be still emerging (Gaiha, 2003). Do these two orientations need to stand in opposition to each other? Is it possible for organizations, and those that lead them, to be profitable and simultaneously help improve or at a minimum not create or worsen social and environmental issues?

This chapter considers the importance of leadership as a central and vital resource to address global social, environmental, and economic problems, and underscores the importance of leadership to any conversation concerning how organizations are to successfully practice responsible global management (Lawrence and Beamish, 2012). Yet, with so many important leadership theories, it is difficult to determine which theory is best suited to guide and develop global leaders who are able to balance organizational financial sustainability (profits) with environmental and social concerns. One possible answer is to begin with a notable commonality among most leadership theories, that being they inculcate the importance of ethical behavior (Johnson, 2011; Kanungo, 2001; Trevino *et al.*, 2003).

Ethical behavior, or others-directed behavior, however, is motivated by a specific set of human values, and these are the motivation behind all prosocial behavior (Rokeach, 1973; Schwartz, 1994). This chapter explores how prosocial leadership can be used to strengthen and reframe our understanding of leadership. The chapter argues that prosocial leaders are best suited to embrace and fulfill the UNGC principles and that prosocial leadership provides a perspective that helps leaders to balance profits and sustainability, and ultimately act as global stewards who take responsibility for the world's economic and social issues. The chapter concludes with possible approaches and alternative strategies for developing prosocial leadership, both within and outside the classroom.

The Interconnectedness of Global Communities

Organizations and the individuals that lead them arguably have little incentive to abandon profitable methodologies that result in wealth creation and directly contribute to raising society's standard of living. The result is that there is still considerable weight given to the belief that organizations, specifically businesses, have as their primary responsibility profit maximization (Friedman, 1970). This belief is problematic for societies, economies, and the environment since it does not consider the systemic connections between society, the environment, and self-interested organizations' negative impacts from business operations – that is, negative externalities, which are byproducts, or outputs an organization has on its surrounding environment, such as pollution, gentrification, or worker displacement. The reality of environmental degradation was predicted by Hardin (1968) as the coming tragedy facing the natural environment if unfettered access to natural resources continued. Specifically, he warns of the elimination or degradation of some commonly accessible natural resources if there is a continuance of unlimited consumption of these natural resources, wherein everyone has free access to take as much as they need, and give little thought to how the environment will be sustained (Berry, 2015). For example, the global whaling industry, which sought to meet the demand for whale oil beginning in the 17th century and concluding in the early 20th century, decimated the Baleen, Bowhead, and Right whale populations (Daniel, 2010). One proposed solution to this conflict of interests is to institute economic systems and national or international polices that mandate limited resource use, with what has become recognized as a Global Commons (Feeny *et al.*, 1990). Anecdotally, the issues surrounding the Commons represent the nature of the modern problem: self-interest and independence verses an interconnected global community.

The reality is that the interconnectedness of communities worldwide has created a Global Commons (Nordhaus, 1994), and correspondingly the challenge has shifted from fostering a locally engaged citizenship to one that is global. It is clear that in today's increasingly pluralistic and globalized world, priorities and strategies must change. Barber (2002) calls for a redefinition of "citizen" to indicate: "The person who acknowledges and recognizes his or her interdependence in a neighborhood, a town, a state, in a nation, and today, in the world" (p. 27). More directly to the point of this chapter, Tichy *et al.* (1997) apply the idea to corporations, asking these organizations to consider their global citizenship, which "recognizes businesses as key players in building active responsive communities" (p. 36). Organizations that are good global citizens, like Starbucks, have initiatives that recognize their interdependence with their local and national communities through community-improvement projects as well as their international interdependence through specific initiatives to ensure their international suppliers are paid fairly and are raising coffee crops sustainability (Sanford, 2011).

Recognizing the active roles and impacts corporations play in society and communities makes good business sense. In many instances, it is in the best interest of organizations to watch, plan for, or reverse ongoing resource degradation. For example, degradation of fish stocks has led to the collapse of the fishing industry in portions of the world and resulted in regulation of numerous fisheries. The degradation of Alaskan fish stocks, for instance, was met with regulation to maintain fish stocks and thus preserve the positive economic impact of fisheries (Layman *et al.*, 1996). The types of issues and the corresponding consequences for organizations depend upon the market in which organizations compete, as well as the environmental resources upon which they depend. For example, a car manufacturer that ignores or averts greenhouse gas emissions standards may be met with new governmental regulations (e.g., Volkswagen). Or a cosmetic company that uses phthalates in production may run the risk of lawsuits or brand image loss (e.g., L'Oréal). But, for all organizations, it should be apparent that if managers ignore an organization's connection to the environment and society, it may ultimately jeopardize financially sustainable operations and/or threaten increased profits (Laszlo, 2008; Werther Jr. and Chandler, 2010).

But citizenship, even if it abides by the aforementioned definition, does not ensure these "aware or knowledgeable citizens" will take responsibility for global issues where there is no apparent connection between the organization and the wider environment. What if connections between the organization and the aforementioned global environmental and social issues are not apparent, and resolution of these issues will involve personal and/or organizational cost? Do the individuals who lead these organizations have personal core values that prioritize concern for social and environmental global issues enough that they will effectively guide their companies in addressing these issues?

For example, the connection between local regulatory practices in Detroit and the Great Garbage Patch in the Pacific Ocean may not be readily apparent. Yet, local policies may be partially responsible for allowing water companies to take unlimited amounts of water from public sources, as in the case of Nestle Co. in Michigan. Nestle is allowed, via local policy, to take unlimited amounts of public water, generating sales of plastic water bottles, some of which end up in the Pacific Garbage Patch (Webb, 2009). In this case, the water bottling company's management and local municipal policies may ignore the water bottling company's delayed impact on, and interdependence with, the ocean. And, if the local plant manager or municipal administrator acted to address this issue, it could be at a professional cost and possibly local community financial expense. The ideas surrounding citizenship are important for initially conceptualizing the responsibilities leaders and their organizations have within communities where there is no apparent direct connection with the larger environment and the broader society.

Stewardship

The concept *stewardship* was first used in popular business literature by Peter Block in his book *Stewardship* (1993) to define taking responsibility for oneself and for governance of institutions. Similarly, stewardship has been developed as an academic theory (Davis *et al.*, 1997; Haskins *et al.* 1998; Hernandez, 2008; 2012) stressing both corporate social responsibility and the importance of individual leadership. Hernandez (2008), whose work is seminal in the academic field of stewardship theory, states:

> Stewardship is defined here as the attitudes and behaviors that place the long-term best interests of a group ahead of personal goals that serve an individual's self-interests. It exists to the extent that organizational actors take responsibility for the effects of organizational action on stakeholder welfare. The issue of balance is a key part of taking personal responsibility (p. 122)

This definition clearly supports two basic components needed to address global issues: personal responsibility that transcends self-interest in relationships (prosocial leadership) and organizational responsibility regarding stakeholder welfare, which fosters its relationship to the global community (stewardship).

Therefore, generally speaking, stewardship as a concept is the result of others-directed leadership, or prosocial leadership, and corporate governance that involves responsibility to stakeholders as well as for the organizations' social and environmental impacts. This model suggests that global stewardship begins with individuals taking responsibility for ensuring the welfare of others, which in turn enables them to lead the organization to ensure that organizational goals are in balance with societal and environmental issues. When these two conditions are met, the result is global stewardship. See Figure 1.1.

Figure 1.1 **The Stewardship Model**

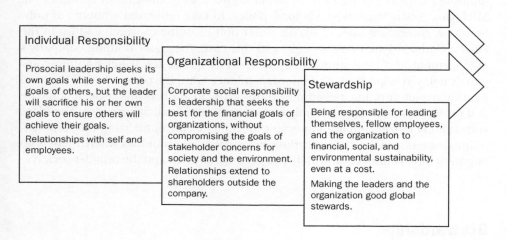

These basic components are recognized by numerous initiatives. The Globally Responsible Leadership Initiative (GRLI, 2005) is an attempt to help leaders on all three levels proposed by the stewardship model: individual, organizational and systemic. Another example is The Center for Creative Leadership (Van Velsor *et al.*, 2010), which has supported the efforts of creating responsible global leaders. The center has found that leaders who seek to take responsibility must realize their important role in supporting organizational culture because it shapes leadership competencies and capabilities. Conscious Capitalism is another good example of an initiative that emphasizes the importance of combining leadership responsibility and managing organizational performance for local shareholders as well as global connections (Mackey and Sisodia, 2014). Finally, germane to this chapter is the UNGC initiative, which recognizes the important role leaders and their organizations can and should play in taking responsibility for the world's social, environmental, and economic problems (UNGC, 2007). Although individual and organizational responsibility are both vital aspects of stewardship, this chapter focuses on the seminal aspect of prosocial leadership development.

The Importance of Leadership

Why put so much emphasis on leadership? In 2007, a survey was conducted by the American Management Association to aid in understanding and evaluating sustainability efforts of organizations that successfully implemented sustainability strategies. One of the major findings of the survey was that organizations that practiced sustainability had top management who visibly supported their organization's sustainability practices and did so because of deeply embedded personal core values (Russell and Lipsky, 2008). Apparently, more and more organizational leaders may be accepting and implementing sustainability practices. According to the McKinsey global survey on sustainability in 2014, the trend for CEOs is to move toward, not away from, sustainability practices (Bonini and Bove, 2014). The conclusion from this research suggests that when the CEO or key leaders in the organization are driven by core personal or prosocial values that transcend personal interests, the creation of a sustainable organization is the likely result. However, without a leader's personal commitment to global responsibility, organizations are likely to fail to have any significant sustainability practices and thus expose themselves to associated risks and may in turn jeopardize revenue (Ferdig, 2007; Lawrence and Beamish, 2012). But when a leader commits to taking responsibility for the global community, there can be dramatic results.

Take, for example, Yvonne Chouinard, the founder of Patagonia. Chouinard began his business in 1966 and by 1970, Chouinard's company was the largest supplier of climbing hardware in the United States. By 2000, Patagonia was grossing about $200 million in net sales. Chouinard has at his core values of responsibility for the people and the planet, values connected to his beliefs as a Zen Buddhist (Chouinard, 2006). Chouinard distilled philosophical elements from Zen Buddhism into his company's mission: "Build the best product, cause no unnecessary harm, and use business to inspire and implement solutions to the environmental crisis" (p. 78). In turn, Patagonia is regarded as a leader in green management practices, inspiring small companies like Clif Bar and advising some large companies including Levi Strauss, Gap, and Walmart (Reinhardt *et al.* 2010). The centrality and importance of leadership in addressing the world's social, environmental, and economic problems are widely accepted (Astin and Antonio, 2004; Deardorff *et al.*, 2005; Yardibi, 2014).

Prosocial Leadership

Prosocial values are uniquely suited to develop global stewards for two reasons. First, prosocial values are intrinsic motivators, being considered a fundamental aspect of what it means to be human, representing our core personal convictions. In fact, all ethical leadership behavior is motivated by a specific set of human values, and these values are the antecedents behind all prosocial or others-directed behavior (Rokeach, 1973; Schwartz, 1994). If we can focus on the values that motivate others-directed behavior, then we are considering what has been demonstrated to be vital in sustainable organizations; leaders who are motivated at a personal level to care about others, even at personal cost. Second, prosocial, or others-directed behavior is a healthy means to correct the aforementioned need to behave selflessly when no direct connection between the organization and its environment or society exits.

Two human motivational values, empathy and altruism, when present in a leader's actions, make behavior prosocial and thus not purely self-interested (Schwartz, 1994). An empathetic act ensures the welfare of some other person in everyday life by progressing toward one's own goals without violating the legitimate goals of other people, because the person desires to remain in harmony with others (Beirhoff, 2002; Beirhoff *et al.*, 1991; Hastings *et al.*, 2000; Hoffman, 1982; Omoto and Snyder, 1995). An altruistic act is devoid of self-consideration, focusing solely on the goals or needs of others alone and done so without regard to external personal reward (Beirhoff, 2002). Empathy and altruism are necessary components of motivating prosocial behavior. Therefore, simply stated, when leaders are acting prosocially they act in ways that seek to promote the welfare of others, even at personal cost.

Examples of this type of self-sacrificing leadership abound, but former Walmart CEO and one-time vocal skeptic of climate change H. Lee Scott seemed unlikely to be among them. Scott, however, was willing to sacrifice his professional image by reversing the retail giant's direction and committing Walmart to do its part in reversing global warming (Sanford, 2011). Specifically, prosocial leaders tend to satisfy their own needs, without interfering with the ability of others' welfare, but they will also forego their own needs, if necessary, to make sure the needs of others are met.

Prosocial Leadership and Established Leadership Theories

Prosocial leadership is not intended to supplant other leadership theories. Instead, it is intended to provide a better paradigm to understand, identify, and determine authentic others-directed leadership. Numerous existing leadership theories carry within them others-directed or prosocial behavior (Ewest, 2015). The presence and centrality of empathy and altruism are also found in other leadership theories including: servant leadership (Greenleaf, 1997), authentic leadership (George, 1990), social change (Komives and Wagner, 2012), spiritual leadership (Fry, 2003), and ethical leadership (Brown *et al.*, 2005). See Table 1.1.

Table 1.1 **Prosocial Leadership and Established Leadership Theories**

Leadership theory	Ways they incorporate empathy or altruism
Transformational leadership	"Transformational leaders, empower, listen and help communities to become self-sustaining" (Kouzes and Posner, 1998, p. 37).
Servant leadership	"Make sure that other people's highest priority needs are being served" (Greenleaf, 1997, p. 7).
Authentic leadership	"Service before self; mission and the organization supersede self-interest" (George, 1990, p.12).
Social change	"Understanding perspectives other than your own are crucial components to participating in community" (Komives and Wagner, 2012, p. 165).
Spiritual leadership	"Altruistic love is a sense of wholeness, harmony and well-being produced through care, concern, and appreciation for both self and others" (Fry, 2003, p. 117).
Ethical leadership	"Treating others fairly, honestly and considerately so followers want to emulate others" (Brown *et al.*, 2005, p. 119).

The presence of prosocial values within leadership theories provides a necessary vehicle for change, moving the conversation about leadership from simple behavioral expectations, toward understanding and examination of core personal motivational values that have been demonstrated as vital to sustainability programs within organizations. If organizational leaders can be intentional in fostering prosocial values in their lives, and in turn develop and instill those prosocial values within the organizations they lead, global stewardship may become a reality. However, intentionally developing such leaders will involve changing and adapting practices, systems, and processes within organizations. These changes will ensure that international initiatives such as the UNGC and PRME will foster leaders who are driving change because of core personal values.

Prosocial Leadership and the UNGC

The following is suggestive of strategies and practices that can be adopted for fostering prosocial leaders who support the UNGC and its accompanying principles. These strategies are intended to help organizational leaders who want to cultivate personal prosocial values within themselves and other organizational leaders, since the leaders' core values are essential in creating sustainable organizations.

The first strategy in developing prosocial leaders is to focus corporate training programs on those leadership theories and their corresponding behaviors, ideas, and aspects that are prosocial in nature – that is, leadership theories that include empathy and altruism. Well-established leadership researchers Avolio and Locke (2002) suggest, "The most effective moral leaders are those who transcend their own interests for the good of their group, organization or society" (p. 228).

The importance of focusing training programs on those leadership theories and behaviors that have prosocial values as motivators will help to ensure that leaders will be attentive to the reality that others-directed behavior is not simply adherence to normative principles but instead an intrinsic human value. The leadership theories in Table 1.1 are good examples of theories that can foster prosocial behavior. If this were done, a significant step forward could be taken in supporting the UNGC goals, considering that leadership education commands 21 percent of all training dollars (Bares, 2008), making it the largest share of investment in corporate learning and development. Total dollars spent on learning and development in 2010 was more than $171.5 billion (Green and McGill, 2011).

Another strategy is socialization within an organizational culture around values that are prosocial in nature. Prosocial development research indicates that an individual's values are conditioned and formed by the groups in which he or she resides (Fiske, 2009; George 1990). This suggests that groups, associations, departments, civic groups, or whole organizations, that have normalized prosocial behaviors and corresponding motivational values, will engender and foster those values and behaviors within all their group members and beyond. Departments known for their prosocial activities can act as an incubator and example for other individuals and departments. This strategy could also involve using CEOs and executives as examples of prosocial leaders. Research indicates that employees may perceive that their CEO is not concerned with social and environmental issues when she or he actually has deeply rooted concerns regarding the environment and society (Russell and Lipsky, 2008).

Prosocial Leadership and Responsible Management Education

The PRME also seeks to develop leaders who take responsibility for the welfare of people, planet, and profit (UNGC, 2007). Certain concepts can be applied to management education and be supportive of fostering prosocial leadership within educational institutions and thus initiate the process of corporate social responsibility and global stewardship.

The first strategy for developing prosocial leadership is encouraging service learning or volunteerism within higher educational activities, with a critical reflection component that involves a moral test. The same type of volunteerism can be part of organizational development strategies, although the critical-reflection component may be harder to execute. Research indicates that those individuals who engage in volunteerism or service learning tend to develop prosocial-related reasoning (Batchelder and Root, 1994). It should be noted that the meaning of "volunteerism" is variable because it is socially constructed and thus its specific meaning varies from culture to culture. However, if understood and implemented correctly, volunteerism does carry with it cultural connections and significant relations to prosocial behavior (Hart and Sulik, 2014). The volunteerism or service-learning activity that is followed with a critical self-reflection, which asks developing leaders to reflect on what the personal resonances they found with their personal values during the service or volunteering activity, would heighten awareness of empathy within the individual (Tomkins and Ulus, 2015).

A second strategy for the classroom is using case studies that present economic, social, and environmental problems, with proposed solutions explored with a simple moral test to determine what a prosocial leader would do. The cases should involve examples of organizations where their operations have direct impacts on the environment and society, as well as organizations whose impacts are indirect. The simple prosocial moral test can be applied by asking, "Is this a moral decision that allows for myself, or the organization to pursue its goals without interfering with the goals of the other?" If the answer is "yes," the action may be prosocial (Ewest, 2016).

These two strategies align well with the PRME that directly ask educators to foster capabilities to create a sustainable global economy by revisiting the role of business in society (Principle 1), through incorporation of values of global social responsibility (Principle 2) using various educational frameworks (Principle 3). Alternatively, the second strategy supports the development of partnerships (Principle 5) and would also tacitly involve dialogue (Principle 6). Yet, it is important to recognize that these as well as other strategies need to be researched (Principle 4) and further creative and innovative methods (Principle 3) can and should be developed to enhance development of leaders and gain a greater understanding of how prosocial leaders are developed.

A consistent alignment with the PRME will help both business practitioners and management educators attain a better understanding of the importance of leadership as a vital resource for individuals and the organizations they lead to practice responsible global management. It will also help demonstrate that prosocial behavior, when understood not as a set of normative principles to be followed, but as intrinsically rooted in personal motivational prosocial values, can lead to a global stewardship.

This will enable reframing of the whole conversation to be more germane to the issues facing humanity. Leadership, to be certain, is a vital resource, but the conversation must be reframed to be more germane to the issues facing humanity. Without leaders who are willing to make personal sacrifices for the sake of the other, our global commons will continue to degrade, as will the global community.

References

Adler, N.J., & Bartholomew, S. (1992). Managing globally competent people. *The Executive*, 6(3), 52-65.

Appleton, S., Song, L., & Xia, Q. (2010). Growing out of poverty: Trends and patterns of urban poverty in China 1988–2002. *World Development*, 38(5), 665-678.

Astin, H., & Antonio, A. (2004). The impact of college on character development. *New Directions for Institutional Research*, 12(122), 55-62.

Avolio, B.J., & Locke, E.E. (2002). Contrasting different philosophies of leader motivation: Altruism versus egoism. *The Leadership Quarterly*, 13(2), 169-191.

Barber, B.R. (2002). The educated student: Global citizen or global consumer? *Liberal Education – Washington D.C.*, 88(2), 22-27.

Bares, A. (2008). Companies spend an average of $1202 per employee on training. (Blog). Retrieved from http://compforce.typepad.com/compensation_force/2008/02/companies-spend.html

Bass, B.M., & Steidlmeier, P. (1999). Ethics, character, and authentic transformational Leadership Behavior. *The Leadership Quarterly*, 10(2), 181-217.

Batchelder, T.H., & Root, S. (1994). Effects of an undergraduate program to integrate academic learning and service: Cognitive, prosocial cognitive, and identity outcomes. *Journal of Adolescence*, 17(4), 341-355.

Beirhoff, H.W. (2002). *Social Psychology: A Modular Course (prosocial behavior)*. New York: Psychology Press.

Beirhoff, H.W., Klien, R. & Kramp, P. (1991). Evidence for the altruistic personality from data on accident research. *Journal of Personality*, 59, 263-280.

Berg, D.H. (2003). Prospective leadership development in college and universities in Canada: Perceptions of leaders, educators, and students. Unpublished doctoral dissertation, University of Saskatchewan–Saskatoon.

Berry, W. (2015). *The Unsettling of America: Culture & Agriculture*. Counterpoint.

Block, P. (1993). Stewardship: Choosing service over self-interest. Berrett-Koehler Publishers.

Bonini, S., & Bove, A.T. (2014). Sustainability's strategic worth: McKinsey Global Survey results. New York: McKinsey & Company.

Brown, M.E., & Trevino, L.K. (2002). Conceptualizing and measuring ethical leadership: Development of an instrument. *Academy of Management Proceedings*, D1-D6.

Bruce, J.R. (2014). Risky business: How social psychology can help improve corporate risk management. *Business Horizons*, 57(4), 551-557.

Chouinard, Y. (2006). *Let My People Go Surfing: The Education of a Reluctant Businessman*. Penguin Books.

Daniel, F. (2010). *Whaling, The Canadian Encyclopedia*. Historica Dominion Institute.

Davis, J.H., Schoorman, F.D., & Donaldson, L. (1997). Toward a stewardship theory of management. *Academy of Management Review*, 22(1), 20-47.

Deardorff, M., Kolnick, J., Mvusi, T., & McLemore, L. (2005). The Fannie Lou Hamer National Institute on Citizenship and Democracy: Engaging a curriculum and pedagogy. *History Teacher*, 38(4), 441-456.

Ewest, T. (2015). The relationship between transformational leadership practices and global social responsibility. *Journal of Leadership Studies*, 9(1).

Ewest, T. (2016). Leadership and moral behavior. In *Leadership Today: Practices for Personal and Professional Performance*. Springer Publications.

Feeny, D., Berkes, F., McCay, B.J., & Acheson, J.M. (1990). The tragedy of the commons: twenty-two years later. *Human ecology*, 18(1), 1-19.

Ferdig, M.A. (2007). Sustainability leadership: Co-creating a sustainable future. *Journal of Change Management*, 7(1), 25-35.

Fiske, S.T. (2009). *Social Beings: Core Motives in Social Psychology.* John Wiley & Sons.

Friedman, M. (1970). *The Social Responsibility of Business Is to Increase Its Profits.* Berlin, Heidelberg: Springer.

Fry, L.W. (2003). Toward a theory of spiritual leadership. *The Leadership Quarterly,* 14(6), 693-727.

Gaiha, R. (2003). Are millennium goals of poverty reduction useful? *Oxford Development Studies,* 31(1), 59-84.

George, J.M. (1990). Personality, affect, and behavior in groups. *Journal of Applied Psychology,* 75(2), 107.

Green, M. & McGill, E. (2011). The 2011 state of the industry: Increased commitment to workplace learning. T + D. Retrieved from http://www.astd.org/TD/Archives/2011/Nov/Free/Nov_11_Feature_State_of_the_Industry.htm.

Greenleaf, R.K. (1977). *Servant Leadership: A Journey into the Nature of Legitimate Power and Greatness.* Paulist Press.

GRLI (2005). Globally responsible leadership: A call for engagement. *The Globally Responsible Leadership Initiative.* Brussels: EFMD (The International Network for Excellence in Management Education). Retrieved from http://www.grli.org/grli/

Hardin, G. (1968). The tragedy of the commons. *Science,* 162(3859), 1243-1248.

Hart, D., & Sulik, M.J. (2014). The social construction of volunteering. *Prosocial Development: A Multidimensional Perspective,* 393-409.

Haskins, M.E., Liedtka, J., & Rosenblum, J. (1998). Beyond teams: Toward an ethic of collaboration. *Organizational Dynamics,* 26(4), 34-50.

Hastings, P.D., Zahn-Waxler, C., Robinson, J., Usher, B., & Bridges, D. (2000). The development of concern for others in children with behavior problems. *Developmental Psychology,* 36, 531-546.

Hernandez, M. (2008). Promoting stewardship behavior in organizations: A leadership model. *Journal of Business Ethics,* 80(1), 121-128.

Hernandez, M. (2012). Toward an understanding of the psychology of stewardship. *Academy of Management Review,* 37(2), 172-193.

Hoffman, M.L. (1982). Development of prosocial motivation: Empathy and guilt. In N. Eisenberg (Ed.), *The Development of Prosocial Behavior* (pp. 281-313). New York: Cambridge University Press.

International Forum for Human Development. (2006). Social Justice in an Open World: The Role of the United Nations.

Johnson, C. (2011). *Meeting the Ethical Challenges of Leadership: Casting Light or Casting Shadow.* Thousand Oaks, CA: Sage Publications.

Kanungo, R.N. (2001). Ethical values of transactional and transformational leaders. *Canadian Journal of Administrative Sciences,* 18(4), 257.

Komives, S.R., & Wagner, W. (2012). *Leadership for a Better World: Understanding the Social Change Model of Leadership Development.* John Wiley & Sons.

Kouzes, J.M. & Posner, B.Z. (1998). *Student Leadership Practices Inventory: Facilitator's Guide.* San Francisco: Jossey Bass Inc.

Laszlo, C. (2008). *Sustainable Value: How the World's Leading Companies Are Doing Well by Doing Good.* Stanford: Stanford University Press.

Lawrence, J.T., & Beamish, P.W. (2012). *Globally Responsible Leadership: Managing According to the UN Global Compact.* SAGE.

Layman, R.C., Boyce, J.R., & Criddle, K.R. (1996). Economic valuation of the Chinook salmon sport fishery of the Gulkana River, Alaska, under current and alternate management plans. *Land Economics,* 113-128.

Mackey, J. & Sisodia, R. (2014). Conscious capitalism: Liberating the heroic spirit of business. *Harvard Business Review.*

Monfreda, C., Wackernagel, M., & Deumling, D. (2004). Establishing national natural capital accounts based on detailed ecological footprint and biological capacity assessments. *Land Use Policy*, 21(3), 231-246.

Nordhaus, W.D. (1994). *Managing the Global Commons: The Economics of Climate Change* (Vol. 31). Cambridge, MA: MIT Press.

Omoto, A.M. & Snyder, M. (1995). Sustained helping without obligation: Motivation, longevity of service, and perceived attitude change among AIDS volunteers. *Journal of Personality and Social Psychology*, 68, 671-686.

Palazzo, G., & Scherer, A.G. (2008). Corporate social responsibility, democracy, and the politicization of the corporation. *Academy of Management Review*, 33(3), 773-775.

Reinhardt, F., Casadesus-Masanell, R. & Jin Kim, H. (2010). *Patagonia*. Boston: Harvard Business School Publishing.

Rokeach, M. (1973). *The Nature of Human Values*. New York: Free Press.

Russell, W.G., & Lipsky, D. (2008). *The Sustainable Enterprise Fieldbook: When It All Comes Together*. J. Wirtenberg (Ed.). AMACOM Div American Mgmt Assn. Greenleaf Press.

Sanford, C. (2011). *The Responsible Business: Reimaging Sustainability and Success*. John Wiley & Sons.

Schwartz, S. (1994). Are there universal aspects in the structure and contents of human values? *Journal of Social Issues*, 50(4), 19-45.

Sloane, W.C. (2004). *Credo: William Sloane Coffin*. Louisville, KY: Westminster John Knox Press.

Stackhouse, M.L. (1995). *Introduction: Foundations and Purposes*. In M.L. Stackhouse, D.P. McCann, S. Stahl, K. Gijnter, N.M. Pless, and T. Maak. Responsible global leadership. *Global Leadership: Research, Practice, and Development* (2013): 240-259.

Tichy, N.M., McGill, A.R., & Clair, L.S. (1997). *Corporate Global Citizenship: Doing Business in the Public Eye*. Lexington Books.

Tilt, B. (2013). *The Struggle for Sustainability in Rural China: Environmental Values and Civil Society*. Columbia University Press.

Tomkins, L., & Ulus, E. (2015). Is Narcissism undermining critical reflection in our business schools? *Academy of Management Learning & Education*, 14(4), 595-606.

Treviño, L.K., Brown, M., and Hartman, L..P. A qualitative investigation of perceived executive ethical leadership: Perceptions from inside and outside the executive suite. *Human Relations*, 56(1), 5-37.

Van Velsor, E., McCauley, C.D., & Ruderman, M.N. (Eds.). (2010). *The Center for Creative Leadership Handbook of Leadership Development* (Vol. 122). John Wiley & Sons.

Ward, C., Yates, D., & Song, J.Y. (2015). Leadership and undergraduate students: A study across disciplines and a plan for the future. *Business Education Innovation Journal*, 7(2).

Webb, R.J. (2009). Michigan Citizens for Water Conversation v. Nestle Waters North America Inc. and Public Trust Doctrine: A Moral Approach.

Werther Jr., W.B., & Chandler, D. (2010). *Strategic Corporate Social Responsibility: Stakeholders in a Global Environment*. Sage Publications.

Xu, B. (2014). China's Environmental Crisis. Council on Foreign Relations.

Yardibi, N. (2014). Ethics and leadership. *Chaos, Complexity and Leadership* 2012 (333-337).

Timothy Ewest is an Associate Professor of Management at Houston Baptist University and a Visiting Research Collaborator at Princeton University's Faith and Work Initiative. Ewest completed his doctorate in management and organizational leadership at George Fox University. His research focuses on prosocial leadership, religion in the workplace, and social entrepreneurship.

tewest@hbu.edu

2

Listening and Engaging to Lead Responsibly

Jyoti Bachani
Saint Mary's College of California, USA

Mary E. Vradelis
Saint Mary's College of California, USA

Introduction

The Principles for Responsible Management Education (PRME) support the Sustainable Development Goals (SDGs) articulated by the United Nations Global Compact (UNGC), by laying out the need to teach future business leaders about sustainable values for business and society. This chapter offers a framework and an exemplar case study suitable for discussing PRME topics in class exercises to build new skills. It follows the career change of a successful Silicon Valley corporate leader to a new position as head of a mission-driven nonprofit organization, showing the role of a leader in shaping the purpose of an organization in society. The study illustrates how individuals organize in negotiation with key stakeholders to influence the purpose of the organizations they cocreate. Using the differences between leading nonprofits and for-profits, it shows how a leader shapes an organization's purpose and how individual values ultimately impact society. To achieve alignment, the leader must learn to listen to and engage with individual values to shape the organizational mission. The experiential role-play exercises at the end of this chapter are developed for leaders who wish to implement the UNGC goals for their organizations.

The Role of Organizations in Society

Traditionally, nonprofit organizations have existed to serve those needs in society that are not met by other organizations, such as businesses or governments. New nonprofits are created by people who are inspired to address an unmet need and do so regardless of whether it is profitable or not. In this era of environmental and economic crises, society has more unmet needs (both traditional and emerging) than existing nonprofit organizations can address. Nonprofit organizations thus prioritize the most urgent needs and are guided by their mission to maintain focus on these.

In the past decade, the need for solving societal problems has taken center stage. Now even business organizations are willing to consider moving beyond the profit motive to become a force for change and address these social problems. Previously, business leaders preferred to stick with the profit motive alone. To address the social needs of the world outside their role as business leaders, they simply relied on their corporate social responsibility initiatives on the side, or by serving on the boards of nonprofit organizations.

This convergence between for-profits and nonprofits has led to organizational innovations such as benefit corporations, social enterprises, and conscious capitalism. These organizations claim to focus beyond the bottom-line profit motive, which rewards only the owners and shareholders, to become purpose-oriented and serve the greater good for humanity. Their purpose includes the needs of customers as well as considerations for the environment, their local communities, and the planet. In his *Harvard Business Review* article "What Businesses Can Learn from Nonprofits," Peter Drucker looks to nonprofits as role models for businesses of all kinds, urging them to engage their staff with "management by objectives and self-control, high demands but corresponding responsibility, and accountability for performance and results" (Drucker, 1989, p. 6).

From Strategy Structure Systems to Purpose, Process, and People

The book *The Individualized Corporation* proposed that organizations are not merely economic entities for profit maximization but are also social institutions where people come together for shared collective action to accomplish goals that individuals cannot fulfill alone (Bartlett and Ghoshal, 1999). Bartlett and Ghoshal offered up a new manifesto for management with the core idea that a Strategy-Structure-Systems (SSS) approach to managing is not adequate. They exhort leaders to also focus on shaping the Purpose-Processes-People (PPP) approach for building truly successful organizations. This idea, inspired the Nonprofit Management Model, described below, addresses social as well as economic aspects of an organization. Figure 2.1 illustrates this model.

Figure 2.1 **The Nonprofit Management Model**

Source: Bachani and Vradelis, 2012, p. 7.

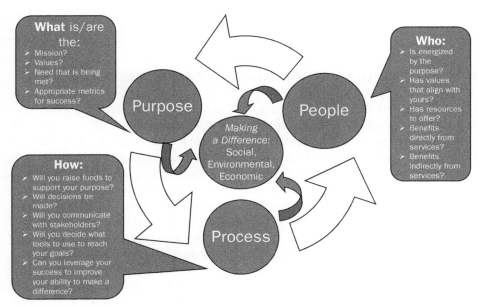

Profit-making organizations that go beyond the bottom line are mission-driven as they go further than a narrow economic focus. Such organizations require managers who have different skills than those being taught currently. The two new management skills proposed by a shift from the SSS approach to the PPP approach are (1) the ability to listen, and (2) the ability to build engagement using consultative practices. The case study in this chapter explicates these.

Organizational structure is one way to coordinate collective activity. Structure is created to align people's specialized skills with jobs and complex tasks that together constitute organized activity. Structure is necessary, but in practice, it tends to stifle. This is so because organizational structures are rarely concerned with an alignment between individual values and the organizational mission. Such an approach seldom creates engagement, which is left to parallel activities that may by chance align the individual values and organizational mission. When engaged, individuals go the extra mile to creatively further the goals.

Consider the case of Hopeful Frontiers[1], a social-services organization under new leadership. The new leader came from a business background and brought a bottom-line orientation to the nonprofit. By listening and engaging, the new leader demonstrates how managers can develop practices that are sustainable for

---

1 Based on a case study first published in *Strategy Making for Nonprofit Organizations* (Bachani and Vradelis, 2012). Names of the organization and its leaders have been changed.

themselves, their teams, the organization, and the external stakeholders. The case offers lessons in the pervasive dilemmas of balancing growth and pacing change while dealing with conflicting demands.

Hopeful Frontiers: A Mission-Driven Organization

Hopeful Frontiers (HF) was founded in 1987 in Madison, Wisconsin, by Marty Carray as a response to the growing problem of bullying in schools. Bullying hurt individual students and impacted teachers' and schools' abilities to help all students learn. HF's mission is to create positive school communities where students succeed both personally and academically. HF partners with schools to provide one-day retreats that train both educators and students to build trust, develop systems for mutual support, and be motivated to make schools a better place for everyone. HF's dedicated and talented staff members use music, storytelling, and interactive exercises to encourage kindness, courage, and respect amongst students. Marty and HF's staff utilize research that demonstrates that when students feel safe in a welcoming environment, they learn more.

By 2000, the project had grown to be a successful and effective program in the greater Madison area. Marty aspired to reach more students by expanding the program. HF had excellent programs but needed more operational expertise to help the organization expand while maintaining high-quality programming. Over the years, Marty had been consulting with her long-time friend Jeff Leeds for business and operations advice. Jeff had a leadership role at a large and successful Silicon Valley company. As Jeff began to seriously consider a mid-life career transition, Marty convinced him to join HF. Jeff was excited by the opportunity to apply his business skills and corporate experience to support HF's mission and grow its impact in schools and communities. The transition was consistent with his personal values, and the chance to work with his friend, a well-respected founder, sealed the deal.

In 2001, Jeff joined HF as its COO. At the time, HF served 80,000 students annually with a staff of 15 people and a stable budget of $1 million annually. Jeff saw the opportunity to utilize his management skills to establish policies, procedures, and systems to raise the organization's level of professionalism. He also wanted to ensure that all schools received the same high-quality programs. Despite minimal staffing and resources, he was ready to serve more students and make HF even more successful.

Early in his career at HF, Jeff had to learn the difference between working for a large corporation versus a far smaller nonprofit organization. At his previous job, he could take for granted that there would be funds invested in professional development of staff. At HF, he found that he often had to turn down good ideas and suggestions from the staff as there were no funds or resources to implement them. Jeff also experienced a different organizational culture. Sometimes his business-oriented management experience clashed with the nonprofit orientation of people he managed. HF's staff were passionate about the program, but to Jeff, they seemed resistant to growth and quality-assurance systems. Jeff began to hire new staff with more corporate experience. Like him, the new hires were drawn to the mission and the commitment to quality but were frustrated by the lack of resources and slow growth.

Jeff took it upon himself to bridge the gap between his corporate experience and the nonprofit operations he was now handling. He started attending nonprofit networking events. He joined a year-long leadership-development program for community-serving leaders, recommended by Marty, a former graduate of the program. The program challenged community leaders to redefine their work's purpose and clarify their core values. In the year-long process, the program offered ways for the participants to identify changes needed to their own behavior in order to sharpen their focus and increase their commitment to community change.

At the end of the year, Jeff had a clearer understanding of the nonprofit culture in addition to a keener understanding of his own core values of quality, caring, and growth. During this time, Jeff built a strong rapport with staff. He learned more about their approach to their work and was able to make incremental changes to the program. In seven years, Jeff worked with Marty to successfully grow the organization's staff to 20. The number of students served each year likewise grew, to 100,000, and the annual budget to $2.5 million. Jeff had successfully adapted to his role in the nonprofit organization.

Growth for Growth's Sake

Jeff and Marty agreed to expand the program to reach more students by expanding beyond its existing region. Jeff's considerable experience in Silicon Valley and the training program to clarify his values to lead a mission-focused organization brought renewed energy and focus to his role. He started by defining the issues at hand. He made plans to get everyone involved. He created an expanded growth strategy for the organization. The new strategy had a clear quantified goal of replicating the program to serve 1 million students across 20 cities by the year 2020. When Jeff presented this strategy to top management, Marty, HF's Board of Directors, and key donors, they were all excited by the ambitious plan.

Jeff made plans to announce the new plan at an upcoming staff meeting. He expected the staff to love it just as the senior management and board members had. Jeff's previous business experience had taught him that a target-oriented growth strategy motivated employees. It offered new opportunities for advancement. It helped align the employees' actions to corporate objectives. HF's staff was dedicated to the mission and would surely welcome the opportunities created by the growth strategy. Jeff was certain that his plan would inspire and energize the employees and that they would be excited to seize the new career growth and opportunities it would provide.

When he presented his vision of growth, Jeff was shocked to discover that instead of being met with enthusiasm, his ideas were opposed by the staff. He had anticipated some resistance to change, but he was surprised that what he faced was more like an act of rebellion. No one showed any excitement about his vision. To the contrary, there were many who were openly critical of this plan. They spoke up in the meeting and openly called it "growth for growth's sake." The employees voiced their concerns about the negative impact of this growth plan on the quality of the programs. Instead of being excited about advancement, many employees feared that a promotion might negatively impact their work-life balance and take them away from valued time with their families. Others saw potential relocation away from their hometown as a form of hardship, if not punishment.

Jeff was unprepared for this opposition to his plans for growth and for the open confrontation he faced in the meeting. The employees' strong opposition to Jeff's expansion plans required him to take a step back and reassess. He also realized that he needed time to rebuild trust with the staff. To create a sustainable growth plan, he realized that he had to ask himself what motivated the staff. In his own words, "We forgot that the staff was there for the mission" (Bachani and Vradelis, 2012, p. 49). Jeff had to find a way to align the organizational goals with the personal motivations of the people who worked for the institution. He understood that HF's key component of structure was actually the people who cared about serving youth.

Jeff and the management team created new processes to regularly listen to the staff. He discovered common ground with others in their shared motivation to make a difference in the world. He learned that his strategy needed to be refocused on HF's purpose and related societal impact metrics rather than the number of students or cities reached. Together, Jeff and the staff reformulated the growth strategy to be more consistent with the purpose and societal impacts that the staff cared most about, which went beyond the metrics.

Input Metrics versus Impact Measures

Nonprofit organizations often have missions that relate to making some sort of societal impact. This takes priority over being accountable for their financial bottom line. Measuring societal impact is not as easy to track and understand as financial metrics that measure profit and loss, or return on investment. Societal impact can be on people, environment, health, education, or other desired outcomes. To measure their effectiveness, nonprofits can initially use evaluative data that serve as tangible proxies for the softer deliverables: for example, the number of students participating in a year, the number of sessions offered each week, or the number of counseling hours provided per patient.

However, nonprofits also have learned that they need to go beyond inputs (number of participants or service hours provided) to outcomes and impact measures (the results of those services) that help social enterprises track their effectiveness in accomplishing their mission. Nonprofits can measure their societal impact with some objective measures that can be tracked, such as graduation rates, decreased number of emergency room visits, increased productivity at work, and so on. In instances where objective measures are not possible, subjective information collected from the populations served can provide indirect metrics. Subjective output measures focus on the impact of services provided, such as reports of increased confidence for students or satisfaction for people receiving health care. Some government agencies, such as Impact Reporting and Investment Standards in the United States, can help nonprofits develop relevant measurements.

For HF, Jeff modified the strategy to be better aligned with the mission that motivated the people. It was rolled out with an initial test-pilot process. It was decided that the programs would be expanded to only three cities, where an additional 20,000 students would be served. The goal of bringing the program to more students was consistent with its mission so student numbers were adopted as a part of the strategic metrics. The goal of growth was not compromised, and neither was the clarity of having quantified targets. The modification to the initial plan was to have socially relevant targets that demonstrated impact in a manner that furthered the mission. Thus, HF's staff members were ready to serve the organization's purpose with processes that engaged them.

Leadership by Listening and Engaging

Responsible leadership is different from traditional notions of leadership. Leading responsibly requires engaging everyone in the organization in a manner that allows them to act responsibly, too. The leader's job is not just to be responsible, but to also nurture a culture of acting responsibly, which becomes a part of what everyone in the organization does. This can happen only if the leader is able to engage everyone to volunteer this responsible behavior. It cannot be dictated or controlled by the traditional stick-and-carrot approaches to shape desired behaviors. Leadership is a dynamic reciprocal relationship between the leader and so-called followers or constituents.

Jeff's traditional leadership style, developed through his experiences in the Silicon Valley company, with its emphasis on the bottom line, proved to be ineffective when he initially led HF. In this nonprofit organization where the majority of people were mission-focused, Jeff needed new skills. He had to learn how to engage his staff in a dynamic reciprocal relationship. He achieved this by listening to the people who worked there and were committed to the mission. He learned what the staff valued. He had clarity on his goal of growth for HF. His prior experiences and training made him value growth and pursue it more readily than the rest of HF's staff. However, he learned quickly that despite support from the top, in order to successfully deliver growth, he had to find a way to build shared value for it among everyone at the organization. The personal values of the staff are just as important, if not more important, than those of the leader. Collectively, they constitute and shape the organizational values and purpose. He had to listen to learn about their values as well as share his, and through the process of sharing, implement and shape the organizational strategy to be consistent with these shared values.

Listening is a crucial leadership skill that is often left out of the typical leadership course curriculum. Current leadership training focuses on communication models where the leader broadcasts his or her message by choosing an appropriate channel. If the followers do not receive the message, it is an indication that there is noise in the process, which can be reduced by simplifying the message. The notion of communication as a dialogue between the leader and followers is almost never included. Even the concept of followership is missing. This needs to change for organizations that want to lead responsibly. The leader can only be a representative spokesperson if he or she can listen to key stakeholders as an essential precursor to the component of developing the message.

In the book *The Starfish and the Spider: The Unstoppable Power of Leaderless Organization* the authors identify the qualities of a deep interest in people and the ability to listen and understand as essential skills for decentralized organizations (Brafman and Beckstrom, 2006). Listening as a skill is going to gain importance as new technologies and social media create a world with more democratic participation of diverse voices. A leader who does not listen cannot hope to lead effectively and is more likely to fail in delivery due to lack of engaged followership.

Listening is a prerequisite to building engagement. Engaged stakeholders cocreate an organization's mission through shared values. To go beyond the bottom line, leaders have to listen in order to provide what the various stakeholders ask for and build consensus on shared values. They have to listen in order to pay attention, in order to empathetically understand what the respective real concerns are. They have to do the work to find different ways to address the identified concerns without compromising on the main goal, vision, and values.

Engaging different stakeholders in a shared dialogue is a key part of leadership. Listening offers the leader a mechanism to understand the collective aspirations of the followers to shape and articulate the zeitgeist. Effective leaders do not have special skills like clairvoyance or wizardry. They just know how to listen intentionally. They articulate the collective aspirations of their followers to capture and spark their collective imagination.

Jim Collins (2005), the author of the monograph *Good to Great and the Social Sectors* articulates that the sources of a leader's power in for-profit and nonprofit organizations are fundamentally different. He offers a distinction between executive and legislative powers, proposing that for-profit leaders have executive powers whereas nonprofit leaders have legislative powers. The executive power is the ability to reward and punish based on being higher up in the hierarchical structure of a business organization. The legislative power does not rely on material rewards or positional ability to impose punitive measures. It relies on influence that comes from being able to engage a large network that is built around shared meaning of values.

In the same monograph, Frances Hesselbein, the CEO of the Girl Scouts of the USA, describes her position as being "in the center of an organization, as opposed to being at the top" (Collins, 2005, pp. 9-13). Without a concentrated executive power, she explains that she accomplished her goals using the "power of inclusion, the power of language, the power of shared interests, and the power of coalition." Nonprofit leaders often do not have access to the same hierarchical or reward power that corporate leaders have access to. Thus they must rely on processes to cultivate influence, such as listening, that responsible leaders can also adopt.

Listening does not mean that the leaders are merely doing the bidding of their followers and are devoid of original thought, ideas, or goals to direct the organization. Effective leaders must have clear personal values along with an appreciation for their organization's mission. This is needed to convert listening into a dialogue. Modeling engagement, the leaders are able to inspire followers to engage energetically and as such there is no risk of ending up as pushovers. Effective listening is not an end in itself but the precursor to creating engagement, which leads to the possibility of successful outcomes through everyone taking a responsible position. Listening and engagement are the two pillars of responsible leadership.

Suggested In-Class Discussion Activities

This chapter relates to the purpose of business in society (Principle 1), values (Principle 2), and the processes/methods (Principle 3) that enable effective learning experiences to promote responsible leadership. Some suggested exercises for participants to learn about themselves and from each other by relating issues from the chapter and their previous experiences are:

1. Ask participants to each identify his/her core values. Ask people to pair up and have a dialogue about how their core values are expressed in their work. Ask participants to explain what they learned about their partner's values and how these were expressed in their partner's work. Close the exercise by asking participants to share reflections on what they learned about synergy and/or conflicts between individuals and their organization's values.

2. Create two groups and simulate the organizational meeting in which management presents the original strategy Jeff created. Ask the participants to react to the strategy in a manner consistent with their own personal values, as in the first exercise. Debrief on the meeting at the end for how

individuals might handle similar situations in their experiences and join organizations that are well-aligned with their values, or how their individual values may be shaped by the mission of the organization they choose to work for.

3. Try role-play exercises in two groups, for management to listen to staff and vice-versa. Ask the listeners to demonstrate good and poor listening in order to compare and contrast. Then ask how presenters felt in the two different experiences, in order to give participants a way to experience the impact of listening. Ask participants if in their work experiences they have ever felt that they were not listened to.

4. Following a substantive discussion of the case in a class, delve into the broader implications that can be drawn from the case study. What did you learn from the case about going beyond the bottom line? How are these lessons transferable to other contexts? What would you do differently based on this chapter?

5. In a case discussion in a classroom, consider the leadership approaches described in the case study, and ask participants to reflect on the lessons for their respective or prospective workplace. Ask if their employer is managed by the Strategy-Structure-Systems (SSS) or the Purpose-Process-People (PPP) approach? How might it change if managed by the other approach?

Suggested Supplementary Reading

Kaner, S. interviewed by Wright, D. (2009). "Working Effectively in Groups: Developing Your Collaborative Mindset." In B. Tracy, K. Blanchard, and S. Covey (Eds.), *Discover Your Inner Strength*, Ch. 15. Sevierville, Tenn.: Insight Publishing.

Gislason, M. and Wilson, J. (2010). *Coaching Skills for Nonprofit Managers and Leaders*. San Francisco: Jossey-Bass.

References

Bachani, J. and Vradelis, M. (2012a). "Nonprofit Leaders and Listening," *Great Lakes Herald*, September. 6(1-18).

Bachani, J. and Vradelis, M. (2012b). *Strategy Making in Nonprofit Organizations: A Model and Case Studies*. New York: Business Expert Press.

Brafman, O. and Beckstrom, R. (2006). *The Starfish and the Spider: The Unstoppable Power of Leaderless Organization*. London: Penguin Books.

Collins, J. (2005). *Good to Great and the Social Sectors: A Monograph to Accompany Good to Great.* Boulder, CO: Jim Collins.

Drucker, P. (1989). *Harvard Business Review,* July-August, p. 6.

Ghoshal, S., & Bartlett, C. (1999). *The Individualized Corporation.* New York: HarperCollins.

Jyoti Bachani is an Associate Professor of Strategy and Innovation at Saint Mary's College of California and a former Fulbright Senior Research Scholar. She earned a PhD from London Business School and a master's in management science and engineering from Stanford University.

Jb19@stmarys-ca.edu

Mary Vradelis is Adjunct Faculty in the School of Economics and Business at Saint Mary's College of California. In addition, as a consultant with Sequoia Consulting Associates, she works as a facilitator, coach, and trainer for nonprofit organizations. Her education includes an executive MBA from Saint Mary's College of California.

mvradelis@sequoiaconsulting.com

3

Cross-Sectoral Solution-Finding and Policy Dialogue on Information and Communication Technologies for Sustainable Development

The Case of the Global Alliance for Information and Communication Technologies and Development

Julia M. Puaschunder[1]

Schwartz Center for Economic Policy Analysis, USA

Public-Private Partnerships

In the age of sustainable development[2], global governance entities create public-private partnerships (PPP) that enhance institutional, political, and judicial

1 Financial support of the Austrian American Educational Fulbright Commission, Eugene Lang Liberal Arts College of The New School, Fritz Thyssen Foundation, Maxwell School of Citizenship and Public Affairs, New School for Social Research, Tishman Environment and Design Center, and University of Vienna is gratefully acknowledged. The author declares no conflict of interest. The author thanks Professor John Mathiason and the students of the 2008 MPA class at the Maxwell School for Citizenship and Global Affairs for helpful comments on the presented ideas and/or earlier versions of this chapter. All omissions, errors, and misunderstandings in this piece are solely the author's.
2 http://www.un.org/sustainabledevelopment/summit/

infrastructures. Legislative frameworks aim at corporate social value creation. International public policy-makers ratify social responsibility declarations that are in sync with societal goals and advocate for the adoption of social responsibility policies.

The United Nations plays a key role in advancing PPPs. The UN Global Compact (UNGC) initiative is an entry point for corporations to engage in social partnership projects featuring operational flexibility and to focus on pragmatic solutions. In addition, the UNGC Secretariat promotes corporate social responsibility (CSR) to the corporate world as a competitive advantage and PPP-administered social responsibility as a corporate success factor beyond the boundaries of legal compliance and philanthropy. Proactive CSR reporting gains public recognition for sustainable development. In networking events, public and private partners are brought together to find a consensus on social responsibility. A fruitful dialogue of UNGC partners and stakeholders aids in the successful implementation of CSR partnerships. International conferences serve as CSR vision councils in which governmental representatives, business executives, financial professionals, non-governmental organization (NGO) representatives, and academics share insights on CSR success factors to advance PPPs. Summits produce a constant stream of literature on PPP best practices that must be made accessible on the internet to further CSR in PPPs.

This chapter analyzes PPP for sustainable development using the example of the Global Alliance for Information and Communication Technologies (ICT) and Development (GAID).

The Global Alliance for Information and Communication Technologies and Development

In the wake of globalization leading to an intricate set of interactive relationships between individuals, organizations and states, GAID was established by the UN in 2006. As a multi-stakeholder cross-sectoral platform, GAID provides a forum for worldwide consultations on ICT with governments, the private sector, civil society, the new media community, and academia.[3] In light of the growing importance of new media and social platforms in instant communication but also education and crisis coordination potential, ICT is prospected to be playing a continuously rising role in sustainable development.

With the greater goals of achieving international civil-society progress, global-crises prevention, and societal-deficiencies alleviation, the UN GAID international platform was aimed at cross-sectoral solution-finding and policy dialogue on ICT for development. Within the private sector, GAID represents workers' associations, producers, and suppliers of ICT and the media community. In the public sphere, governmental representatives institutionalize ICT for development. Within the civil

---

3 Retrieved from the internet October 10, 2016 at http://close-the-gap.org/discover-us/united-nations/un-gaid/

society, GAID engages NGOs, private foundations, and consumers. Scientific and academic ICT advocates, and also individuals and institutions providing oversight on information issues are also part of the GAID network. Agencies implementing ICT programs for development contribute to GAID.

Within the UN system, GAID is a think tank on ICT for development-related issues and an advisory group to the UN Secretary General. GAID enhances intercultural and cross-sectoral dialogues among stakeholders to globally address and facilitate the transfer of knowledge on ICT. As an umbrella organization, GAID promotes the use of ICT for the achievement of the UN Sustainable Development Goals (SDGs) (World Economic Forum Report 2015). The various GAID stakeholders contribute to advocacy and the policy debate on the role of the information society in international development. In a multi-stakeholder attempt, GAID facilitates PPPs to foster the dissemination of technological solutions for the achievement of development. As a networking governance platform, GAID steers the dissemination of innovations on ICT for development. The partners of the alliance have the overarching goal of tackling societal challenges in a knowledge-based information society. Partners demonstrate leadership on ICT and mainstream the global ICT agenda for the accomplishment of UN endeavors. Best-practices knowledge on ICT is shared in policy dialogues and presentations of innovative business models for community investment, economic growth through access to new media technologies and the ICT empowerment of people living in poverty.

In recent decades, ICT revolutionized the availability and access to information. In the wake of the IT revolution, ICT has gained importance as a means of information dissemination in e-newsletters, blogs, and e-forums. As a multidimensional knowledge-brokerage tool, ICT has enhanced information synthesis and transparency. New-media sources granted unprecedented accountability and benchmarking opportunities to stakeholders. Since the inception of GAID, the communication-technology sector has been developing rapidly. The whole world, including economic actors, various national and international institutions and organizations as well as other stakeholders, has been trying to cope with the dynamics of instant communication transfers and technological reach around the globe. As of today ICT has strengthened global governance by improving the performance and efficiency of markets and governments and thereby has directly contributed to society.

Regarding the UN SDGs,[4] which were introduced in September 2015, ICT has become an essential tool for the alleviation of societal deficiencies. As for the eradication of hunger, the IT revolution has perpetuated efficiency in the information flow on drought, hunger, and crises. As an innovative avenue for fighting poverty, ICT provides access to capital online and by mobile phones. Information flow is key to medical assistance of underserved communities and an essential prerequisite for effective epidemiology. As an essential feature of preventive medical assistance, ICT helps educating on maternal health and combating child mortality, HIV,

4 http://www.un.org/sustainabledevelopment/summit/

malaria, and other diseases. ICT has led to groundbreaking insights on the decay of natural resources and climate change. Information and communication foster environmental protection and sustainability.

New media technologies are pivotal to preventing environmental crises and managing risk in the domain of climate change. Access to information and the reduction of information-transfer costs have helped in educating underserved groups, an essential ingredient for societal development and the empowerment of minorities. Web-based communication has developed into an innovative teaching and learning method that features fast interactivity, cooperative learning arrangements, and richness in content. As a communication and information tool for education, ICT is also key for minority advocacy and empowerment, but lack of accessibility may cause problems in low-income countries. Within corporations, ICT develops competencies necessary for lifelong learning and employee empowerment. In the implementation of policies, ICT links minorities and local aid with global umbrella organizations. Overall, ICT strengthens policy-making bodies on a national and global level in collaboration with the UN. ICT fosters development progress throughout the world through instant communication opportunities and access to information (Reinfried *et al.*, 2007). The following section features an exploratory analysis of the GAID initiative start.

Empirical Analysis

The author and assistants conducted a qualitative analysis of GAID in order to derive recommendations for the improvement of PPPs. The evaluation covered web content, publications, interviews, e-mails, and blog responses collected from February to April 2008 and again in 2016. A total of ten partnerships were selected for the analysis including four flagship initiatives, two regional networks, and four communities of expertise. The analysis focused on the global activities of GAID with special attention to the endeavors outlined in the 2006 business report. At the global level, inception conferences were screened, which took place during 2007 and 2008. Information was retrieved from web pages, featuring workshop reports and handbook material then and in 2016. Additional knowledge was sought by e-mails and individual expert interviews with executives who implemented GAID in 2008 and in 2016. With regard to the "think tank" function of ICT for development, a question on the success of GAID was posed onto the GAID internet discussion list to which considerable responses were received.

Regarding the SDGs, an additional follow-up analysis was staged given contents that were presented during the 2016 International Conference on Sustainable Development hosted at Columbia University and The New School in New York City.[5]

5 http://ic-sd.org/

Results of GAID PPP Implementation Analysis

In February 2002 an inauguration meeting planned the setup of the GAID initiative to be officially approved by the UN Secretary General on March 2006. GAID comprises multiple partners in the setup meeting with a bias toward the private sector and academia compared to other UN meetings (Mathiason, in speech, April 2008).

Flagship Partnership Initiatives, Regional Networks and Communities of Expertise promote ICT for development at the national, regional, and ground levels. A summary of the GAID initiatives' progress, deficiencies, and recommendations is exhibited in Tables 3.1–3.4.

Operational Phase of GAID

When GAID was analyzed in 2009, its precise direction remained unclear, and the added value per stakeholder group was often not obvious (ICT4D Report, 2009). Certain funding streams were lacking for implementing substantial initiatives based on the goals and outlines of the initiative (ICT4D Report, 2009). A detailed, evidence-based analysis of the status of GAID was performed through scanning online data sources in order to shed light on what had happened since the program began in 2006.

Since the inception of GAID, changing technologies have been introduced in the age of the digital, big-data revolution and information transition. Updated information on how the program has evolved helps us draw conclusions about lessons learned. Findings are that GAID has brought together many of the organizations previously central to ICT for development, such as the World Bank, the Swiss Agency for Development and Cooperation, the Global Knowledge Partnership (GKP), Canada's International Development Research Center (IDRC), and governmental stakeholders (ICT4D Report, 2009). Embracing partners from the private sector, global governance institutions, national governments, civil society organizations, and research institutions may have blurred the focus of the initiative.

In 2012 a feasibility study of GAID assessed the demand of its services, support for the organizational development, and aid for its new programming (UNGAID, Feasibility Study & Strategy Development for the United Nation's GAID, 2012).[6] The results helped to retool the program to make it more responsive to its mission in stakeholder communication at additional conferences and online presence (UNGAID, Feasibility Study & Strategy Development for the United Nation's GAID,

---

6 Retrieved October 12, 2016 at http://internationalsolutionsgroup.com/project/feasibility-study-strategy-development-for-the-united-nations-gaid/

2012).[7] In 2012 the International Solutions Group (ISG)[8] carried out a feasibility check of GAID that provided strategic advice and assistance to GAID in assessing its current structure and programming; informed GAID about future development strategies; and helped GAID to be more responsive to its mission. In particular, the study assessed the demand of GAID's services and support for the organizational development of the organization. In addition, it examined new programming that will allow the organization to become more responsive to its mission.[9] A further current search for the GAID program's most recent reports and website updates reveals a stop in new initiatives. This could be a sign of declining interest in ICT for development. For instance, while there seems to have been a fair amount of writing on communication and technology for development about ten years ago (e.g., Heimeriks and Duysters, 2007; Kotlarsky and Oshri, 2005; Leye, 2007); relatively little attention seems to have been paid to the role of ICT for sustainable development. Little seems to be known about the concrete impact of ICT-related programs and respective PPP efforts for reaching sustainable development. More concrete insights on ICT for development, however, would help better understand the lessons learned from the GAID initiative to overcome similar challenges. The chapter therefore also includes a recent analysis of ICT for development in light of the SDGs that lie at the heart of the UN 2030 Agenda including goals to end extreme poverty, fight inequality, and build peaceful societies on a healthy planet (SDGs Report, 2016).

The SDGs Report 2016 distributed at the 2016 International Conference on Sustainable Development hosted by Columbia University and The New School New York[10] highlighted ICT playing a key role for SDG implementation. The technology revolution has enabled innovative and cost-effective methods based on mobile phones, mapping, sensors, and satellite imagery to collect and improve data for development. But use of these advances was found to require "new partnerships and collaboration between companies, institutions and civil society" (p. 14).

The SDGs Report 2016 also addresses the major challenge posed by a paucity of data and poor information on ground work systems that make it difficult to monitor and assess implementation of networking systems. There needs to be a routine of follow-ups about the functioning of programs and a vital data collection and analysis over time to ensure the sustainability of long-term ICT for development strategies. The variety of contexts, good investment in information collection and processing requires a broad approach covering all contextual and economic factors relevant to universal ICT for development utilization. Incomplete essential information in the past has hampered development.

Table 3.1 **Qualitative Analysis of the GAID Start-up Process and Flagship Partnership Initiatives**

Positive progress	Deficiencies	Recommendations
· Innovative PPPs have been set up, extended, and made public. · Secretariats have been set up to work on progress. · Some flagship partnership initiatives are active and visibly linked with GAID, indicating a strong commitment to being a part of GAID. · Private sector sponsorships have been established. · ICT partners have forged a consensus on the harmonization and standardization of priorities. · International conferences and summits fostered information dissemination, networking, and funding. · Some of the flagship initiatives report working groups representing policy makers, NGOs, and the private sector attending initial global forums to present findings. · Regional forums and plenary sessions have been organized by the local multi-stakeholder partners that brought together key constituents. · Minutes of regional forums were made available to the public via websites featuring blog entries showing a high level of transparency and engaging experts worldwide. · Progress has been made accessible to a range of constituents. Global forums on ICT accessibility have been launched. Partnership best practices have been openly shared.	· During the start-up period, the setup has been slower than expected and outlined by the business plan. · Website linkages with GAID are not extensive. Missing web-information and internet references hinder the communication and networking of multiple stakeholders.	· GAID needs to develop a strong networking relation with international organizations. Thereby GAID faces the challenge of distinguishing itself from larger member organizations by offering niche services. · Engage experts that add further value to GAID and flagship initiatives. · Identify opportunities for proactive collaboration and substantive linkages between GAID and other initiatives without losing attention to specificities of local constituents. · GAID should improve access to financial means and information resources as well as training services. · The slower-than-expected progress should be monitored by accountability control and goal-accomplishment checks. · Create web portals and setup centers that help promote ICT for development in local communities. · Irregular and limited communication with GAID could be overcome by regular and mandatory conferences, summits, and meetings. Minutes of the meetings should be made easily accessible in order to enhance best-practice advancement among multiple stakeholders. · The website linkages with GAID have to be intensified to increase the visibility of the multiple connections of the initiative to the wider GAID network.

Table 3.2 **Qualitative Analysis of the GAID Regional Networks**

Positive progress	Deficiencies	Recommendations
· Partnerships have been built with organizations of regional partners. · Diverse stakeholders comprising public and private constituents have attended conferences, workshops, and seminars. These networking events were staged to identify and tackle regional needs, serve as an information brokerage platform, and help implement programs for development. The events were geared toward building and expanding multi-stakeholder networks to better implement policies and raise awareness and funding for respective causes. · A variety of stakeholders engage in information transfer and partnering in networking initiatives. · Websites were launched to foster partnerships and disseminate information.	· Difficulties in obtaining funding for the implementation of the program are apparent. · The approval of working plans is delayed, which puts implementation at stake. · The incorporation of resolutions in policies and practices is not streamlined. · The network executives appear to hold onto ambiguous goals in terms of the scope of projects. The role of the partners is not clear to several constituents. · Some websites are not operational, which limits the information flow on the network's activities and discussion possibility for the network. · A lack of official network conferences is apparent, which degrades the likelihood and quality of the multi-stakeholder communication.	· Resolutions must be facilitated by clear strategies and policies negotiated in interagency meetings. · The agreed-upon policy models, network scope, and focus must be communicated throughout all layers of the network. · Regional policy-makers and local administrators have to work closely on the implementation of respective policies. · Conferences and summits are key for multi-stakeholder initiatives during the start-up phase. Innovative and new media means of information exchange should be explored. · Additional sources of funding should be investigated.

Table 3.3 Qualitative Analysis of the GAID Communities of Expertise

Positive progress	Deficiencies	Recommendations
· Public- and private-sector constituents were brought together to address and solve ICT for development problems.	· The lead partners do not feature extensive networks.	· Goals and responsibilities have to be made transparent and accountable. For the outlined goals, respective achievement measurement and performance control must be installed.
· Respective websites were launched and web- based networks established. Weblinkages outline networking and collaboration engagements.	· The initiatives have difficulty in connecting the global with the local level in activities.	· The connection to GAID has to be strengthened. The communities of expertise have to develop a unique proposition within the wider GAID network. GAID has to establish itself in respective local communities and further advance related activities and grassroots initiatives.
· Official linkages to the UN have fortified the strength of the PPPs.	· There seems to be a weak relationship between the GAID community of expertise board and the current members, who facilitate the ICT solutions in developing countries.	
· ICT training programs and workshops have been organized and launched through PPPs.	· The connection between GAID and the communities of expertise is partial and irregular. The entrepreneurship community of expertise indicates problems of maintaining a connection between the partners and motivating them to engage in their initiatives.	· Multi-stakeholder means to create a vital dialogue between all constituents involved have to be considered. Regular conferences and meetings are recommended.
· Capacity-building developed user-friendly e-governance tools.		
· Trainings have improved ICT skills and fostered social development		
· Open surveys were conducted to identify areas of concern.		· At these gatherings, common goals have to be discussed and transparency of goals and goal-achievement measurements must be agreed upon.
· Additional communities of expertise were formed in workshops.	· There is a lack of funding and expected assistance from GAID, which imply start-up deficiencies.	· Further meetings, summits, and conferences should be launched as for fostering a more vital stakeholder dialogue, extending networks, and revitalizing the stakeholder dialogue.
· Factors that could inhibit the spread of the use of ICT within areas of expertise were identified.	· The activities developed by the partners are taking place without GAID's direct involvement.	
· Work plans and goal-setting as well as measurable output criteria have been defined.		
· Future endeavors were planned and outlined.	· The overall business plan of the community of expertise was reported to be vague about the creation, the strengthening, and the expected outcomes of the alliance.	· To overcome financial constraints, the communities of expertise must continuously look for innovative sources of funding ensured by promoting the successes already accomplished.
· Community and constituent engagement events have served networking purposes.		
· GAID community of expertise have helped ensure that specificities are kept in mind when ICT for development is discussed within the UN and GAID networks.		

Table 3.4 **Summary of GAID Qualitative Analysis**

Positive progress	Deficiencies	Recommendations
· Launch of innovative PPPs. · Network extensions. · Linkages to the UN. · Transparent information-sharing worldwide. · Private-sector sponsorships. · Secretariat for work on progress. · Harmonization of priorities. · Standardization of processes. · International forums, conferences, and summits for information dissemination, networking, and funding. · Networking events to identify and tackle regional needs and help implement programs. · Surveys to identify areas of concern. · Trainings to improve ICT skills to foster development. · Goals and accomplishment plans for future endeavors.	· Work plan and implementation delays. · Multi-stakeholder networking deficiencies · Lack of linkages with GAID. · Missing web-information and internet references hinder communication and networking of multiple stakeholders. · Funding constraints. · Inconsistent policies and practice implementation. · Role and goal ambiguity of partners. · Vague business plans and undefined outcomes.	· Develop a strong networking relation with international organizations and local communities. · Identify networking opportunities. · Accountability control and goal accomplishment checks. · Regular and mandatory conferences, summits, and meetings. · Transparency on best practices. · Promote ICT in local communities. · Engage experts. · Improve funding. · Set clear strategies and policies. · Innovate information exchange. · Foster a vital dialogue between all constituents.

Finally, the report assures that reliable and accessible data remain high on the agenda for governments, civil society, and other stakeholders. By engaging diverse actors and data sources, countries can better track progress, while deepening the ownership people and governments have of the results (p. 55). The digital age is acknowledged to offer potential to generate data that can inform government policies. The rapid growth of new technologies improves the possibilities to understand the world and expand communication across borders.

Today's decision-makers have a more diverse array of facts easily available at hand. Yet for many of the poorest countries in the world this luxury remains inaccessible. As the SDG Report indicates, huge data gaps persist. The data deficit is partly a consequence of a lack of resources, especially when governments are struggling with inadequate budgets to invest in the latest data technologies. Data collection costs money, time, and human effort, which may be scarce, especially in the developing world. Nevertheless, investments in data collection pay off as information is invaluable for governmental executives for their decision-making in the allocation of scarce resources.

Making resources available for the poorest countries would be key in improving data systems. Donors and other partners play an essential role. According to the Sustainable Development Report 2016, making the most of the new opportunities presented by technology to make data faster, more accurate, and more useful will take more than money. It will mean governments, researchers, the private sector, NGOs, and multilaterals working together to see how new data can solve old problems. Improving data collection and shared access to data thus needs to become a collective effort. New data at the same time will raise questions about privacy protection and with whom to share information. Public- and private-sector institutions will have to come together on a larger scale to provide, use, and streamline information flows. The Sustainable Development Report advocates for further partnerships bringing together governments, companies, NGOs, UN agencies, and other multilaterals determined to improve production and increase the use of data to address sustainable development.

Discussion

This case study on GAID and PPPs discusses cross-sectoral solution-finding and policy dialogue on ICT for sustainable development. The UN partnership network GAID is analyzed as an example of an international PPP with focus on social development. The GAID inception, setup, and initiative focus, and also implementation problems have been addressed in order to derive improvement recommendations for other UN-led PPPs.

Overall, GAID leveraged its position as a UN-related PPP network that advocates for ICT for development on a global basis. GAID introduced ICT for development in the international dialogue. Given the information retrieved online and from stakeholder reports, public and private actors have engaged in advocacy and policy dialogue, corporate social entrepreneurship, and philanthropy on ICT for development.

On a partnership level, the results are mixed. GAID has supported existing networks and embraced new stakeholders. Novel ICT initiatives were developed under GAID's guidance, and several of these have been quite successful. Most of the partners have demonstrated an ability to achieve results but – after ten years of GAID's inception – the results are somewhat sobering. As vibrant parts of the GAID network, the successful partners have advanced the use of ICT for development on the regional, national, and international levels. Some preexisting partnerships visibly linked with GAID have meetings to streamline actions for the advancement of common endeavors. While the setup of GAID features positive results, the evaluation also identified areas for improvement. For instance, a stronger emphasis on long-term goals and endeavors pursuit could connect ICT to accomplishing the SDGs and the UNGC goals. In this GAID and ICT would pay a broader value for all those who are interested in PPPs and care about the implementation of the SDGs and the UNGC around the world.

At the same time, the analysis reveals difficulties in establishing the network in terms of integrating individual partnerships with GAID and facilitating information exchange. Some preexisting partnerships have continued their own endeavors with little attention to GAID. These agencies have merely agreed to be associated with the GAID, but have neither used the network nor contributed extensively to the community's goals. Other partners have experienced problems during the start-up phase – foremost in connecting with GAID and extending the network – mainly due to resource limitations and a lack of stakeholder interest and networking expertise. In some cases the partners overestimated the extent to which GAID could mobilize resources or facilitate networks with the constraints of GAID's own budget. A few of the preexisting members are still not linked very well with GAID and have become almost inactive or even ceased to function. The overall situation of the GAID network implies areas for improvement regarding sustainable development, stakeholder management, regional goal-accomplishment strategies, and accountability control.

From the initiative's own sustainability point of view, GAID's long-term financial sustainability should be ensured by securing multi-year donations. In order to tap into new sources of funding, GAID should build additional alliances with international organizations – foremost the UN and the World Bank – as well as with corporate professionals, trade unions, NGOs, and academic communities. These entities should be asked for capital, in-kind contributions, and collaborative support to further develop the initiative. Increasing the visibility of the initiative would help GAID to reach out to new donors. Providing access to information on GAID by the use of new media tools – that is, e-newsletters, blogs, and Facebook – would foster engagement of a broad audience. Internet information portals need to position GAID as a network hub for information exchange that attracts stakeholders' attention and raises participants' commitment.

In terms of stakeholder management, in its "think tank" function, the GAID Secretariat should play an active role in the coordination of the partners' endeavors and fortify the networks' connectivity by launching stakeholder events. As UN-led networking forums, conferences would bring together executives from international organizations and corporations, government officials, and the civil society to discuss ICT for development interests. Agreement on common goals would implicitly coordinate partners' activities and fortify the impact of the entire GAID network. Social gatherings are expected to build a mutual understanding about ICT for development and promote a trust-based, supportive environment throughout the network. For the longer-term planning of the network, stakeholder meetings could also help in identifying emerging issues of concern and foster information exchange on future endeavors.

Regarding regional goal-accomplishment strategies, the partners should agree on implementation strategies and align activities accordingly. By committing themselves to specific goal-accomplishment strategies, the partners need to specify how their activities will contribute to the GAID goals. Transparency on such strategies would help monitor the partners' contributions and work in progress. The degree to which partners feature standardized or local ownership of goals should be outlined to all stakeholders at early stages of the partnering process. The GAID constituents need to work closely on implementing collectively shared goals. Corporate partners should incorporate GAID goals into business plans that become the basis for respective training programs. Local meetings need to gather participants to coordinate and govern the implementation of ICT for development. Regional campaigns would root ICT for development in the cultural context and thereby support the network extension. Regional seminars and workshops should create learning experiences to foster the overall effectiveness of GAID in local networks. Regional dialogues could strengthen the transfer of knowledge on local success patterns and generate applicable problem-solving capabilities. Information-sharing on ICT best-practice standards would lead to contemporary ICT solutions and prepare for future challenges.

Accountability of the partners' commitments could counterbalance a lack of clarity about the purpose of the initiative. Based on transparent activities and monitoring, benchmarking of impact assessments could identify best-practice learning models for future PPPs. Accountability control should also feature assessment of progress on external goals. External audits should become the basis for rewarding positive results and providing assistance in case of defaults. Noncompliance with goal accomplishment and communication deficiencies of the partners should be sanctioned – for instance, by warnings, de-linking partners from the GAID internet portal or exclusion from the network. As for a long-term development, a reintegration into the GAID must be made possible to steer partner behavior into a favorable direction.

Conclusion

Overall, GAID has shown positive results at the global and partnership levels. At the same time, improvement has taken place in some areas. On the global level, GAID has attracted attention and gained participation from multiple stakeholders on ICT for development, in particular the private sector and academia. GAID has brought ICT considerations into the mainstream of intergovernmental debate. Given the nature of the relative novelty of GAID, the initiatives are sometimes stuck in planning future endeavors and opportunities rather than in implementing concrete management actions immediately.

Evaluation of partnerships developed as a consequence of GAID at various networks found mixed results. Some new partnerships have been quite successful and shown strong progress. Other previously existing initiatives were revitalized by the GAID partnering. Some initiatives successfully organized GAID conferences, summits, and meetings. Other accomplishments comprised the advancement of ICT at the ground level by fostering accessibility and technology use.

In summary, GAID showed some significant results in implementing its mission in its early days. GAID launched innovative PPPs, extended its network, and secured funding in the beginning. At the start, GAID's global activities were particularly successful in leveraging its position as a UN-related organization that focused on keeping ICT for development on the global agenda. GAID has also been successful in raising and supporting a number of constituent partnerships. Most of these partnerships have demonstrated an ability to achieve start-up results. For rising partnership initiatives, goals and accomplishment plans have been defined and future endeavors were outlined. Numerous international forums, conferences, and summits have strengthened the network. Networking events also have identified and tackled regional needs and helped implement programs. Information on ICT has been spread worldwide. ICT accessibility and harmonization of best-practices standards have been fostered along the way. Training and workshops have fostered ICT skills and social development on the ground level.

Based on this analysis, recommendations include linking the global network with partnership networks. For GAID and its partners, recommendations comprise improving GAID's planning, strengthening resource mobilization and setting up clearer business plans with outcome control mechanisms such as goal accomplishment checks and accountability.

The GAID partnership network needs to secure long-term financial sustainability by strengthening existing alliances and fostering extensions. Stakeholder networking activities will help find consensus and support the network. Regional initiatives should coordinate local action and govern the implementation of ICT for development. Transparent goal-accomplishment strategies will monitor partners' contributions. Benchmarking and impact assessments will derive best-practice learning models for future PPPs.

For the future, GAID is advised to continue developing a strong networking relation with international organizations and local communities. Further opportunities to network and engage with a wider range of constituents in regular conferences, summits, and meetings need to be explored. Innovations in ICT for development should be fostered and promoted to constituents.

References

Heimeriks, K.H. & Duysters, G. (2007). Alliance capability as a mediator between experience and alliance performance: An empirical investigation into the alliance capability development process. *Journal of Management Studies*, 44(1), 25-49.

ICT4D Report. (2009). *Information and Communication Technology for Development*. Cambridge: Cambridge University Press.

International Conference on Sustainable Development. (2016). Columbia University and The New School, New York, September 21-22.

Kotlarsky, J. & Oshri, I. (2005). Social ties, knowledge sharing and successful collaboration in globally distributed system development projects. *European Journal of Information Systems*, 14(1), 37-48.

Leye, V. (2007). UNESCO, ICT corporation and the passion of ICT for development: Modernization resurrected. *Media, Culture & Society*, 29(6), 972-993.

Reinfried, Y., Schleicher, A. & Rempfler, A. (2007). Geographical views on education for sustainable development. *Geographiedidaktische Forschungen*, 42, 243-250.

Sustainable Development Goals Report: The People's Agenda (2016). UNA-UK.

United Nations Global Alliance for ICT and Development (UNGAID). (2012). Feasibility Study & Strategy Development for the United Nation's GAID, 2012. Retrieved October 12, 2016 at http://internationalsolutionsgroup.com/project/feasibility-study-strategy-development-for-the-united-nations-gaid/

World Economic Forum 2015 Report. Davos, Switzerland: World Economic Forum.

Julia Margarete Puaschunder studied philosophy/psychology, business, public administration, social and economic sciences, natural sciences, law, and economics. Her research projects on four continents were presented at several Ivy League universities. After having captured social responsibility in corporate and financial markets, Puaschunder currently researches intergenerational equity on climate justice, overindebtedness, and demographic aging.

julia.puaschunder@newschool.edu

4

Off-Grid Solar Energy and the UN Global Compact

Inara Scott
Oregon State University, USA

United Nations (UN) secretary-general Ban Ki-moon has said, "Sustainable energy is the golden thread that connects economic growth, increased social equity and an environment that allows the world to thrive" (UN, 2014). Although energy access is not explicitly identified in the Universal Declaration of Human Rights, it is closely associated with a number of rights, including the right to a standard of living adequate for health and wellbeing (Article 25) (UN, 2016b). Access to affordable and reliable energy is one of the new Sustainable Development Goals (SDGs) that were adopted in September 2015 and came into force in January 2016 (UN-DESA, 2016) and is widely recognized as key to improving conditions for people living in poverty. Despite its importance, in 2015 more than 1.2 billion people lacked access to electric service (IEA, 2015a). The bulk of these individuals reside in the developing world, many in remote rural areas that are unlikely to be served by grid-connected electricity any time soon.

While energy access is essential to community development and economic growth, the use of nonrenewable fuels – particularly kerosene, which is widely used for lighting in the absence of electricity – can be environmentally damaging as well as threatening to human health and safety. One way for people without access to the electric grid to obtain basic electric service is through off-grid solar products, including solar lanterns, solar charging stations, and small solar home systems. These basic products may provide light for cooking, reading, and studying, or economic activity like harvesting food or making goods. They may also provide life-saving access to cellular phones and the ability to communicate with distant medical personnel.

Three of the Ten Principles of the UN Global Compact address environmental responsibility, which is a central issue of sustainable development (UN, 2016a). Principles 8 (undertake initiatives to promote greater environmental responsibility) and 9 (encourage the development and diffusion of environmentally friendly technologies) emphasize the importance of businesses engaging in sustainable enterprises that promote environmental responsibility and encourage the diffusion of environmentally friendly technologies. Principle 7 (business should support a precautionary approach to environmental challenges) stresses the need for business to enact the precautionary principle in their activities by seeking to prevent rather than remediate environmental challenges. The importance of Principle 7 cannot be overemphasized in the face of climate change, which represents an existential threat to low-lying coastal communities and cultures.

Off-grid solar lighting represents a unique combination of a thriving market, an environmentally beneficial technology that has the potential to avoid or eliminate significant greenhouse gas emissions, and a tool for promoting sustainable development. The market thus provides a uniquely powerful example of an opportunity for firms to profitably engage in the UNGC. However, while off-grid solar products represent a significant business opportunity and a key step in the achievement of the SDGs, introducing products in subsistence markets can be extremely challenging for businesses accustomed to working in developed economies.

In recognition of both the promise and complexity of off-grid renewable energy access, this chapter offers concrete recommendations and insights into best practices and business models that have led to commercial success in the off-grid solar lighting field. Using a combination of theory-based research and case studies, this chapter examines how successful ventures incorporate local entrepreneurs in their supply chain and work in partnership with a variety of other entities. It considers the importance of broadening business models and building local capacity to fill institutional voids. Ultimately, by providing real-life examples of how businesses can successfully enact the UNGC, it offers powerful lessons for business schools and a concrete platform for engaging students in the Principles of Responsible Management Education (PRME).

Why Off-Grid Solar Energy?

The prominence of energy in the SDGs and in almost every sustainability initiative is no accident. Globally, energy use and production are responsible for two-thirds of greenhouse gas emissions (IEA, 2015a). At the same time, energy is essential for development. Numerous studies have linked energy access to improved outcomes in education and economic growth (Modi *et al.*, 2005; Bhattacharyya, 2006; Casillas and Kammen, 2010; Nania and Vilsack, 2010). Access to electricity can create a virtuous cycle of improved health and education; increased gender equality, life expectancy, and productivity; and enhanced economic development (Casillas and Kammen, 2010; Lahimer *et al.*, 2013; van de Walle *et al.*, 2013; Alstone *et al.*, 2015). Although energy access is not *sufficient* to ensure human rights and lift communities out of poverty, it may be considered a necessary step along that path.

The need for greater energy access is profound. In sub-Saharan Africa, almost 70% of the population lacks access to electricity, while 20% of the population in India is without electricity (IEA, 2014). Besides slowing economic growth and development, the lack of access to electricity creates a number of other problems. The pollution from kerosene lamps and biomass, the primary alternatives for lighting, creates substantial negative health effects, including death (Centurelli, 2011; Africa: A Brightening Continent, 2015). Kerosene lamps also present significant risks for home fires. Importantly, kerosene, biomass, and petroleum (used for diesel generators, another common alternative) emit significantly more greenhouse gasses than their renewable counterparts, contributing to climate change (Akella *et al.*, 2009).

While reliable, grid-connected electric service may be considered a goal for all communities, in many rural areas connecting to an electric grid is economically infeasible (IEA, 2011; Mainali and Silveira, 2013). An example helps to illustrate the problem of extending the electric grid. A recent study of grid-connection in Senegal found that it would cost approximately $650 to connect a single home to the grid less than 30 meters away (Nania and Vilsack, 2010). Distances to rural villages are substantially further, measured in kilometers, not meters, while average household income in many African nations is less than $2,000 annually (Global Issues, 2016). Due to the prohibitive cost, the International Energy Agency (IEA) has estimated that 55% of new electricity-generating resources will have to come from off-grid or micro-grid projects in order to provide universal access to energy services (IEA, 2011).

In isolated rural areas, off-grid solar products can provide an interim solution that can truly change lives, without creating an accompanying environmental cost or contributing to climate change. For less than $20, solar lights can provide up to 1,000 nights of illumination, while less than $10 can provide reliable charging for cell phones and radios. Solar energy may also help eliminate the "energy premium" suffered by individuals in economically disadvantaged rural areas, wherein they pay more for access to fuels like kerosene and petroleum than their urban counterparts. In many high-poverty areas, kerosene represents a significant portion of monthly household expenses. In contrast, because they do not have recurring fuel costs, solar lamps can be 24% less expensive than kerosene, which allows individuals to recoup initial costs in a matter of a few months (IFC, 2012b).

Solar lighting can undoubtedly change lives and contribute substantially to the achievements of the SDGs. It also represents a growing business opportunity. Just as the market for cellular and mobile phones has grown exponentially, so has the market for small solar lighting and charging units and small solar home systems since 2012 (Davies, 2013; Alstone *et al.*, 2015). From 2009 to 2015, the percentage of homes in nonelectrified Africa with solar lighting grew from 1% to nearly 5%

(Africa, A Brightening Continent, 2015). Conservative estimates of the growth of firms selling solar home systems range from 40% to 70% (The Climate Group and Sachs, 2015). The potential market for solar lights and solar home systems is estimated at $31 billion (IFC, 2012a).

Example of LED solar light with USB mobile charging port

Off-grid solar products thus represent a significant business opportunity for companies engaging in the UNGC. Renewable energy brings improved health and education, supports economic development within local communities, and improves environmental outcomes, while also offering the potential for profitable business models. Unsurprisingly, given the potential for growth, a number of enterprises both large and small have sought to fill this niche. However, organizations working in remote and undeveloped areas often face significant challenges in managing supply chains, gaining trust and acceptance from local populations, and overcoming the financing barriers presented by individuals living in poverty.

Best-Practices for Enterprises Serving the Base of the Pyramid

From 2006 to 2012, almost half of the world's population lived on less than $2.50 a day (Phelps and Crabtree, 2013). Businesses seeking to serve these subsistence, or poverty markets, dubbed the "base of the pyramid" (BOP) to represent their prominence and relative size in the world's population, face unique challenges. First, these markets are generally characterized by a lack of formal structures and institutions, making it difficult for an outside entity to enter into financial and legal arrangements with individuals or communities. (London *et al.*, 2010; Rivera-Santos and Rufin, 2010). The farther the community is from urban areas the more difficult it may become to conduct business transactions.

Another common characteristic of BOP markets is the existence of so-called "institutional voids," which refers to the absence of structures necessary to support production, marketing, financing, and distribution of goods (Parmigiani and Rivera-Santos, 2015). Entities seeking to serve BOP markets need to consider how to address fragmented supply chains, a lack of distribution networks, and little formal infrastructure to service and repair goods. A similar challenge for entities seeking to market solar lighting products is the population's discomfort, mistrust, or simple lack of familiarity with more advanced products and technology. A final key barrier to serving subsistence markets is the lack of financing available for purchases that represent multiple months of income. Even if the investment in a solar lantern will pay back within a short time, coming up with the initial investment can present an insurmountable challenge. A lack of formal institutions for individuals to save, lend, and transfer money exacerbates this problem.

To overcome these challenges, studies have found a number of factors are essential to the success of venture capital serving subsistence markets: entities must create strong partnerships with a variety of individuals or organizations, fill institutional voids, build local capacity, and widen their business model to offer a greater breadth of services. In many cases, strategies for addressing these challenges work in tandem. For example, a best practice for filling institutional voids is to build local capacity.

Create Partnerships

To work within the informal economy of the BOP, it is essential that enterprises partner with local individuals and organizations (London *et al.*, 2010; Rivera-Santos, 2010; Reficco and Marquez, 2009; Hahn and Gold, 2014). These partnerships aid the organization in building trust, gaining knowledge of local customs, and becoming embedded in informal economic arrangements. Partnerships with community members often go beyond purely economic arrangements to become personal relationships, and these relationships may be crucial to the success of the firm.

The characterization of subsistence markets as an "informal economy" is crucial for businesses to understand. Where developed markets rely on formal contracts and legal arrangements to guide and shape business transactions, in a subsistence market individuals may rely on trust and relationships. Individuals may be reluctant to enter into transactions without gaining the approval of respected community members, while a lack of banking or financial institutions may require individuals to develop informal arrangements for contracting and payment. In addition, communities may have traditions, rituals, or unspoken arrangements for trans-acting business that require local knowledge to navigate. For this reason, without a community-based partner or guide, outside businesses may struggle. The local partner may include an individual or an NGO or nonprofit agency familiar with the region and its customs. The key is finding an entity with established roots and ties to the community.

Besides working with local individuals and organizations, successful entities serving subsistence markets will generally form networks that include a larger, financially stable outside organization. Serving the BOP is unlikely to result in quick profits or high profit margins. In order to be sustainable, enterprises serving this population must be prepared for longer horizons for establishing the business and seeing profitability. Yet by the same token, a highly profitable and stable multi-national corporation may be unable to create relationships and establish trust with the community. The most successful networks often involve a social enterprise to help establish legitimacy, an anchor organization to create financial stability, and a local community-aid organization to help provide knowledge of local customs and begin the process of establishing relationships with local individuals (Webb *et al.*, 2009; Sakarya *et al.*, 2012).

Fill Institutional Voids & Build Local Capacity

Another key to serving subsistence or BOP markets is finding a way to fill institu-tional voids, ideally also building local capacity. The concept of institutional voids represents the lack of formal structures, relationships, and entities used to con-duct business transactions that are typically assumed to be present in developed markets. For example, the lack of transportation infrastructure and long distances between rural villages leaves firms without established routes to distribute their goods or commercial establishments within which to offer them. The lack of edu-cational and marketing channels makes it difficult for rural populations to gain familiarity with technology and may create mistrust for individuals seeking to sell unproven and unfamiliar goods. A lack of access to repair or service professionals may inhibit people from purchasing unfamiliar and complex goods.

Successful enterprises serving the BOP must find ways to fill these voids. Research suggests this is best done by building local capacity to engage in business functions. Engaging and training local entrepreneurs to provide support for distri-bution, sales, marketing, and repair efforts creates benefits for both the buyers and the sellers of goods (Chesbrough *et al.*, 2006; Van den waeyenberg and Hens, 2012; Sodhi and Tang, 2014). Enterprises can fill distribution voids by training entrepre-neurs in neighboring communities to transport goods from central distribution hubs. Local entrepreneurs can market products and demonstrate their benefits to local communities. While residents of remote rural communities may not trust the reliability of a solar light presented by an outside salesperson, they may believe a community member who has had personal experience using the same product. For more complex products such as solar home systems and small solar panels, individuals may need training on upkeep and maintenance, and assistance with routine troubleshooting. To perform these services, enterprises need to form ongoing relationships with individuals who can answer questions and provide basic product support.

When community members are trained as partners in the sales of off-grid solar lighting products, they bring profits into the community and create ongoing business opportunities. Successful local entrepreneurs create a positive cycle of building economic growth that brings more financial resources into impoverished communities.

Expand Business Model

While a narrow business model focused on manufacturing or distributing a product may work in urban settings, it is unlikely to be successful in a BOP. Rather than just manufacturing a product, successful off-grid enterprises may offer financing or build relationships with local organizations that can; train local entrepreneurs to act as distribution, sales, and repair forces; and care for products at the end of their useful lives by offering disposal and/or recycling of nonfunctioning products, which may contain hazardous materials.

This full life-cycle approach to the enterprise business model may be inefficient or disfavored in developed markets, but may be essential to serving the BOP. Financing in particular is a key barrier to adoption of technology that may pay for itself in a matter of months, but is prohibitively expensive for individuals with little or no disposable income. Operating within the BOP cannot be approached with a "business as usual" mindset. It requires different processes and, for enterprises already established in developed markets, new business models.

Successful Enterprises Serving the Off-Grid Solar Market

The elements of successful firms serving BOP markets are well illustrated by a number of firms operating successfully in the developing world. These enterprises rely heavily on partnerships with a number of institutions, use local entrepreneurs in a variety of ways to build capacity and fill institutional voids, and offer a breadth of services to replace those that may be absent in rural communities.

For example, in rural India, the Lighting a Billion Lives (LABL) Initiative has adopted a model that includes significant community involvement (Chaurey *et al.*, 2012). Before providing solar lighting products in a community, the LABL Initiative trains local entrepreneurs to manage, operate, and repair a solar charging station. SELCO, a large solar lighting firm operating in India, believes so strongly in the importance of local community involvement that it made the decision to cap the size of the business in order to maintain individual connections and involvement (Mukherji, 2011).

Grameen Shakti, a well-established and highly regarded nonprofit that installs solar home systems in Bangladesh, also relies heavily on local ownership and participation (Sovacool and Drupady, 2012). To fill institutional voids and connect patchy distribution systems, Grameen Shakti trains local female entrepreneurs to educate customers, and to install and repair its solar home systems (Grameen Shakti, 2016).

Grameen Shakti has also been at the forefront of helping find ways for individuals to finance the cost of solar home systems. It offers a popular micro-credit program, which includes a down payment, installments, and a service charge (Asif and Barua, 2011). By pairing with rural banks, credit cooperatives, and microfinance agencies, SELCO has made it possible for many individuals to secure credit, without offering financing services themselves (Mukherji, 2011). Tata Solar, the largest integrated solar company in India, provides engineering, procurement, and construction, and also offers a monthly installment plan that is partially financed by the company, and partially financed through government assistance (IFC, 2012a).

Many of the enterprises serving the off-grid lighting market use local entrepreneurs as a key aspect of their business model. Barefoot Power, a for-profit social enterprise that operates globally, has a "business in a bag" training program to support entrepreneurs and establish micro-franchises (Barefoot Power, 2016). Sunny Money, a social enterprise that is working toward a long-term strategy of becoming a self-sustaining for-profit enterprise, also works with local entrepreneurs to market and distribute its products (Sunny Money, 2016). D.light, one of the most well-established solar lighting enterprises operating in Africa and internationally, is also a for-profit social enterprise that works with local entrepreneurs (D.light, 2016).

While there are many examples of social enterprises working in these markets, there is also room for larger for-profit corporations, serving either as anchor institutions or as a stand-alone enterprise. Philips and Sinoware are both large for-profit enterprises offering off-grid solar lighting products in India.

Concluding Remarks and Implications for Management Education

The UNGC encourages businesses to use economic power to advance sustainable development and the development of new enterprises that are both profitable and provide long-term benefits to communities. Off-grid solar lighting is an area of significant need and a core business opportunity that will only grow in the future. However, businesses entering this space need to do so thoughtfully, and be prepared to establish a new set of business practices. By working closely with communities, building local capacity, creating partnerships with other organizations, and filling the inevitable institutional voids that appear in developing markets, enterprises can successfully bridge the gap between opportunity (or local demand) and enterprise (or supply), for the benefit of individuals, their communities, and the environment.

Management students are typically taught how to work within established markets, within an existing commercial infrastructure that allows them to segment production and outsource nonessential functions. Before these students can effectively build and manage enterprises to serve subsistence markets, they need exposure to the unique business models that will be required. Using examples of successful off-grid solar lighting enterprises and related research on the BOP markets provides students with exposure to unfamiliar business models, while at the same time preparing them to enact the UNGC in whatever type of business they ultimately join.

Many of the skills needed to serve subsistence markets will benefit students regardless of where they practice. In particular, partnering with local communities, building relationships with complementary organizations, and building the economic sustainability of communities in which a business operates are key to any organization's success. Students may also benefit from illustrations of the way organizations have adapted to the challenges posed by working in the BOP, which are instructional for any type of organization, all of which must ultimately adapt to changing market conditions.

Principle 1 of the PRME pledges to "develop the capabilities of students to be future generators of sustainable value for business and society" (PRME, 2016). To become effective agents for building sustainable value in vulnerable and difficult-to-serve subsistence markets, students need to develop unique competencies and have the opportunity to learn from successful enterprises. Students may also be skeptical that for-profit businesses can find opportunities to build financial value while also reducing greenhouse gas emissions, increasing economic self-sufficiency of nonurban, remote communities, and providing for basic human rights. Yet the case studies and research offered in this chapter show that this is possible. Studying enterprises offering off-grid solar lighting products can therefore be inspirational as well as instructional.

Traditional business models focused on developed markets ignore millions of potential customers. In the field of energy access, ignoring this market represents a missed opportunity to provide for basic human rights, reduce environmental impacts and greenhouse gas emissions, and build economic and sustainable value. Off-grid solar lighting represents a unique story that business schools should be encouraged to tell.

References

Africa: A Brightening Continent. (2015, January 17). *The Economist*. Retrieved from http://www.economist.com/news/special-report/21639018-solar-giving-hundreds-millions-africans-access-electricity-first.

Akella, A.K., Saini, R.P., & Sharma, M.P. (2009). Social, economical and environmental impacts of renewable energy systems. *Renewable Energy*, 34(2), 390-396.

Alstone, P., Gershenson, D., & Kammen, D.M. (2015). Decentralized energy systems for clean electricity access. *Nature Climate Change*, 5(4), 305-314.

Asif, M., & Barua, D. (2011). Salient features of the Grameen Shakti renewable energy program. *Renewable and Sustainable Energy Reviews*, 15(9), 5063-5067.

Barefoot Power (2016). 'BRAC and Barefoot: Impact in Uganda', http://www.barefootpower. com/index.php/social-impact/74-impact-in-uganda, accessed 21 April 2016.

Bhattacharyya, S.C. (2006). Energy access problem of the poor in India: Is rural electrification a remedy? *Energy Policy*, 34(18), 3387-3397.

Casillas, C.E., & Kammen, D.M. (2010). Environment and development. The energy-poverty-climate nexus. *Science*, 330(6008), 1181-1182.

Centurelli, R. (2011). Energy poverty: Can we make modern energy access universal? Focus on financing appropriate sustainable technologies. *Colorado Journal of International Environmental Law & Policy*, 22, 219-250.

Chaurey, A., Krithika, P.R., Palit, D., Rakesh, S., & Sovacool, B.K. (2012). New partnerships and business models for facilitating energy access. *Energy Policy*, 47, 48-55.

Chesbrough, H., Ahern, S., Finn, M., Guerraz, S. (2006). Business models for technology in the developing world: The role of nongovernmental organizations. *California Management Review*, 48(3), 48-61.

D.light (2016). 'For Dealers: Join d.light in the Growing Off-Grid Solar Market', http://www. dlight.com/dealers/, accessed 21 April 2016.

Davies, G. (2013, March 4). Building an African market: Solar energy entrepreneurs on the rise. *Renewable Energy World*. Retreived from http://www.renewableenergyworld.com/rea/ news/article/2013/03/building-an-african-market-solar-entrepreneurs-on-the-rise.

Global Issues. (2016). Social, Political, Economic and Environmental Issues That Affect Us All. Retrieved from http://www.globalissues.org/article/26/poverty-facts-and-stats

Grameen Shakti. (2016). Diversification and Scaling Up GS Activities through Entrepreneur Development. Retrieved from http://www.gshakti.org/index.php?option=com_content &view=section&layout=blog&id=6&Itemid=57.

Hahn, R., & Gold, S. (2014). Resources and governance in "base of the pyramid"-partnerships: Assessing collaborations between businesses and non-business actors. *Journal of Business Research*, 67(7), 1321-1333.

International Energy Agency (IEA). (2011). Energy for all: Financing access for the poor, World Energy Outlook 2011. Retrieved from http://www.iea.org/media/weowebsite/ energydevelopment/weo2011_energy_for_all-1.pdf

International Energy Agency (IEA). (2014). Africa Energy Outlook. Retrieved from http://www. iea.org/publications/freepublications/publication/WEO2014_AfricaEnergyOutlook.pdf.

International Energy Agency (IEA). (2015a). Energy and Climate Change. Retrieved from https://www.iea.org/publications/freepublications/publication/WEO2015SpecialReporton EnergyandClimateChange.pdf.

International Energy Agency (IEA). (2015b). World Energy Outlook 2015 Executive Summary. Retrieved from http://www.iea.org/publications/freepublications/publication/WEB_ WorldEnergyOutlook2015ExecutiveSummaryEnglishFinal.pdf.

International Finance Corporation (IFC). (2012a). From gap to opportunity: Business models for scaling up energy access. Retrieved from http://www.ifc.org/wps/wcm/connect/topics_ ext_content/ifc_external_corporate_site/ifc+sustainability/learning+and+adapting/ knowledge+products/publications/publications_report_gap-opportunity.

International Finance Corporation (IFC). (2012b). Lighting Africa Market Trends Report 2012. Retrieved from http://www.dalberg.com/documents/Lighting_Africa_Market_ Trends_Report_2012.pdf.

Lahimer, A.A., Alghoul, M.A., Yousif, F., Razykov, T.M., Amin, N., & Sopian, K. (2013). Research and development aspects on decentralized electrification options for rural household. *Renewable and Sustainable Energy Reviews*, 24, 314-324.

London, T., Anupindi, R., & Sheth, S. (2010). Creating mutual value: Lessons learned from ventures serving base of the pyramid producers. *Journal of Business Research*, 63(6), 582-594.

Mainali, B., & Silveira, S. (2013). Alternative pathways for providing access to electricity in developing countries. *Renewable Energy*, 57, 299-310.

Modi, V., McDade, S., Lallement, D., & Saghir, J. (2005). Energy services for the millennium development goals. Retrieved from http://www.undp.org/content/dam/aplaws/publication/en/publications/environment-energy/www-ee-library/sustainable-energy/energy-services-for-the-millennium-development-goals/MP_Energy2006.pdf.

Mukherji, S. (2011). SELCO: Solar lighting for the poor. Retrieved from http://www.inclusivebusinesshub.org/forum/topics/selco-india-solar-lighting-for-the-rural-poor-1.

Nania, J., & Vilsack, D. (2010). Put out the fire: Developing sustainable energy policy for all Namibians. *Colo. J. Int'l Envtl. L. & Pol'y*, 21, 287-339.

Parmigiani, A., & Rivera-Santos, M. (2015). Sourcing for the base of the pyramid: Constructing supply chains to address voids in subsistence markets. *Journal of Operations Management*, 33-34, 60-70.

Phelps, G. & Crabtree, S. (2013). Worldwide, median household income about $10,000. Retrieved from http://www.gallup.com/poll/166211/worldwide-median-household-income-000.aspx.

Principles for Responsible Management Education (PRME) (2016). 'About Us, Six Principles', http://www.unprme.org/about-prme/the-six-principles.php, accessed 23 April 2016.

Reficco, E., & Marquez, P. (2009). Inclusive networks for building BOP markets. *Business & Society*, 51(3), 512-556.

Rivera-Santos, M., & Rufín, C. (2010). Global village vs. small town: Understanding networks at the base of the pyramid. *International Business Review*, 19(2), 126-139.

Sakarya, S., Bodur, M., Yildirim-Öktem, Ö., & Selekler-Göksen, N. (2012). Social alliances: Business and social enterprise collaboration for social transformation. *Journal of Business Research*, 65(12), 1710-1720.

Sodhi, M.S., & Tang, C.S. (2014). Supply-chain research opportunities with the poor as suppliers or distributors in developing countries. *Production and Operations Management*, 23(9), 1483-1494.

Sovacool, B.K., & Drupady, I.M. (2012). *Energy Access, Poverty, and Development: The Governance of Small-Scale Renewable Energy in Developing Asia*. Burlington, VT: Ashgate.

Sunny Money (2016). 'Partners: Become a Sunny Money Agent', http://sunnymoney.org/index.php/become-an-agent/, accessed 21 April 2016.

The Climate Group & Goldman Sachs. (2015). The business case for off-grid energy in India. Retrieved from http://www.theclimategroup.org/what-we-do/publications/the-business-case-for-off-grid-energy-in-india.

United Nations (UN). (2014). Sustainable energy "golden thread" connecting economic growth, increased social equity, secretary-general tells ministerial meeting. Retrieved from http://www.un.org/press/en/2014/sgsm15839.doc.htm.

United Nations (UN). (2016a). The Ten Principles of the UN Global Compact. Retrieved from https://www.unglobalcompact.org/what-is-gc/mission/principles.

United Nations (UN). (2016b). The Universal Declaration of Human Rights. Retrieved from http://www.un.org/en/universal-declaration-human-rights.

United Nations Division for Sustainable Development (UN-DESA). (2016). Transforming our world: the 2030 agenda for sustainable development. Retrieved from https://sustainabledevelopment.un.org/post2015/transformingourworld.

Van de Walle, D., Ravallion, M., Mendiratta, V., & Koolwal, G. (2013). Long-term impacts of household electrification in rural India. Policy Research Working Paper Series. Retrieved from http://ideas.repec.org/p/wbk/wbrwps/6527.html.

Van den waeyenberg, S., & Hens, L. (2012). Overcoming institutional distance: Expansion to base-of-the-pyramid markets. *Journal of Business Research*, 65(12), 1692-1699.

Webb, J.W., Kistruck, G.M., Ireland, R.D., & Ketchen, Jr., D.J. (2009). The entrepreneurship process in base of the pyramid markets: The case of multinational enterprise/nongovernment organization alliances. *Entrepreneurship Theory and Practice*, 34(3), 555-581.

Inara Scott teaches courses on environmental law and sustainable business at Oregon State University's College of Business. Professor Scott's research at Oregon State centers on energy regulation, the legal and policy implications of climate change, and sustainable business practices. Professor Scott received her JD, *summa cum laude*, from Lewis & Clark Law School in Portland, Oregon, and her BA from Duke University, *summa cum laude*. Prior to teaching, she practiced law for over a decade, specializing in energy and administrative law.

Inara.Scott@bus.oregonstate.edu

Section 2
Organizational Challenges and Strategies

5

New Collaborative Ways of Organizing Corporate Social Responsibility

Inger Jensen
Roskilde University, Denmark

Introduction

This chapter describes the evolving perception and understanding of corporate social responsibility (CSR) in general and its related empirical evidence based on the United Nations Global Compact (UNGC) longitudinal surveys. It includes analysis of how CEOs of UNGC signatories have responded to related challenges as responsible managers. They call for necessary regulatory frameworks that further facilitate existing/emerging willingness and capacity and provide innovative solutions where either market conditions or regulations are not in place. The chapter illustrates active collaborative approaches and innovative solutions implemented by two Danish companies, Maersk and Novo Nordisk. They are among those transformational organizations (UNGC LEAD group) that are not waiting for markets to demand sustainability or governments to regulate it. Maersk, a shipping company, has facilitated trade in developing countries through logistic knowledge and digital solutions and has supported a ship recycling supplier working toward sustainable practices; Novo Nordisk, a pharmaceutical company, has invented a global project to identify city lifestyles that could be changed to prevent diabetes and organized a way to prevent price-up processes of insulin in Kenya. These cases are based on in-depth understanding of global and local regulation, markets and market failures related to sustainability, and they demonstrate a capacity to collaborate with governments, civil society organizations and other partners in the private sector. The companies illustrate innovative approaches that actively transform and improve conditions for sustainability. The chapter also describes a new regulatory framework that has recently been put in place in Denmark. In such a way the chapter relates to an overall expectation that the 17 UN Sustainability Development Goals (SDGs) provide further steps to involve national governments in taking care of the world for the next generation.

From Individual Corporate Responsibility to Collaborative Initiatives

The theoretical discussion about CSR started in the 1950s. One of the movement's pioneers, H.R. Bowen, wrote the book *Social Responsibilities of the Businessman* (Bowen, 1953). The author noted that "businessmen are responsible for the consequences of their actions in a sphere somewhat wider than that covered by their profit-and-loss statements" (p. 44). It was a noteworthy precursor of what would later be called the business's impact on society and environment. Further discussion about CSR in the second half of the 20th century mainly focused on the individual company and its responsibility (Frederick, 1960; K. Davis, 1960; K. Davis, 1967; K. Davis, 1973; K. Davis *et al.*, 1966; Freeman, 1984; Carroll, 1999). From the beginning of the 21st century, however, the focus developed from a company-oriented approach to more collaborative and institutional approaches. The initiative taken by Kofi Annan, secretary-general of the UN in 2000 to establish the UNGC, underscores the importance of fostering global collaboration on corporations' social responsibility. As an initiative by the UN, the Global Compact has neither the legislative power to regulate global corporate responsibility nor the legitimate force to control and sanction offenses. The fundamentally new suggestion created by the UNGC was to develop common policies to operationalize processes, where responsibility in praxis can be described transparently and legitimized. By 2016, with more than 8,000 companies and 4,000 non-businesses as signatories, the UNGC is the largest voluntary corporate responsibility initiative in the world. (UNGC, 2016a)

How Responsible Managers Experience Challenges and Opportunities

The UNGC has initiated a series of studies that gives insight into the experience and perspectives of CEOs who are signatories. Since 2007 a UN global CEO study has been carried out and published every three years. The 2007 study is referred to in the following studies that are available at UNGC's online library (UNGC, 2016b). The studies of 2010, 2013, and 2016 were commissioned by the UNGC and carried out by Accenture (UNGC-Accenture, 2010, 2013, 2016).[1] These studies dealt with issues related to business's responsibility and sustainability and offered statistical data on various issues of concern to CEOs all over the world. This chapter uses these studies to present managers' understanding of how the relationship between business and corporate sustainability has changed over this period.

In 2007 the CEOs were optimistic regarding the possibility of the individual company practicing the principles of sustainability. The impression was that consumers and the market would demand and support sustainability. In 2010 CEOs were still confident that markets would align business success with sustainability-related objectives. In the context of continued recessionary pressures from 2008, however, social and environmental issues had become secondary in importance in shaping the future success of their companies. By 2013 the survey indicated that although CEOs understood the importance of social and environmental sustainability to their business, many had shifted their focus back to traditional metrics of short-term financial concerns, and market forces were not aligning in the way that had been predicted in 2010. As Accenture concludes:

> During our conversations this year, business leaders described a plateau beyond which they cannot progress without radical changes in market structures and systems, driven by a common understanding of global priorities (UNGC-Accenture, 2013, p. 5)

The 2013 study concludes that market forces fail to incentivize global sustainability practices. It is important, however, to note that the CEO survey responses are from more than 100 countries all over the world, including both developed and developing countries. Therefore, survey results reflect a very generic concept of the market. It would be helpful to have a more in-depth analysis of markets and market failures in different parts of the world to better understand the implications for market structures and systems and their impact on sustainability practices.

The 2013 CEO study notes that 83% of CEOs believe that government policymaking and regulation will be critical in harnessing sustainability as a transformative force (UNGC-Accenture, 2013). Some CEOs expressed the need for regulation and taxation; some were worried about too much regulation or unforeseeable regulation; and others recommended that corporations collaborate with governments to make relevant regulation and/or to partner with peers, nongovernmental organizations (NGOs) and local authorities to find new systems and solutions. These CEOs are from nations worldwide with a huge variety of national regulations and

---

1 These studies were based on in-depth interviews and supplemented by online surveys. The 2010 survey was completed by 766 out of 7,000 signatories from nearly 100 countries, and the 2013 survey by 1,000 out of 8,000 signatories from 103 countries. In 2016, interviews with 50 CEOs of leading innovators supplemented the online surveys completed by signatories from more than 150 countries.

standards. The political and ideological attitudes toward market regulations vary widely across the globe, thus making it difficult for the international community to derive a consensus about needed regulations. In 2015, however, the 193 member states of the UN agreed on 17 SDGs over the next 15 years to end extreme poverty, fight inequality and injustice, and protect our planet (UNGC, 2015). These are broad goals and plans, not tied to specific governmental approaches.

The 17 SDGs transcend the principles of the Global Compact that the signatories committed to follow, but in the 2016 CEO study the UNCG signatories are incited to collaborate and make partnerships that will extend the network's efforts to support the SDGs.

The focus of the 2013 CEO study was to find out what characterized successful and responsible companies. Throughout the report are categories of companies' approaches to sustainability from relatively passive to highly proactive approaches. These include:

- A reactive and adaptive approach adjusting to societal expectations and regulative demands

- An approach focused on philanthropy, compliance, mitigation, and license to operate

- An approach characterized by individual business initiatives for sustainability through new products, services, and business models

- An approach based on collaboration, looking beyond the firm, and creating new systems to contribute to a new global architecture of sustainability. This approach is also called transformational as it contributes to transforming the conditions for sustainability.

Toward Transformational Approaches

This section illustrates active and innovative approaches that contribute to transforming the conditions for sustainability. The two cases involve Danish companies that are among those that are not waiting for markets to demand sustainability or governments to regulate. They are solving problems with innovative solutions and collaborative approaches. As such, they belong to an advanced group of sustainable companies, called the UNGC-LEAD. To become a LEAD participant the company must be committed to taking an active part in projects that go beyond the Global Compact and that support the SDGs. There are 43 LEAD participants from 22 countries *(UNGC-LEAD, 2016)*.

The case companies, the Maersk Group and Novo Nordisk, were chosen to illustrate transformational approaches to moving beyond the bottom line and contributing to the advancement of the respective SDGs.

Maersk Group: Addressing Systemic Issues

The Maersk Group is a worldwide conglomerate operating in 130 countries. In addition to owning one of the world's largest shipping companies, the group is involved in a wide range of activities in ports and logistics, and in the oil and gas industries. Based on an interview by the author with Annette Stube, director of group sustainability, and on the company's sustainability report, this section illustrates how systemic issues can be addressed and changed (Maersk-Group, 2015).

Change at a systemic level is the only way to effectively address and solve certain sustainability issues. Maersk's sustainability report notes that systemic issues require leadership and collaboration. To accomplish this many actors have to move in the same direction at the same time. The report describes five systemic issues (Maersk-Group, 2015, pp. 6-13):

- Enabling trade through projects

- Exploring solutions for ship recycling

- Taking the lead on climate change

- Tackling corruption

- Establishing global partnerships for change

To provide examples of systemic solutions when existing markets fail to support sustainability, the following sections focus on the issues related to enabling trade and to ship recycling.

Enabling Trade

Maersk states that "Trade is a key driver of growth and development and a core element in our sustainability strategy to unlock growth for countries and communities" (ibid., p. 8). The projects are related to SDG 8, Good Jobs and Economic Growth, and SDG 9, Innovation and Infrastructure.

Maersk's Enabling Trade initiative includes three pilot projects:

- A digital shipping information pipeline in East Africa

- Developing a trading hub in East Indonesia

- Educating traders through ConnectAmericas

This chapter will describe the digital shipping information pipeline in East Africa and developing a trading hub in East Indonesia as illustrative examples of systemic solutions.

A Digital Shipping Information Pipeline in East Africa

The overall objective of this project is to enable East African business participation in regional and global trade. Together with Trademark East Africa, in 2014 Maersk mapped 200 different and often paper-based communication interactions between 30 individuals or organizations involved in the transport of goods from East Africa to Europe. This mapping showed that the cost of time spent on documentation processes is equal to the actual shipment costs. Transport and logistics costs in East Africa are on average 50% to 60% higher than in the United States and Europe. To remove this documentation barrier to trade, Maersk is piloting a shared, cloud-based digital document-exchange infrastructure (the shipping information pipeline). Trademark East Africa secured broad engagement with relevant stakeholders in 2015, allowing Maersk to create ownership and a governance structure for the project. With this in place, Maersk began piloting the shipping information pipeline.

Developing a Trading Hub in East Indonesia

The government of East Indonesia has decided to establish Bitung as a hub port for shipping commodities to global markets. In 2015 the Alliance for the Economic Development of Bitung was signed between relevant ministries and the Maersk Group. The alliance intends to document the challenges in the exporting of products, including clearance, terminal handling, and regional as well as global connectivity of the Bitung area. It is also designed to improve the port, support local manufacturing, create jobs, and possibly invest in infrastructure. When the Bitung project is documented and the effects established, it should be possible to replicate the actions in other locations.

Ship Recycling

Another initiative of Maersk is exploring solutions related to ship recycling, which is a heavily debated issue known to attract great stakeholder attention, mainly due to work practices on beaches. To many, ship recycling has become synonymous with negative human-rights impacts and environmental degradation. The ship recycling project relates to SDG 8, Good Jobs and Economic Growth; SDG 13, Climate Action; and SDG 17, Partnerships for the Goals.

According to Maersk, out of a total of 768 ships dismantled globally in 2015, 469 were sold to facilities on the three beaches with ship recycling yards in India, Pakistan, and Bangladesh. Despite Maersk's and other ship owners' insistence on responsible recycling, there has been no change in practices. Currently, responsible recycling is possible only in a limited number of yards in China and Turkey. On average, using one of these yards has an added cost of US$1 to 2 million per recycled vessel (ibid., p. 11). This example illustrates clearly that the existing market conditions do not support sustainability.

In 2015 Maersk decided that:

> The Group should initiate engagement with a number of carefully selected yards in Alang, India. We will work directly with these to upgrade their practices to comply with our standards. We will engage with facilities as they receive our ships for recycling by having Maersk group employed

staff on-site to ensure upgrading of standards and conditions are made. … At the same time, we know that the problem extends far beyond our own vessels. To mitigate this larger problem, we want to involve other ship owners, engage a broader coalition to help upgrade the Alang area to get better waste facilities, hospitals and a general upgrade of all the facilities on the beach. The more ship owners that commit to engaging over this issue, the greater the leverage for change. (ibid., p. 11)

Novo Nordisk: Transformational and Philanthropic

Novo Nordisk is a global healthcare company with more than 90 years of innovation and leadership in diabetes care. Headquartered in Denmark, Novo Nordisk employs 41,600 people in 75 countries and markets its products in more than 180 countries.

Novo Nordisk's sustainability report (Novo Nordisk, 2016b) addresses the 17 UN SDGs, noting that:

> The Global Goals are ambitious, as they should be. It is a tall task to safeguard the world's global health and development challenges. To succeed, governments, civil society organizations and the private sector need to work together as partners in the implementation. (Novo Nordisk, 2015)

As shown in Figure 5.1, Novo Nordisk contributes to SDGs in order of its priority: Good Health (3), Partnerships for the Goals (17), Sustainable Cities and Communities (11), Responsible Consumption (12), and Reduced Inequality (10).

Figure 5.1 **Novo Nordisk's proportional contribution to SDGs**
Source: Susanne Stormer, Novo Nordisk.

Novo Nordisk has a special ownership and voting structure that favors long-term business interest. This explains why the two projects described below are supported by the board although they do not seem profitable from a short-term perspective (Novo Nordisk, 2016c).

The descriptions of the projects Cities Changing Diabetes and Accessibility and Affordability of Diabetes Care illustrate sustainability approaches that actively transform the existing conditions by a variety of collaboration and are based on Novo Nordisk's annual report (Novo Nordisk, 2015) and interviews conducted by the author with Susanne Stormer, vice president for corporate sustainability.

Cities Changing Diabetes

Of the estimated 415 million people worldwide with diabetes, about 50% are diagnosed, about 25% receive care, about 12.5% achieve treatment targets, and about 6% live a life free from diabetes-related complications (Novo Nordisk, 2015, p. 23).

Type 2 diabetes is largely preventable. About nine cases in ten could be avoided by making lifestyle changes. Healthful lifestyle change is the best way to fight the diabetes epidemic. While cities have the potential to bring about significant health benefits for residents, the vast human and economic burden of diabetes is currently being driven by the way people live in cities. Founding partners Novo Nordisk, the University College London, and the Steno Diabetes Center have been joined by the cities of Copenhagen, Houston, Johannesburg, Mexico City, Shanghai, Tianjin, and Vancouver in the effort to identify, understand, and address the root causes of diabetes in cities. The project has a three-phase strategy: to map the challenge, to share learnings with cities around the world, and to act as a catalyst for action to defeat the rise of diabetes in cities. This first-of-its-kind research found that vulnerability to diabetes in cities around the world is influenced far more than previously thought by social and cultural factors. The ongoing project can be followed online (Novo-Nordisk, 2016a).

Because the Cities Changing Diabetes supports preventing diabetes, it seems at first glance to reduce the market for diabetes care. However, the knowledge obtained about the social and cultural factors involving diabetes will increase awareness of the individual and societal consequences of diabetes that is left untreated or whose treatment is delayed. Thus, over the long-term the company can improve its partnership with stakeholders. In that sense it can be called transformational and philanthropic.

Accessibility and Affordability

In each of the countries of India, Nigeria, Ghana, and Kenya, Novo Nordisk has applied business models adapted to the local environment in order to increase access to care for the working poor. The aim is to develop sustainable solutions that create value for people with diabetes, their communities and Novo Nordisk.

Since 2012, Novo Nordisk has partnered with the Kenyan Ministry of Health and faith-based organizations that manage approximately 1,000 health facilities in Kenya. At the time the project was initiated, the price of a vial of insulin could be as high as 1,800 Kenyan shillings (approximately US$18), and insulin was often out of stock at pharmacies. The partnership with faith-based organizations has succeeded in limiting price markups, ultimately controlling the price that the patient has to pay at the pharmacy, and ensuring that insulin is more accessible in Kenya. Today, the price of a vial of insulin has been reduced to 500 Kenyan shillings (approximately US$5), and insulin is available in 184 facilities compared to only 53 in 2012. In 2015, the project covered 28 of Kenya's 47 counties. In collaboration with the faith-based organizations and the Kenya Defeat Diabetes Association, diabetes patient-support groups have been established; 1,100 healthcare professionals have received training in diabetes care; and centers of excellence for diabetes care have been established in connection with large public hospitals. This project has enhanced accessibility and affordability and is an example of a partnership that helps society, patients, Novo Nordisk, and its pharmaceutical peers.

The differential pricing policy is another part of Novo Nordisk's global initiative to promote access to healthcare for the least developed countries (LDCs, as defined by the UN) by providing insulin at or below 20% of the average market price for human insulin in the western world (Novo Nordisk, 2015). In 2015 the total number of patients treated with insulin through this initiative was about 411,000 in 23 of the world's 48 poorest countries.

Novo Nordisk's customers in the global world compose a complexity of national governments, health authorities, assurance companies, and private agencies in developed and developing countries. The projects discussed in this chapter integrate various management disciplines that do not operate independently in the organization. A recent doctoral dissertation by Novo Nordisk global advisor Lykke Schmidt, "Making Partnership Worthwhile - A Case of Valuing in Practice," analyzes how different value perspectives are balanced within departments of the organization (Schmidt, 2016). The need to balance different value perspectives goes beyond different departments of an organization and even the organization's partnerships with its respective business partners and other stakeholders.

National Regulations Supporting UNGC Initiatives

As discussed in the section based on the CEO studies and illustrated by the case studies, sustainability also depends on regulation and supporting mechanisms.

One can distinguish between regulation that defines substantial obligations, limits, and taxes related to corporate responsibility and regulation that contributes to transparency of CSR. This section focuses on the latter, illustrating the approach taken in Denmark.

According to the Danish Auditors' organization FSR, the Nordic countries, France, the Netherlands, the United Kingdom, and South Africa are pioneers in developing regulations that support the Global Compact initiatives (FSR, 2015).

Since 2009, the Danish Financial Statements Act has required large companies to indicate in their annual report whether they have a CSR policy. The demands on reporting have developed gradually since then, and in 2015 the national parliament of Denmark updated the Financial Statements Act[2] to incorporate the EU directive on disclosure of nonfinancial information[3]. By 2018, 1,100 Danish large companies must comply with the new legal demands, which include:

1. Description of the business model

2. Policies regarding:

   o Climate and environmental matters

   o Social and employee matters

   o Respect for human rights

   o Anticorruption and bribery matters

3. For all four fields of responsibility the company must *follow* or *explain*.

4. To *follow* means to comply with the directive and report on all four fields of responsibility about:

   o Policy

   o Actions

   o Due diligence processes – when relevant

   o Risks of negative impact

   o Use of nonfinancial key performance indicators (KPIs)

   o Results

5. To *explain* means that the company must indicate why it has not reported on some of the four fields of responsibility.

The new demands increase focus on how CSR is integrated into the policies and internal management of the company. To explore how prepared Danish companies are to comply with the new rules, the Confederation of Danish Industry (DI) and Carve Consulting[4] have examined the CSR and Communication of Progress (CoP) reports for 2014 of all Danish companies that are members of the UNGC.

The Carve Consulting study concludes that most companies still have a long way to go in integrating CSR systematically into practice and creating transparency regarding the companies' positive and negative impacts in all four responsibility fields. The main findings are that the largest companies are the most prepared to meet the new demands (Carve Consulting, 2016a).

---

2 § 99a and § 99b
3 Directive 2014/95/EU.
4 http://carve.dk/

Concluding Remarks and Further Reflections

The business leaders in the 2013 CEO study described a plateau beyond which they could not progress without radical changes in market structures and systems, driven by a common understanding of global priorities. The LEAD case companies described above are at the forefront of the Danish regulation regarding integrating sustainability in their strategies. They have contributed in the global context to create new sustainable solutions where markets and local regulation have failed to support sustainability. To support the SDGs by partnerships with governments, civil society organizations, and business partners – even competitors – companies need to balance different value perspectives that go beyond various departments of an organization and traditional business models.

The Danish regulations described in this chapter contribute to transparency and focus on how CSR is integrated into the policies and internal management of the company. They also demand that the companies critically reflect on their positive and negative impacts on society and environment. As the Carve Consulting study concluded, the largest companies are the most prepared to meet the new demands. An important further study would be to explore sustainability approaches of small or medium-sized enterprises.

In the 2013 study, the CEOs noticed that many investors had shifted their focus back to traditional metrics of short-term financial concerns. In contrast to this the LEAD case company Novo Nordisk has a special ownership and voting structure that favors long-term business interests. Further research could address how different kinds of ownership influence sustainability approaches.

To contribute to these changes, business schools supporting the UN PRME should educate managers of the next generation to make more in-depth analysis of markets, market barriers, and failures in different parts of the world. Managers should also understand the relations between companies' innovative solutions and national regulatory frameworks' impact on sustainability practices.

References

Bowen, H.R. (1953). Social responsibilities of the businessman. NewYork: Harper & Row.

Carroll, A.B. (1999). Corporate social responsibility: Evolution of a definitional construct. *Business & Society*, 38(3), 268-295.

Carve-Consulting. (2016a). *CSR reports - danske virksomheder.* Retrieved from http://csrrapport.dk.

Davis, K. (1960). Can business afford to ignore social responsibilities? *California Management Review*, 2, 70-76.

Davis, K. (1967). Understanding the social responsibility puzzle: What does the businessman owe to society? *Business Horizons*, 10, 45-50.

Davis, K. (1973). The case for and against business assumption of social responsibilities. *Academy of Management Journal*, 16, 312-322.

Davis, K., & Blomstrom, R.L. (1966). *Business and Its Environment.* New York: McGraw-Hill.
Frederick, W.C. (1960). The growing concern over business responsibility. *California Management Review,* 2, 54-61.
Freeman, R.E. (1984). *Strategic Management: A Stakeholder Approach.* Boston: Pitman.
FSR. (2015). Nye krav til redegørelse for samfundsansvar. Retrieved from http://www.fsr. dk/~/media/Files/Faglig%20viden/Publikationer/99a%202015/brochure%2012%20 sider%20med%20skemaer%20web3.ashx.
Maersk-Group. (2015). Sustainability Report 2015. Retrieved from http://www.maersk. com/~/media/the%20maersk%20group/sustainability/files/publications/2016/files/ maersk_group_sustainability_report_2015_a3_final.pdf.
Novo-Nordisk. (2015). Novo-Nordisk Annual Report 2015. Retrieved from http://www. novonordisk.com/content/dam/Denmark/HQ/Commons/documents/Novo-Nordisk-Annual-Report-2015.PDF.
Novo-Nordisk. (2016a). Cities Changing Diabetes. Retrieved from http:// citieschangingdiabetes.com.
Novo-Nordisk. (2016b). Communication on Progress 2015. Retrieved from http://www. novonordisk.com/content/dam/Denmark/HQ/Commons/documents/Novo-Nordisk-UN-Global-Compact-2015.pdf.
Novo-Nordisk. (2016c). Ownership. Retrieved from http://www.novonordisk.com/ about-novo-nordisk/novo-nordisk-in-brief/ownership.html.
Schmidt, L. (2016). Making partnership worthwhile: A case of valuing in practice. (PhD dissertation), Aalborg University, Denmark.
UN-Global-Compact. (2015). 17 goals to transform our world. https://www.unglobalcompact. org/sdgs
UN-Global-Compact. (2016a). Retrieved from https://www.unglobalcompact.org/.
UN-Global-Compact. (2016b). Explore our library. Retrieved from https://www. unglobalcompact.org/library.
UNGC-Accenture. (2010). A new era of sustainabiity. Retrieved from https://www. unglobalcompact.org/docs/news_events/8.1/UNGC_Accenture_CEO_Study_2010.pdf.
UNGC-Accenture. (2013). Architects of a better world. Retrieved from https://www. unglobalcompact.org/docs/news_events/8.1/UNGC_Accenture_CEO_Study_2013.pdf.
UNGC-LEAD. (2016). LEAD Commitment, Retrieved from https://www.unglobalcompact. org/take-action/leadership/gc-lead/what-is-lead.

Inger Jensen is Associate Professor emeritus in Social Psychology and Sociology at the Department of Social Sciences and Business at Roskilde University. Her research focus is on the societal processes that define legitimacy of organizational activities and on institutionalization of managing CSR. She has authored several texts on corporate responsibility and legitimacy, is author and editor of "The Balanced Company" (Gower), and has recently authored contributions to methodological and epistemological reflections on supervising master students. She has chaired a pan-European PhD seminar for several years and has management experience as member or head of several organizational boards. She has previously served as Deputy Vice-Chancellor of Roskilde University.

inger@ruc.dk

6
Embedding the Human Rights and Labor UNGC Principles
A Tata Steel Case Study

Sunil Bhaskaran
Tata Steel, India

Priyadarshini Sharma
Tata Steel, India

Context

Corporations spanning international boundaries in their operations and sourcing must increasingly factor in cross-border realities in the conduct of business. These include social and environmental aspects and call for framing of policies and responses that translate globally accepted norms and practices on the ground. The United Nations Global Compact (UNGC) provides guidelines based on its Ten Principles that have gained widespread acceptance in building effective governance practices across sectors and geographies. Even as we classify the contextual landscape as related to the developed, developing, underdeveloped, and emerging economies, the underlying significance of these principles for organizations irrespective of the stage of the economic growth they may be operating in remains uncontested.

About Tata Steel
Tata Steel Group is among the top global steel companies with an annual crude steel capacity of nearly 30 million tons per annum (MnTPA). It is now

the world's second-most geographically diversified steel producer, with operations in 26 countries and a commercial presence in over 50 countries. The group's vision is to be the world's steel industry benchmark in value creation and corporate citizenship.

Tata Steel India: Established in 1907, Tata Steel founded and developed India's first industrial city, now Jamshedpur, where the company established one of Asia's first integrated steel plants. The Jamshedpur Works currently comprises a 9.7 MnTPA crude-steel production facility and a variety of finishing mills. Tata Steel has a significant presence in allied and downstream areas through its various strategic business units. The company also possesses and operates captive iron ore, coking coal, and chrome ore mines.

The company dedicated the first phase of the 6 MnTPA greenfield steel project at Kalinganagar to the state of Odisha on November 18, 2015.

The corporate social responsibility (CSR) activities of the company have expanded to more than 800 villages in the states of Jharkhand, Odisha, and Chhattisgarh.

The first six principles of the UNGC framework pertain to human rights and core labor compliances. The rationale for the emphasis on embedding human rights and labor-related aspects is seemingly two-fold. First, human rights and labor issues have become increasingly central to business sustainability, and frameworks such as the UNGC principles aim to contribute to identification and mitigation of risks irrespective of a company's location or size. Secondly, the UNGC principles' voluntary profile serves as an incentive for forward-looking adapters to mainstream their practices and gauge impending footprints.

From a practitioner's perspective, the integration of the UNGC principles into everyday business operations has always merited analysis. At Tata Steel, one of the founding signatories of the UNGC, the legacy of pioneering work practices and community welfare provides the context for adaptation of the compact's principles. This chapter discusses the philosophical underpinnings, policy framework, management system, partnerships, and resultant learning for continual improvement involved in the application of the UNGC, with spotlight on Principles 1–6, at Tata Steel's Jamshedpur Works.

The Overarching Framework

At Tata Steel, the overarching framework of the Tata values and the Tata Code of Conduct (TCoC) has long upheld respect for stakeholders' rights. The Universal Declaration of Human Rights, International Labour Organization (ILO) Conventions, and International Convention on the Rights of the Child, among others, serve to guide business decisions. Respect for the rights of indigenous communities with special emphasis on women and children; creation of decent work; and quality of life has also fostered many initiatives. The company's policies on social accountability (human rights at the workplace), corporate responsibility, affirmative action, and HIV/AIDS are other manifestations of its commitment to human rights and their evolving application in the workplace.

Tata Steel's affirmative action policy, for instance, holds that diversity in the workplace positively impacts business. It guides initiatives directed at improving employability. It seeks to encourage business entrepreneurs from socially disadvantaged communities and increase access of talented youth from marginalized backgrounds to quality higher education. The HIV/AIDS policy ensures non-discrimination of affected personnel. The core principles of the TCoC similarly state that the company must "respect the human rights and dignity of all our stakeholders." As an equal opportunity employer, Tata Steel upholds that it will engage in "no unfair discrimination on any ground." The TCoC further articulates that "We don't employ children at our workplace" and "We don't use forced labour in any form."

> "In a free enterprise the community is not just another stakeholder in the business but in fact the very purpose of its existence."
>
> J.N. Tata, Founder, Tata Steel

Figure 6.1 **Principles 1–6 of the Ten Principles of the UNGC**

UNGC Principles 1–6

Human Rights

Principle 1: Businesses should support and respect the protection of internationally proclaimed human rights; and

Principle 2: make sure that they are not complicit in human rights abuses.

Labour

Principle 3: Businesses should uphold the freedom of association and the effective recognition of the right to collective bargaining;

Principle 4: the elimination of all form of forced and compulsory labour;

Principle 5: the effective abolition of child labour; and

Principle 6: the elimination of discrimination in respect of employment and occupation

Furthering Voluntary Initiative: SA8000 as a partnering tool

In its existence over a century, Tata Steel has a history of pioneering practices, which include implementation of the eight-hour workday (1912), provision of free medical aid (1915), and the workers' provident fund scheme (1920), to cite a few examples. With the objective of comparing performance over time, generating transparency, and driving improvement, Tata Steel (India) in 2003 sought to apply the global Social Accountability 8000 (SA8000) standard. The company's steel works was certified to SA8000 in 2004 and continuously recertified every three years thereafter. In 2016, it was recommended for recertification. The elements of the Universal Declaration of Human Rights and ILO Conventions encompass the SA8000 clauses. In sync with the UNGC labor principles, SA8000 covers core elements.

SA8000 is a global, auditable, and voluntary certification standard for decent working conditions that stipulates various provisions for workers, including those in the supply chain, through its nine clauses addressing the following:

- Child labor
- Forced or compulsory labor
- Health and safety
- Freedom of association and right to collective bargaining
- Discrimination
- Disciplinary practices
- Working hours
- Remuneration
- Management system

The voluntary standard comprises provision for external, third-party surveillance audits at half-yearly intervals. It has served as a partnering tool in ensuring the UNGC labor clauses are implemented on the ground in letter and spirit. Awareness-raising and continual improvement on these aspects is a vital part of deploying human rights and labor principles addressing the workforce – a key stakeholder. Tata Steel started its journey on raising awareness and compliance on social issues in supply chains by initiating third-party audits of the vendors it engages. The management commitment toward respecting human rights and elements of the UNGC and SA8000 is expressed in the company's social accountability policy, which is dedicated to upholding human rights at the workplace.

The Tata Steel Human Rights-Business Interface Domain

Tata Steel employees, guided by the TCoC, adhere to international conventions and national as well as local laws. A number of forums are in place for capturing and addressing concerns. The illustrated Human Rights-Business Interface (Table 6.1) lists indicative operations, supply chain, and community interfaces where due diligence may be warranted, depending on the degree of business involvement. The appropriate corrective and preventive steps can be taken accordingly.

Table 6.1 **The Tata Steel Human Rights-Business Interface Domain**

Operations	Supply chain	Community
· Employment terms and working conditions including health and safety (also see supply chain) · Child rights · Consumer issues including health and safety in product usage · Security practices · Right to privacy	· Sourcing practices including sourcing from conflict zones · Applicable legal compliances such as no child or forced labor, payment of wages, hours of work, health and safety, etc.	· Economic, social, cultural, and property rights · Health, safety, and security · Indigenous people and child rights

Freedom of Association and Right to Collective Bargaining

Tata Steel has respected the right of employees for freedom of association and collective bargaining. Tata Workers' Union (TWU) serves as the representative body for workers. The company does not interfere with the functioning of the TWU. The TWU representatives are elected through a free and fair election process. It is ensured that there is no discrimination, harassment, or retaliation for being members or participating in trade-union activities.

Among union-management consultative forums, the SA8000 Management Review Committee includes active roles being played on deliberations regarding labor and workplace issues by the TWU leadership. The wide-ranging agenda for management–union meetings encompasses targets and reviews of various functions.

Tata Steel's joint consultative process between management and union has contributed to its industrial harmony of over 85 years.

No Forced or Compulsory Labor

Tata Steel does not engage in or support the use of forced or compulsory labor. It is ensured that employees work voluntarily. No work is demanded from the workforce as a means of repayment of debt of any kind.

Original documents are sought for verification at the time of joining and returned immediately. Tata Steel or any entity providing services to it does not engage in or support trafficking in human beings and condemns the same.

No Child Labor

Tata Steel does not engage in or support the use of child labor. No employee in Tata Steel is less than 18 years of age. Documentary evidence of proof of age is verified at the time of recruitment. Relevant external authorities or referral doctors may also be consulted for verification in this regard as and when required.

This policy toward child labor is also communicated to all contractors and suppliers. A written commitment from all contractors and suppliers for complying with SA8000 requirements is taken. The age for the workforce engaged by the contractors is verified. All vendors in business with Tata Steel are required to give a declaration that they are not engaging child labor. This is also verified at the time of third-party vendor audits. Tata Steel urges all stakeholders to honor the commitment of not engaging in or supporting the use of child labor through its internal/external communication and dialogue.

The company facilitates many educational initiatives in the communities where it operates to support school programs through CSR projects. These include interventions in early childhood education, mid-day meals, school infrastructure, scholarships and aid, residential schools for tribal children, initiatives to improve quality of education in schools, and the 1,000 Schools Program in the state of Odisha.

No Discrimination

Tata Steel does not engage in or support any discrimination in hiring, remuneration, access to training, promotion, termination, or retirement based on race, caste, birth, national or social origin, religion, disability, gender, sexual orientation, family responsibilities, marital status, union membership, political opinions, or age.

The company has formulated guidelines that promote equal access to employment, promotion, and training. It pays equal remuneration to men and women for the same category of work per the Equal Remuneration Act of 1976. There is a system in place to provide redressal for grievances of employees who may be affected by discrimination.

No discrimination is made toward employees who become disabled during the working period with consideration given for rehabilitation.

Supported by policy intent, the UNGC framework's human rights and labor principles find regular reiteration in decision-making.

Implementation Challenges, Solutions, and Opportunities

Implementing the UNGC principles in managing workplace issues, including the supply chains, has offered Tata Steel many opportunities to create multiple forms of value, such as human, social, environmental, and economic. Sustainability approaches involve moving away from the linear progression of individual bottom lines and moving toward drawing value from their inter-linkages (Sharma, 2009). The expectations of business on labor, human rights, due diligence, and social inclusion call for multifaceted program design wherein dialogue across internal and external stakeholders assumes a vital role and is a prerequisite for forging sustainable solutions. Review of effectiveness and efficiency points of these programs on an ongoing basis is also a must. In the course of implementing UNGC Principles and SA8000, a major lesson has been in breaking functional silos. This has been achieved through regular monitoring, reviews, and interactive approaches. The collective experience for the company and its partners on the somewhat intangible domain of social compliances has resulted in formalizing expectations and delivery mechanisms. The awareness-raising and shared learning has generated new ideas resulting from a better understanding across functional domains (Table 6.2). A detailed review of the company's social, environmental, and ethical approaches is available in its corporate sustainability reports.[1]

A submission for further reading is the Tata Steel case in the Centre for Private Enterprise-Social Accountability International study, "From Words to Action: A Business Case for Implementing Workplace Standards," which reflects on continual improvement through workplace aspects.[2] The study posits that "fulfilling an employer's responsibility for all its workers, including contracted ones, is a major issue for every business in today's global economy." And that "by using the building blocks of specific programs and solutions developed in the

1 The corporate sustainability reports can be accessed at http://www.tatasteel.com/sustainability/csr-reports.asp.
2 CIPE-SAI study, "From Words to Action: A Business Case for Implementing Workplace Standards," http://www.cipe.org/sites/default/files/publication-docs/SAI.pdf.

process of attaining SA8000 compliance, Tata Steel can continue to improve its internal stakeholder relations and be an example of good corporate citizenship to others" (p. 34).

Table 6.2 **Implementation of the UNGC at Tata Steel**

Implementation Strengths and Milestones
· Improvement in statutory compliances resulting from greater focus
· Support from union in social dialogue
· Improvement in supply-chain engagement through third-party audits
· Overall collaborative and cross-functional thrust within steel works in creating systems and processes

Focus Area
· Enhancing compliances company-wide, especially in supply chains

Capacity-Building and Management Education Implications

Sustainability frameworks with specific and defined clauses offer structure and building blocks. However, the task of developing blueprints in letter and spirit in alignment with the frameworks' intent rests with the organization that adopts them. Gearing the personnel to meet the requirements of such frameworks, which may be global and call for local adaptations of their clauses, puts forth the need for awareness and learning for forging business-operations alignment with environmental, social, and governance (ESG) issues. As a process, all recruits at Tata Steel undergo orientation classes that include SA8000 and CSR modules. This exercise enables the company to communicate at the onset its expectations regarding the kind of cultural norms that are to be upheld. Orientation programs provide the sounding board to initiate newcomers, among them new graduates, on challenges that emerge in ensuring social compliances. The company's internship program serves the purpose of preparing managers and leaders of tomorrow. The interning students' project work during such engagement seeks to address solution-finding and also involves research work.

Summary

The UNGC provides a globally relevant framework through its principles for organizations operating across borders in diverse socio-economic and cultural terrains. Progression along the domain of labor and human rights and social inclusion calls for identification and mitigation of vulnerabilities. It also presents many opportunities for differentiation and good practices in addressing ESG challenges. The voluntary nature of the framework facilitates adaptation of responsible mechanisms by organizations at their own pace and in keeping with their stage of growth. The principles provide support toward creating an internal climate of transparency, commitment, and continual improvement. Driving synergies between shop-floor systems and workplace aspects embodied in global approaches necessitates reflection on both the what and the how of programs to be implemented. Clear articulation of policies helps guide the quest for proactive and long-lasting solutions in the course of embedding sustainability frameworks.

At Tata Steel, the path for UNGC implementation is to go beyond compliance and seek opportunities to create a lasting footprint of social value. Cross-cutting elements of the National Voluntary Guidelines of the Government of India and the Global Reporting Initiative as well as non-discriminatory practices such as Affirmative Action and Equal Employment Opportunity, among others, are references in building upon the operational blueprint. The intent to embed and enhance the perspective of these systems in the labor and human-rights approach of the company, and generate best practices of the standard the Tata brand upholds, guides the implementation agenda.

References

Kaufman, E.K. (2009). The case of Tata Steel: Including contract workers as India's integral business stakeholders. In CIPE and SAI, *From Words to Action: A Business Case for Implementing Workplace Standards. Experiences from Key Emerging Markets.* Retrieved from http://www.**cipe**.org/sites/default/files/publication-docs/**SAI**.pdf.

Sharma, P. (2009). SA8000 in Tata Steel. In D. Leipziger (Ed.), *SA8000: The First Decade* (pp. 24-34). Sheffield: Greenleaf.

Tata Steel Corporate Sustainability Reports. Retrieved from http://www.tatasteel.com/sustainability/csr-reports.asp

Sunil Bhaskaran is Vice President of Corporate Services at Tata Steel Limited. He oversees procurement of materials and services, sustainability, security, medical services, delivery and administration of civic infrastructure, and provides leadership to drive human-development initiatives of Tata Steel toward the realization of its corporate citizenship vision. He holds a BTech in chemical engineering from the Indian Institute of Technology, a PGDM from the Indian Institute of Management, and a GMP from Cedep INSEAD in France. He is a member on the Global Advisory Board of Social Accountability International (SAI) in New York.

sunilbhaskaran@tatasteel.com

Priyadarshini Sharma is a Senior Manager at Tata Steel Limited. She holds master's degrees in communication studies and public administration. She is a Tata Administrative Service officer.

priyadarshini.sharma@tatasteel.com

7

Our Need, Your Interest
Responsible Decision-Making in Private Equity[1]

Dianne Lynne Bevelander
Erasmus University Rotterdam, The Netherlands

Michael John Page
Bentley University, USA

Background

The Karmijn Kapitaal case presented in this chapter is primarily focused on socially responsible decision-making when raising investment capital. It encourages debate around the responsibility that investment professionals have when accepting investment commitments from individuals. Readers are invited to consider the extent to which *caveat emptor* should apply when a conflict exists between capital needs of the fund being managed and the true interests of a prospective investor, particularly when all legal requirements are comfortably met. A number of broader issues relevant to the UN Global Compact (UNGC) principles are surfaced throughout the case to encourage readers to look beyond the bottom line when making decisions that are responsible and just. The context of the firm and its philosophy also encourages a dialogue around diversity and inclusion as sources of economic and social advantage for organizations.

1 This case could not have been completed without the encouragement, support, and active engagement of Hadewych Cels, founding partner of Karmijn Kapitaal. The authors would like to acknowledge and thank her for help preparing the case. They would also like to express their appreciation to her fellow founding partners, Désirée van Boxtel and Cilian Jansen Verplanke.

From a Principles for Responsible Management Education (PRME) perspective, Karmijn Kapitaal is an excellent example of how the six PRME principles (*purpose, values, method, research, partnership,* and *dialogue*) can be integrated into the development of a single pedagogical instrument. The case was developed with the active support of the company's founding partners to graphically illustrate the conflicts faced by executives when weighing narrower corporate interests against broader societal responsibilities. It has been written in a manner that justifies its use across a variety of courses – *business ethics, entrepreneurship, investments, business strategy,* and *leadership* – to encourage students to think about their wider responsibilities as future business leaders.

Beyond the Bottom Line

It was the summer of 2012. Hadewych Cels was sitting in her favorite chair in Karmijn Kapitaal's fairly minimalist Amsterdam office staring out the window on the Amstel River[2]. She was deep in thought. The last few years had not been easy. She and her partners were struggling to raise a relatively small fund of around 50 million euros (about US$60 million) for what they considered to be a unique investment strategy.

Hadewych thought back to the meeting she had with Ms. Rossum the day before. She knew they needed the capital that Ms. Rossum wanted to invest, but was troubled by the idea of an 81-year-old widow giving Karmijn all of her savings—some 800,000 euros. Ms. Rossum's enthusiasm for the three partners and the proposition that Hadewych had presented, was such that she made an impassioned appeal to invest all her discretionary savings with Karmijn. Ms. Rossum had been a successful businesswoman, she lived in a beautiful home, and her pension was more than adequate for her ongoing needs. However, Hadewych still wondered whether she should accept the investment and whether it would be prudent for Ms. Rossum to commit her entire bank savings given her current monthly income.

Hadewych continued to reflect on the many conversations she had had with her two business partners, Cilian and Désirée, about ethics, moral character, and the questionable behavior of notable financial market participants leading up to the 2008 global financial crisis. Although these conversations often occurred over an evening glass of wine, they were by no means casual. Rather, they led to a commitment to responsibility, transparency, and honesty as core values for Karmijn Kapitaal that would inform how the firm secured funding and would subsequently invest capital. This commitment entailed taking on a wider concern for the wellbeing of their investors than might be considered the norm within the private-equity world. Karmijn would do things differently!

2 http://www.karmijnkapitaal.nl/1-EN-homepage.html.

Hadewych, Cilian, and Désirée believed that investors should not place more funds with the firm than they could really afford to lose. In spite of a conviction that their investment strategy appropriately managed downside risk, the partners understood the risks inherent in private equity. They wanted to be confident that their investors had the financial capacity to cope with possible illiquidity or loss in investment value with Karmijn without undue strain on their quality of life.

Hadewych and Her Partners

Hadewych, a bright, driven and soft-spoken personality, received her doctorandus in economics at Erasmus University[3]. She subsequently earned a master's degree in applied mathematics before starting as a strategy consultant for Nolan, Norton & Co. Although she loved the variety and intellectual challenge of being a consultant, she wanted to be closer to where business decision-making really takes place. Consequently, she decided to complete an MBA as preparation for a career change from consulting.

While studying for her MBA at Harvard Business School Hadewych learned about private equity and discovered that the hands-on role investors play in the sector appealed to her. This led to her accepting a position immediately after graduating in an investment firm that acquired factories of multinationals that were about to be closed down with a view to giving these *redundant assets* a second life. Although not always successful, the creativity and energy required to turn an operation around and save jobs others considered expendable proved to be both invigorating and rewarding. The experience led Hadewych and three colleagues to spin off from the firm and create Plain Vanilla, an investment firm with aspirations not too dissimilar from those of her former employer[4].

What started as a plan to invest in redundant factories morphed into more general "turnaround investing." Plain Vanilla bought a loss-making division of a professional-services firm as well as a number of factories struggling under receivership. In settings where saving jobs was not automatically linked to economic gain, Hadewych started to see the downsides of working on turnarounds. Sadly, she found herself in an environment where opportunism sometimes takes the lead and where the working atmosphere can turn hostile.

---

3 Prior to the introduction of the three-cycle – bachelor, master, doctorate – Bologna process being introduced into the European higher education area, Dutch universities awarded a doctorandus degree as the first degree. This was considered the equivalent of an English or North American master's degree.

4 Two of Hadewych's three partners at that time, Coen Binnerts and Hein Hoogduin, continue to run Plain Vanilla. The third, Andreas Ezinga, left just after Hadewych and is now a partner in a private-equity fund that focuses on ecommerce and leisure.

Karmijn Kapitaal cofounder Désirée van Boxtel, a friend of Hadewych's since their undergraduate university days, had extensive experience in private equity and entrepreneurship. Her nine years as an entrepreneur began when she and a partner started an interior-design company that they sold successfully in 2007. Prior to this, Désirée worked in private equity for ABN AMRO Bank and engaged with innumerable small- and medium-sized enterprises (SMEs). During this period her dream of becoming an entrepreneur flourished, and she developed an appreciation of how her analytical skills, combined with her creativity and ability to think conceptually, provided the needed expertise to build and grow businesses. Not surprisingly, having sold her interior-design business, Désirée wanted to step back into private equity. She was convinced that her personal experience had equipped her to help entrepreneurs grow their own businesses.

The third partner, Cilian Jansen Verplanke, had been a colleague of Désirée's at ABN AMRO Bank. Cilian left ABN AMRO to set up and lead Rabobank's private-equity investment unit. With more than 20 years of private equity and commercial banking experience, including working with entrepreneurs and managing acquisitions, Cilian ended her banking career as executive vice president responsible for Rabobank's large corporation lending division. During this period, while immersed in bank politics, she began to appreciate how much she missed the energy she had previously derived from working directly with entrepreneurs.

Founding Karmijn Kapitaal

Realizing their common aspiration to establish an investment company that each could be proud of, Hadewych, Désirée, and Cilian got together in 2009 to start a private-equity investment fund together. They shared a common desire to work on their own terms, according to their own work ethics, and with entrepreneurs and SMEs that inspired them.

A mutual friend suggested that they could and should do something with women in investing. Following his suggestion, they began researching female leadership and found considerable international evidence that gender-diverse teams perform better than teams that are exclusively or predominantly male (Hunt *et al.*, 2015; Catalyst, 2013; Erhardt *et al.*, 2003). Their research also showed that although more than a quarter of Netherlands-based SMEs are led by a gender-diverse team, less than 2% of the SME portfolio companies in which private-equity firms invest have such leadership. Clearly, SMEs with gender-diverse management teams represented an under-recognized opportunity for a new investment company entrant. The three prospective partners knew from experience that half of the effort in private equity involves finding opportunities that do not have competing funds chasing them. A relative lack of competitor attention enables the firm's principals to cultivate a relationship with the entrepreneurs as well as give them the time to develop a thorough understanding of the market within which the entrepreneurs operate.

Hadewych, Désirée, and Cilian decided that investing in gender-diverse management teams was going to be their unique positioning statement. Karmijn would be a private equity firm that invests *"in companies that are led by a mixed management team, consisting of a balanced combination of women and men"*. The investment philosophy of partners would be informed by the belief that *"diversity of leadership styles leads to better decision making."*[5]

From their prior experiences in the male-dominated private-equity world, the three women knew the impact that a different voice at the table can make. They were convinced that finding SMEs with a diverse mix of leadership styles among the management team could be crucial to its longer-term success. From their almost half a century of collective experience, Hadewych, Désirée, and Cilian were only too well aware that entrepreneurs do not always excel in surrounding themselves with the best leadership teams. Such teams consist of complementary individuals who balance the talents of a deal-oriented entrepreneur with risk and other management skills – some short-term oriented and others longer-term – in a leadership environment of respect where these different personalities and voices cooperate. Based on their experience, they also knew the chances of finding this mix of styles would be higher in gender-diverse management teams.

Karmijn Kapitaal was born in 2011 and its strategy was set: a unique investment approach focused on investing in SMEs with balanced gender-diverse management teams. The firm would establish itself by raising a relatively small fund of between 30 and 50 million euros. It would also invest only in companies with which the partners believed they could "click." They would not invest in SMEs with leaders – whether male or female – who hired only clones of themselves to principally serve as endorsers of the decisions made by the leader. They would also avoid companies that produced products or offered services of which Karmijn's partners could not feel proud. Aside from these key philosophical criteria, Karmijn Kapitaal's investment strategy would be consistent with industry practice globally. It would invest in a diversified portfolio of companies whose overall cash flows, liquidity, and expense controls are understood and for which appropriate, measurable performance metrics existed or could be established.

Challenging Times

After numerous accepted appointments with institutional investors, and just as many refusals to meet, Hadewych, Désirée, and Cilian realized that their

---

5 http://www.karmijnkapitaal.nl/37-EN-diversity.html. Appreciating the need to address the gender composition of their own organization, the three partners subsequently built their team of professionals with gender in mind. At the time of writing the case, the Karmijn Kapitaal investment team was 37.5% male.

proposition was too small and too new to appeal to the traditional fund-of-funds managers who look to invest in more established investment vehicles. In addition to having a unique – that is, unknown – investment strategy, the three partners began to appreciate that they had been labeled a *first-time team* and not a combination of experienced talent in which big institutional parties were ready to invest.

Faced with early rejection from traditional fund sources early in 2011, Karmijn Kapitaal began to widen its scope and look to raise smaller tickets[6] from wealthy individuals and successful entrepreneurs. This shift in emphasis coincided with considerable media attention that the firm began to receive because of its relatively unique investment strategy. Several interested investors responded. Commitments started flowing in, although only 8 million euros had been raised by summer 2011. The three women were decidedly anxious as they were still far short of their target of 30 to 50 million euros, with some early investor commitments due to expire by the end of the year.

It was at this stage of the firm's development that Hadewych received the inquiry from Ms. Rossum. Reacting to a newspaper article that had recently appeared about the fund, Ms. Rossum asked to meet with the Karmijn team to discuss a possible investment. The meeting was scheduled to take place at the home of Ms. Rossum.

Hadewych, Désirée, and Cilian arrived at the appointed time of their meeting and found themselves greeted by a charismatic 81-year-old lady who lived in a beautiful mansion. She welcomed them enthusiastically, offering them tea and traditional Dutch stroopwafels[7]. As they chatted, the team came to learn that Ms. Rossum had retired from her position as CEO of a Dutch family company. She owned her home, had a monthly pension that comfortably met her needs, and considered herself able to do all that she wanted. Beyond this, she had 800,000 euro sitting idle in the bank. After reading a newspaper article on Karmijn Kapitaal, Ms. Rossum had decided that she would like to invest her bank funds with the firm. She considered the value proposition intriguing and, as a retired female CEO, she wanted to invest in SMEs that recognized the value of having women as an integral and equal component of any leadership team.

A Decision to Be Made

The three partners left Ms. Rossum's home somewhat awed by how astute, informed, and independent she was at her age. Ms. Rossum seemed to instinctively

---

6 Many international venture funds at the time required a minimum commitment of between US$500,000 and US$1 million (see www.dividendsandpreferences. com/2009/07/how-to-invest-in-vc-fund.html?m=1, accessed May 14, 2016. Netherlands regulations dictated that the minimum ticket Karmijn Kapitaal could raise was 100,000 euros.

7 A traditional Dutch waffle made from two thin layers of baked dough with a caramel-like syrup filling in the middle.

warm to Hadewych, and thus she was the partner selected to work closely with Ms. Rossum. Consequently, Hadewych found herself faced with leading the decision of whether Karmijn Kapitaal should accept Ms. Rossum's commitment.

Discussion Items

- *Is investing in Karmijn Kapitaal a good idea in the first place?* One might argue that there are sound reasons why institutional investors have not been drawn to the "opportunity" Karmijn presents. Research finds that although early returns for successful private equity funds can be high, they may decline as fund managers become less driven or change investment strategy in order to pursue larger deals (Kaplan and Schoar, 2005; Metrick and Yasuda, 2010; Marquez *et al.*, 2015).

- *How risky is a private-equity investment and what proportion of one's capital should a person invest in private equity?* In general, asset managers advise that private equity investments should constitute no more than 10% of an individual's capital because there is always a chance that all of the investment could be lost (Idzorek, 2007). Some even suggest that investment in this asset class should be no more than 5% of an individual's capital (Pelletier, 2013). Additionally, financial advisors will often argue that even this amount should be spread among various private-equity commitments.

- *What are the mechanics of a private-equity commitment, and what is the usual time horizon involved?* Funds committed to a private-equity fund are not contributed all at once. Rather, they are "called" for over a period time – ten years in the case of Karmijn Kapitaal – as the fund finds appropriate investments. Subsequently, every time the fund exits from an investment, the money is returned to the investors. Most private-equity funds have lives of around ten years. Ms. Rossum's age made it plausible she could pass away before the investment period was over. If this happened, her children would have to pay in the remainder of her commitment when the fund executed a "call."

- *Can/should the team make a judgment about whether this investment is a good fit for Ms. Rossum? As astute as she appears to be, is she making a well-informed decision?*

- *What would be an appropriate investor base structure (gender-wise) for Karmijn Kapitaal and why? And what about the Karmijn Kapitaal partnership structure and management? Why does diversity matter in business development and corporate management?*

What Happened?

Hadewych welcomed a 100,000 euro commitment from Ms. Rossum, but only after ensuring she made an appointment with a reputable asset manager to advise her on an appropriate investment strategy for the funds she had standing idle in the bank. Additionally, Hadewych asked whether she could speak with Ms. Rossum's children about the ten-year commitment she would be making. Ms. Rossum happily agreed, and she became a member in Karmijn Fund I in early 2012. In doing so, she became part of an investor base that was 50% female, and she started to enjoy the company of other strong-willed characters at Karmijn Kapitaal membership meetings.

Karmijn Kapitaal Fund I started with a first close of 11 million euros in October 2011 and was able to subsequently raise a total of 46 million euros. The fund has invested in seven portfolio companies across a variety of sectors: Mediterranean food, medical devices, lingerie, television production, designer shoes and bags, craft beer, and dyslexia treatments.[8] With its seventh investment, Karmijn Fund I became *fully invested*. The fund made its first exit in 2015, generating a 59% internal rate of return. Although other exits have not yet materialized, the gross paper return of the fund is 33% percent – a return considered impressive in the market (Ghai *et al.*, 2014). The second Karmijn Kapitaal fund, Karmijn Fund II, is expected to close at 90 million euros before the summer of 2016.

Ms. Rossum is doing well and was present at the membership meeting of Karmijn Fund I in May 2015.

Concluding Reflections

As a case that explicitly connects business decision-making with ethical and other value-based considerations, Karmijn Kapitaal demonstrates how the six PRMEs – *purpose, values, methods, research, partnerships*, and *dialogue* – can be integrated

---

8 As of June 2016, Karmijn Kapitaal had successfully divested of one of its earlier investments in over-the-counter self-care products, *YouMedical*, to a Swedish healthcare company. It retained an interest in: (1) *Kunst.nl*, a company that rents art to companies for their offices; (2) *Jopenbier*, a specialist and award-winning brewery; (3) *Opdidakt*, an organization that provides research-informed guidance on educational and social-emotional challenges facing children and young adults; (4) *Fred de la Bretonière*, a renowned designer of leather bags, shoes, and belts; (5) *Tuvalu Media*, an award-winning television production company that Karmijn invested in by acquiring the stake previously owned by Sony International; (6) *Marlies Dekkers*, an internationally acclaimed lingerie designer acquired through a bankruptcy restructuring; and (7) *Enrico*, the Dutch market leader in top-quality Mediterranean delicacies supplied to major supermarket chains. Enrico was acquired from its retiring founders.

into a key pedagogy used by business schools to educate future business leaders. As a research-based case (*Principle 4*), it was developed in partnership with the company's executive (*Principle 5*). Furthermore, consistent with the PRME method objective (*Principle 3*), the case effectively enhances pedagogical approaches that facilitate student-led discussion (*Principle 6*) and learning around issues concerning the purpose (*Principle 1*) as well as values (*Principle 2*) of business.

The use of real cases as inductive ways of surfacing theoretical concepts or as grounding supplements in more theory-oriented courses remains dominant in management education worldwide. As such, they should be viewed as key *hidden* opportunities for transforming graduates into engaged, socially responsible leaders.

Although the focus of the case is socially responsible (ethical) capital raising, readers are encouraged to reflect upon other dimensions and create their own teaching approaches when using it across a variety of upper-level undergraduate or graduate courses. Management educators are encouraged to develop further cases in the same vein that create the appropriate level of *decision ambiguity* to stimulate the lively, and at times possibly heated, classroom dialogue that has been experienced when using earlier versions of Karmijn Kapitaal with banking executives.

References

Catalyst. (2013, July). Why diversity matters. *Catalyst Report*. Retrieved from http://www.catalyst.org/system/files/why_diversity_matters_catalyst_0.pdf.

Erhardt, N.L., Werbel, J.D. & Shrader, C.B. (2003). Board of director diversity and firm financial performance. *Corporate Governance: An International Review*, 11(2), 102-111. doi: 10.1111/1467-8683.00011.

Ghai, S., Kehoe, C., & Pinkus, G. (2014). Private equity: Changing perceptions and new realities. McKinsey & Company. Retrieved from http://www.mckinsey.com/industries/private-equity-and-principal-investors/our-insights/private-equity-changing-perceptions-and-new-realities.

Hunt, V., Layton, D. & Prince, S. (2015). Why diversity matters. *McKinsey* & Company. Retrieved from http://www.mckinsey.com/business-functions/organization/our-insights/why-diversity-matters.

Idzorek, T. (2007). Private equity and strategic asset allocation. Ibbotson Associates. Retrieved from https://corporate.morningstar.com/ib/documents/MethodologyDocuments/IBBAssociates/IbbotsonPrivateEquity.pdf.

Kaplan, S.N. & Schoar, A. (2005). Private equity performance: Returns, persistence, and capital flows. *The Journal of Finance*, 60(4), 1791-1823. doi: 10.1111/j.1540-6261.2005.00780.x.

Marquez, R., Nanda, V. & Yavuz, M.D. (2015). Private equity fund returns and performance persistence. *Review of Finance*, 15(5), 1783-1823. doi: 10.1093/rof/rfu045.

Metrick, A. & Yasuda, A. (2010). The economics of private equity funds. *Review of Financial Studies*, 23(6), 2303-2341. doi: 10.1093/rfs/hhq020.

Pelletier, M. (2013, May 27). Know the risks before investing in private equity. *Financial Post*. Retrieved from http://business.financialpost.com/investing/know-the-risks-before-investing-in-private-equity.

Dianne Lynne Bevelander, MBA (Cape Town), PhD (Lulea), is Professor of Management Education at the Rotterdam School of Management of Erasmus University Rotterdam in the Netherlands. She established the Erasmus Center for Women and Organizations and serves as its inaugural executive director. Dianne develops and runs Women in Leadership executive courses, and she is often included in conference organization and invited to give keynote addresses and plenary talks.

dbevelander@rsm.nl

Michael John Page, BSc Engineering (Natal), MBA (Cape Town), PhD (Cape Town) is Professor of Finance and Management at Bentley University in the United States. He serves on the advisory boards of several international business schools and on the governing boards of the EFMD, AACSB International, and South Africa Partners.

mpage@rsm.nl

8

Gender Diversity and Corporate Sustainability
Insights from a German Multinational Company

Christine Naschberger
Audencia Business School, France

Madhumitha Ravikumar
Technical University of Munich, Germany

Introduction and Context

Since the early 1970s, there has been a long and fierce debate on the accountability of businesses to a wider audience than their shareholders (Ackerman, 1975). Previously, the focus of business organizations was mainly on their financial outcomes. Then a wider perspective gained ground and stakeholders were taken into account. By taking a wider perspective, decision-makers and leaders of global corporate organizations are increasingly facing the challenge of meeting the expectations of a broad range of stakeholders, such as employees, customers, creditors, society, and unions while still delivering a return to shareholders (Bansal, 2001, 2005). In 2000, the United Nations introduced a corporate social responsibility (CSR) milestone, the UN Global Compact (UNGC), as an initiative to encourage businesses to implement CSR initiatives and to protect the environment (Post, 2013). Consequently, many corporations and also business schools and universities have become members, applying the Ten Principles of the UNGC. Therefore, corporate sustainability, classified under three main dimensions – economic growth, social responsiveness, and environmental quality (Bansal, 2005) – is increasingly becoming a strategic issue to be dealt with by organizations.

For over 25 years, the advancement of women has been a focus of discussion. Gender diversity has been encouraged as a means of improving organizational performance by inculcating boards with new insights and perspectives (Carter *et al.*, 2003). For the purpose of meeting sustainability challenges, diversity at the board and senior management levels is considered important (Galbreath, 2011; Grayson *et al.*, 2008). A great deal of research has been focused on the "business case for gender diversity" and how it affects an organization's overall financial performance (Terjesen, 2009; Dang and Nguyen, 2016; Dang *et al.*, 2016). See, for instance, the McKinsey & Company report "Women Matter" (2011). Soares *et al.* (2011) found in their study that "gender inclusive leadership delivers sustainable benefits to both companies and societies" (p. 3). However, research examining links between gender diversity and corporate sustainability have yet to be systematically investigated (Boulouta, 2013; Ricart *et al.*, 2005).

This case study discusses the roles that women have on the three dimensions of corporate sustainability – *economic, social, and environmental* – and provides an opportunity to understand the symbiotic relationship between women and the different aspects of corporate sustainability. The German company on which this case study is based believes that taking a proactive approach to increasing the number of women in management positions is an important way to add value to business (Company Sustainability Report, 2015). As such it can act as an inspiration and potential benchmark for others to expand their female workforce and achieve gender-diversity targets or quotas. More generally, the chapter provides insight into gender-diversity programs and empowerment of female executives, as well as some concrete human resource (HR) tools. The aim of the chapter is to analyze how women can act as a driving force behind the economic, social, and environmental performance of an organization. The empirical part of the chapter is based on an online survey of 25 female managers, followed by interviews with a few women managers in order to analyze their perspectives on the three dimensions of corporate sustainability.

The results should be of value to management-development institutions including those that are providing executive seminars and/or are interested in embedding the results into their curricula. By making references to the respective aspects of the UNGC and Principles for Responsible Management Education (PRME), the case could help raise awareness among managers that women's empowerment within organizations positively influences economic growth, social responsiveness, and environmental quality. The underlying assumption is an existing close relationship between participation of women managers and leaders (Grosser and Moon, 2005), gender equality (Lombardo and Forest, 2015), and economic growth. Finally, the chapter may help highly talented women to navigate more effectively through the "labyrinth" of leadership and to achieve their personal career goals and act as a role model to encourage talented young women to climb the career ladder.

Women in Management

In spite of being a key focus area in some multinational corporations, the ratio of women to men in senior level or executive positions for the past ten years has barely changed. For example, in the United States, recent research shows that the progress in women's advancement over the past several decades, has slowed considerably in recent years and that "the pipeline for women is in peril" (Carter and Silva, 2010). According to a recent study by McKinsey & Company and LeanIn.org, "Corporate America is not on a path to gender equality" (McKinsey & Company and LeanIn.org, 2015, p. 3). The study shows that at the current rate of change, it will take at least 100 years to reach gender equality at work. Milligan *et al.* (2014) conclude that organizations globally are far from achieving gender equality.

The situation is quite different in several European countries where legal initiatives have encouraged listed companies to work toward goals of women in top management and board positions. The proportion of women on large European boards increased from 13.9 percent in 2011 to 25 percent in 2015 (De Pril and Roberts, 2016). The same report highlights that very small change is observed in the executive suite. Of the 600 companies studied, only 21 women were in CEO positions in 2004 (3.5% of total employers). By 2011, this proportion had fallen to 3%, and by 2014, the same percentage as ten years prior (3.5%) had just been reached again. In France, Sophie Bellon, CEO of Sodexo, was the first French woman to chair a French Stock Index company (CAC 40), and recently Isabelle Kocher was designated to head ENGIE, an electric utility multinational. Both female CEOs were appointed in 2016. As in the United States, well-known female German top managers are rare. Ines Kolmsee[1] serves as the CEO of AlzChem Hart GmbH, and before that she was the CEO at SKW Stahl-Metallurgie for eight years.

The concept of the "glass ceiling" is persistent in many organizations around the globe (Farrell and Hersch, 2001; Belghiti-Mahut and Naschberger, 2010). Some authors prefer the metaphor of the "labyrinth of leadership" (Eagly and Carly, 2007) because, they say, some female CEOs such as Mary Barra (General Motors) and Marissa Mayer (Yahoo) have shattered the glass ceiling. The glass ceiling metaphor was proposed to account for the scarcity of women in top leadership. On the other hand, the labyrinth is a contemporary symbol that conveys the idea of a complex journey toward a goal worth striving for (Naschberger *et al.*, 2017). "Passage through a labyrinth is not simple or direct, but requires persistence, awareness of one's progress, and a careful analysis of the puzzles that lie ahead" (Eagly and Carly, 2007, p. 64).

Nevertheless, there are numerous obstacles for female managers on the way to the highest levels of a company, the so-called C-suite of executives (Ibarra *et al.*, 2010; Naschberger *et al.*, 2012). According to the McKinsey & Company and

---

1 Edgar, R. (2010). Financial Times Interview with Mrs. Ines Kolmsee: Female CEO stands out in Germany (Nov. 18, 2010): http://video.ft.com/679358761001/Female-CEO-stands-out-in-Germany/World

LeanIn.org study of 2015, only 17% of C-suite positions in American companies were held by women. A lack of family-friendly policies, work-life balance, networking, as well as a lack of female role models are holding women back (Naschberger *et al.*, 2012). Sandberg also notes that women hold themselves back (2013). A recent study of the International Labour Organisation (ILO) shows that even though bigger companies may provide gender- or family-friendly policies, due to a lack of information, employees may not benefit from these policies (ILO, 2015). McKinsey & Company note that "unconscious gender bias" embedded in cultural beliefs also is keeping women back (2011, 2013).

The German Context

The topics of women's empowerment and women's advancement have been on the agenda of many German corporations since March 2015 when Germany passed a law[2] that requires corporate boards be at least 30% women by 2016. Dauer (2014) states that German businesses have shown little enthusiasm for binding targets since decision-makers – mostly men – believe that a quota is more about gender and less about qualifications. Words and expressions like "the quota woman" (*die Quotenfrau*) foster resistance to change. Also, many women feel that they do not want special treatment; rather, they seek flexible solutions for combining their professional and personal lives (ILO, 2015). The quotas for women on corporate boards have been used in other European countries including France, Italy, Spain, Norway, and Belgium. Due in large part to a legislation-based quota system introduced in 2006, Norway has the highest percentage of women on boards of large, listed companies (38.7%), followed by Sweden with 34.6% (De Pril and Roberts, 2016).

The new law in Germany is the latest development in a raging debate over whether voluntary efforts or government mandates are needed to change male-dominated corporate cultures. The early evidence from European countries like Norway shows that the representation of women on boards increases in accordance with the law (Teigen, 2012). But less clear is whether such increases do anything to tackle deeper problems such as the dearth of women in upper-level management positions – in other words, whether they help to fix the leaky pipeline for female talent.

---

2 According to Göpfert and Rottmeier (2015), the German Law on Equal Participation of Women and Men in Leadership Positions in the Private and Public Sector will require an implementation of a 30% female quota on supervisory boards. Furthermore, the law sets a target for the two top levels of management. According to Baker & McKenzie, more than 3,500 German companies will be affected by the latter (http://www.bakermckenzie.com/algermanyequalparticipationmar15/). If a company does not comply with this law, elections that are in breach of the quota might be legally challenged and nullified (De Pril and Roberts, 2016).

Some German organizations acted ahead of the requirements of the law, as for instance the DAX 30-listed company Deutsche Telekom, which announced in 2010 a voluntary goal of 30% female managers by 2015 (Bennhold, 2011). According to the German Institute for Economic Research (DIW Berlin, 2015), in 2014, less than 20% of supervisory board members and directors at the 100 largest multinational German companies were women. German female managers are underrepresented in decision-making positions as the share of women on boards was 16% in 2012 (European Commission, 2012) and 21.3% in 2015 for the 30 German DAX companies (Women on Boards Davies Report, 2015). Traditional gender roles and persisting gender stereotypes hinder German female managers in advancing despite the country's chancellor being female (Bennhold, 2011).

Young educated German women may choose career over a family life as having both does not seem compatible. At 1.44, the German total fertility rate was declining and among the lowest in Europe in 2015 (World Fact Book, 2015; German Federal Statistical Office, 2015). Furthermore, Germany has been identified as one of the countries in critical need of talent (Adema *et al.*, 2014). Increased female labor-force participation is one of the suggested solutions to avoid the looming decline of the German workforce (Adema *et al.*, 2014).

Many German female managers "opt out" of their position for one to three years after childbirth to take care of the child. Small and big companies are impacted by this cultural habit, although many larger firms like Siemens do have childcare centers close to the workplace, offering new alternatives to highly qualified women (Siemens, 2016). Besides a lack of organizational flexibility there is also a lack of governmental childcare facilities in Germany (Bruchhagen *et al.*, 2010).

The Case of a German Multinational Organization

The organization chosen for this case study is the holding company of one of the leading global services providers in insurance, banking, and asset management. With approximately 181,000 employees worldwide, this multinational German company serves more than 80 million customers in about 70 countries. The parent company, a multinational financial services company, is headquartered in Bavaria.

Company Policies and Practices[3]

The organization signed the UNGC in 2002, and this chapter highlights the implementation of UNGC Principle 6 (elimination of discrimination with respect to employment and occupation), showcasing how the organization is seriously

---

3 Unless noted otherwise this section is based on the three most recent company Sustainability Reports (2014, 2015, 2016).

committed to gender diversity. According to the company's Group Global Compact report (2007/2008), the company ranks among the top women-friendly companies. A study conducted by the organization of Corporate Women Directors International (CWDI) in 2007 ranked the parent company as one of three German companies in Europe's top ten for gender equality, with 20% of high-management positions filled by women. In the era of globalization and in light of social changes, the company recognizes that promoting diversity is key to gaining competitive advantage and that promoting women in the workplace will be beneficial to the business in the long run (Company Website, 2016).

The objectives of the company's diversity strategy is to change mentalities, attitudes, norms, and the overall culture of the organization. Diversity is one of the corporate values. The company's diversity statement is as follows:

> We have a wonderfully diverse foundation made up of people of every conceivable background. A person's gender, ethnicity, age, religious belief, sexual orientation, education, disabilities or national identification are differences we value and celebrate. (Company website, 2016)

The company recognizes the importance of an inclusive working environment, and a Global Diversity Council is responsible for driving the success of the diversity strategy. Consistent with its Code of Conduct, the company has a zero-tolerance policy for discrimination or harassment in the workplace.

Since 2008, the company has maintained a strong commitment to increasing the share of women in the talent pool of executive positions. In 2008, the company's supervisory board decided to establish a global target of 30% women in its managerial talent pool by 2015. (Company Website, 2016). In 2015, the company increased this target to 40%. The company confirms the importance of sanctioning diversity programs from the top, while the CEO and women executives act as gender-diversity protagonists. In order to drive cultural change, the company implemented a range of global, regional, and local initiatives. Supporting actions including part-time employment, job sharing, flexible work-life programs, and a top management sponsorship program for women were implemented (Company Annual Report, 2014). To achieve gender targets, new measures including systematic and dedicated coaching programs for women, identification of 200 female vetted successors, flexible working solutions, childcare, and an option to return part-time to the same position after parental leave were introduced (Company HR Factbook, 2015). In addition, to help address the issue of "unconscious bias," the company runs awareness workshops for HR leaders and managers (Company HR Factbook, 2014). The Company's 2015 Sustainability Report specifically notes that 450 training programs were delivered to more than 4,500 employees to combat "unconscious bias" that may arise in situations such as job interviews and employee appraisals. The company also offers mentoring opportunities and networks for women to increase exchanges and to foster the advancement of women. In 2015, staff members participated in eight women's networks, which operated around the world. Furthermore, to improve the balance between work and private life, the company launched new nurseries. And to support employees' careers the organization provides support before, during, and after a parental leave. An innovative initiative is a parental-leave toolkit providing information and steps for parents to smooth the reentry process since maternity or parental leaves are often seen as detrimental to women's careers. Lastly, the company's program Parents in Leadership (*Eltern in Führung*) supports the return of women to their leadership roles after maternity leave.

In 2015, women made up 53% of the company's workforce, and the percentage of female managers reached 37%, up from 34% in 2012 (Company Sustainability Report, 2015). The company has an ongoing commitment to increase the proportion of female managers. At least 20% of all positions in the highest levels of management are to be filled by women by mid-2017 and at least 30% in the longer term (Company Website, 2016). The company's Supervisory Board, composed of 12 members, included four women (33%) in 2016 (Company Website, 2016).

Quantitative and Qualitative Research

To illustrate the influences of gender diversity and corporate sustainability in the organization, quantitative and qualitative research was undertaken. The quantitative part was based on analysis of data collected using a web-based questionnaire. It mainly focused on statistically evaluating the influences of gender diversity on corporate sustainability. The qualitative research was based on one-to-one interviews with three women managers. This component was conducted to shed light on the perceptions of women managers on the relationship between gender diversity and corporate sustainability and how they were able to make positive contributions to the three dimensions of corporate sustainability.

Quantitative Analysis of the Survey Results

A web-based survey was conducted with a group of 25 senior women managers working within various departments of the company including operations, claims and underwriting, human resources, communications, and sustainability. The choice of sampling population is reasonable as senior women managers are flag-bearers for promoting gender diversity topics within the company besides being an integral part of several regional and local initiatives for women's empowerment.

The questionnaire was rationalized based on the Corporate Sustainability Assessment (CSA)[4], conducted annually by RobecoSAM[5], which serves as the framework for measuring corporate-sustainability performance of companies. The case-study

---

4 The CSA is industry-specific and sent out by RobecoSAM to 2,500 worldwide corporations over 58 market sectors to determine the respective sustainability rating of all those corporations. The CSA has a set of industry-specific assessment criteria covering the economic, social, and environmental dimensions of every industry.

5 An international investment company with a specific focus on sustainability investments.

company received the Gold Class Sustainability Award 2014 from RobecoSAM, in recognition of its excellent sustainability performance as assessed in the 2013 Dow Jones Sustainability Index Assessment. Initially, the key assessment criteria set out by CSA[6] for the evaluation of sustainability performance of the case company were listed. The survey questions were designed to evaluate the impact of women managers on these key assessment criteria within the areas of economic, social, and environment issues that have a material impact on the company's ability to generate long-term sustainable value. The survey data were analyzed based on the Weighted Scoring Method (WSM)[7] with three formulated hypotheses[8]. The total weighted scores obtained as the result of the analysis by WSM were: 27.5 (economic), 25.3 (social), and 23.2 (environmental). All three scores confirmed that the three dimensions of corporate sustainability are positively influenced by gender diversity. Women managers have the greatest influence on the economic dimension, followed by the social dimension, with the least influence on the environmental dimension.

Interviews of Women Managers

The interviews with women managers were based on open-ended questions on their perceptions about the influence of women executives on corporate sustainability and how as female managers they are able to make positive contributions to the three elements of corporate sustainability. Three survey respondents who work in three different functional areas (communication, sustainability, and group HR) were interviewed. Their ages ranged from 37 to 40. The answers are presented below verbatim, usually with the functional area noted.

One of the questions asked was "Based on your experience within the company, please explain how women managers are able to make positive contributions to the three elements of Corporate Sustainability?" The interviewed women managers believed that they were contributing – *more so than their male counterparts* – in several areas:

6 Recommendation for further understanding of CSA and a detailed reading of CSA assessment methodology: http://www.robecosam.com/en/sustainability-insights/about-sustainability/robecosam-corporate-sustainability-assessment.jsp
7 Through the WSM, weights were assigned to each of the response options based on their relative relevance to the question. Consequently, for every question, a total weighted score was achieved by multiplying the number of responses for every option with their originally assigned weights. Aggregating the weighted scores on a dimension-by-dimension basis (economic, environmental, and social) resulted in a total weighted score for each of the three dimensions of corporate sustainability. For further details please feel free to contact the authors.
8 H1 - a dimension with a positive score is positively influenced by gender diversity; H2 - a dimension with a negative score is negatively influenced by gender diversity; H3 - a dimension with a neutral score not influenced by gender diversity.

- "Increasing corporate sponsorships and rising donations & volunteering since women managers' entry in the Sustainability & Corporate Responsibility Departments" (sustainability, communication)

- "Ensuring the Code of Ethics is in place to protect shareholder funds" (sustainability)

- "Boosting brand reputation through female empowerment" (communication)

- "Maintaining positive relationships with stakeholders" (sustainability, communication)

- "Establishing of various green initiatives" (sustainability, communication)

- "Increasing employee engagement" (group HR)

- "Pushing for a high quality of Corporate Social Responsibility initiatives" (sustainability, communication, group HR)

The interviewees' perceptions further demonstrated that women are able to positively influence the three dimensions of corporate sustainability. The basis for their argument on how having a gender-balanced senior management team strengthens economic growth (the bottom line), social responsiveness, and environment quality (beyond the bottom line) was "women managers constantly are keen on focusing commitment to all stakeholders of the company and not just the shareholders thus creating a greater possibility for them to positively influence all three dimensions of Corporate Sustainability." Further, women managers also identified themselves

> as a key link for achieving high performance in all Corporate Sustainability areas given their special interests to help the organization be more socially responsible. The advantage of creating a corporate culture of sustainability can have the added benefit of helping employees feel more connected to your organization.

For example, the Group HR representative mentioned that "Corporate Sustainability is frequently used to describe the attempts to motivate employees and leverage employee engagement."

Overall, all three respondents strongly felt that revealing a symbiotic relationship between gender diversity and corporate sustainability would definitely enable companies to have a stronger business case to increase opportunities for women to climb up the corporate ladder and also to perceive gender diversity as a mainstream corporate issue.

Implications for Business Practices and Management Education

Key lessons for corporate decision makers and management students include the following:

Learning for the corporate world: The case study's findings support the overall research premise that women managers' positively influence all three dimensions of corporate sustainability (economic outcomes, social responsiveness, and environmental quality). They suggest that women empowerment and advancement contribute to achieving overall corporate sustainability.

Learning for management education institutions: Academic institutions educating current and future responsible managers could use these findings and the respective innovative management practices to promote a more sustainable view of businesses through their curricula, stimulating PRMEs 1 through 3 (purpose, values, and method). Today's students and managers may think that gender equality is not a relevant topic anymore and that gender parity has already been achieved. The case itself is an example of research (Principle 4) that is needed to get a better understanding of the reality of today's business world and the need to inspire partnerships and dialog (Principles 5 and 6) aimed at fostering gender equality and the advancement of women not only as a fundamental human right but also for achieving the advancement on the three critical dimensions of corporate and overall sustainability.

Suggested Further Reading

Bruchhagen, V., Grieger, J., Koall, I., Meuser, M., Ortlieb, R. & Sieben, B. (2010). Social inequality, diversity and equal treatment at work: The German case. In A. Klarsfeld (Ed.), *International Handbook on Diversity Management at Work: Country Perspectives on Diversity and Equal Treatment.* (pp. 109-138). Cheltenham: Elgar.

References

Adams, R. & Ferreira, D. (2009). Women in the boardroom and their impact on governance and performance. *Journal of Financial Economics*, 94, 291-309.

Adema, W., Ali, N., Frey, V., Kim, H., Lunati, M., Piacentini, M. & Queisser, M. (2014). Enhancing Women's Economic Empowerment through Entrepreneurship and Business Leadership in OECD Countries. OECD Report, 42 pages.

Ackerman, R.W. (1975). *The Social Challenge to Business.* Cambridge, Mass.: Harvard University Press.

Baker & McKenzie. (2015). Law on equal participation of women and men in leadership positions in the private and public sector. Retrieved from http://www.bakermckenzie.com/algermanyequalparticipationmar15.

Bansal, P. (2001). Building competitive advantage and managing risk through sustainable development. *Ivey Business Journal*, 66, 47-52.

Bansal, P. (2005). Evolving Sustainability: A longitudinal study of corporate sustainable development. *Strategic Management Journal*, 26, 197-218.

Belghiti-Mahut, S. and Naschberger, C. (2010). Beauté naturelle: Carrière de femmes et plafond de verre. In F. Chevalier (Ed.), *Pratiques de GRH dans les pays francophones: 48 études de cas* (pp. 62-66). Paris : Vuibert.

Bennhold, K. (2011, June 28). Women nudged out of German workforce. *New York Times*. Retrieved from http://www.nytimes.com/2011/06/29/world/europe/29iht-FFgermany29.html?_r=0.

Boulouta, I. (2013). Hidden connections: The link between Board gender diversity and corporate social performance. *Journal of Business Ethics*, 113(2), 185-197.

Women on Boards Davies Report. (2015). *Improving the Gender Balance on British Boards. Women on Boards Davies Report, Five Year Summary October 2015*. Retrieved from https://www.gov.uk/government/uploads/system/uploads/attachment_data/file/482059/BIS-15-585-women-on-boards-davies-review-5-year-summary-october-2015.pdf.

Bruchhagen, V., Grieger, J., Koall, I., Meuser, M., Ortlieb, R. & Sieben, B. (2010). Social inequality, diversity and equal treatment at work: The German case. In A. Klarsfeld (Ed.), *International Handbook on Diversity Management at Work: Country Perspectives on Diversity and Equal Treatment* (pp. 109-138). Cheltenham, UK: Elgar.

Carter, D.A., Simkins, B.J. & Simpson, W.G. (2003). Corporate governance, board diversity and firm value. *The Financial Review*, 38, 33-53.

Carter, N.M. & Silva, C. (2010). *Pipeline's Broken Promise*. New York: Catalyst. Retrieved from http://www.catalyst.org/publications/372/pipelines-broken-promise.

Catalyst. (2004). *The Bottom Line: Connecting Corporate Performance and Gender Diversity*. New York: Catalyst. Retrieved from http://www.catalyst.org/system/files/The_Bottom_Line_Connecting_Corporate_Performance_and_Gender_Diversity.pdf.

Catalyst. (2014). *Catalyst Census: Women Board Directors*. New York: Catalyst. Retrieved from http://www.catalyst.org/knowledge/2014-catalyst-census-women-board-directors.

Corporate Women Directors International (CWDI). (2007). Corporate Women Directors International 2007 Report: Women Board Directors of the 2006 Fortune Global 200. Retrieved from http://www.globewomen.org/CWDI/2007%20Colloquium/CWDI%202007%20Colloquium%20Archive11-11-08.htm.

Dang, R. & Nguyen, D.K. (2016). Does board gender diversity make a difference? New evidence from quantile regression analysis. *Management International*, 20(2), 163-174.

Dang, R., Houanti, L.H., Naschberger, C. & Tuyên Lê, N. (2016, May). Women on corporate boards and firm financial performance: Evidence from French SMEs. Paper presented at Small business economics, accounting and finance conference, Audencia Business School, France.

Dauer, U. (2014, December 11). Corporate Germany set for gender revolution. *The Wall Street Journal*. Retrieved from http://www.wsj.com/articles/german-cabinet-gives-nod-to-increase-number-of-women-on-boards-1418299350.

De Pril, K. & Roberts, M. (2016). Gender Diversity on European Boards. Realizing Europe's Potential: Progress and Challenges. A European Women on Boards Study Carried out in Partnership with ISS. Retrieved from http://european.ewob-network.eu/ewob-publishes-landmark-report-on-the-progress-of-women-on-the-boards-of-major-european-companies.

DIW Berlin. (2015). Women Executive Barometer 2015: Highest Decision-Making Bodies in German Companies Still Male-Dominated. Retrieved from https://www.diw.de/en/diw_01.c.495406.en/topics_news/women_executive_barometer_2015_highest_decision_making_bodies_in_german_companies_still_male_dominated.html.

Eagly, A. & Carly, L.L. (2007). Women and the labyrinth of leadership. *Harvard Business Review*, 85(9), 62-71.

Edgar, R. (2010, November 18). Financial Times interview with Mrs. Ines Kolmsee: Female CEO stands out in Germany. *Financial Times*. Retrieved from http://video.ft.com/679358761001/Female-CEO-stands-out-in-Germany/World.

European Commission. (2012). The Current Situation of Gender Equality in Germany. Country Profile 2012. Retrieved from http://ec.europa.eu/justice/gender-equality/files/epo_campaign/country-profile_germany_en.pdf.

Europaforum. (2013). Présence des femmes dans les conseils des entreprises – Le Parlement européen a modifié et adopté la proposition de directive de la Commission européenne. Retrieved from http://www.europaforum.public.lu/fr/actualites/2013/11/pe-femmes-vote/index.html.

Farrell, K.A. & Hersch, P.L. (2001). Additions to Corporate Boards: Does Gender Matter, Working paper, 30 p.

Federal Statistical Office. (2015, December 16). Increase in 2014 Fertility Rate to 1.47 Children per Woman. Press Release 468. Retrieved from https://www.destatis.de/EN/PressServices/Press/pr/2015/12/PE15_468_126.html.

Galbreath, J. (2011). Are there gender-related influences on corporate sustainability? A study of women on boards of directors. *Journal of Management & Organization*, 17, 17-38.

Gmür, M. (2006). The gendered stereotype of the good manager: Sex role expectations towards male and female managers. *The International Review of Management Studies*. 17(2). 104-21.

Göpfert, B. & Rottmeier, D. (2015). Die Frauenquote kommt! - Ein Zwischenruf aus dem Arbeitsrecht. Baker & McKenzie. Retrieved from http://www.bakermckenzie.com/files/Publication/0d3c6694-1103-4b4c-a359-533ca21bc367/Presentation/PublicationAttachment/1b8ef8e9-cf81-48f4-a0de-627c070bd3ce/al_germany_equalparticipation_mar15_german.pdf.

Grayson, D., Jin, Z., Lemon, M., Rodriguez, M.A., Slaughter, S. & Tay, S. (2008). A New Mindset for Corporate Sustainability. A white paper sponsored by BT and Cisco.

Grosser, K. & Moon, J. (2005). Gender mainstreaming and corporate social responsibility: Reporting workplace issues. *Journal of Business Ethics*, 62(4), 327-340.

Holst, E. & Wiemer, A. (2010). Women still greatly underrepresented on the top boards of large companies. *Wochenbericht des DIW Berlin*, 7, 45-53.

Ibarra, H., Carter, N.M. & Silva, C. (2010). Why men still get more promotions than women. *Harvard Business Review*. Sept. 2010, 80-85.

International Labour Organisation (ILO). (2015). Women in Business and Management: Gaining Momentum. Global Report. Retrieved from http://www.ilo.org.

Lombardo, E. & Forest, M. (2015). Europeanization of gender equality policies. A discursive-sociological approach. *Comparative European Politics*. 13(4), 222-239.

McKinsey & Company and LeanIn.org. (2015). Women in the workplace 2015 study. Retrieved from http://womenintheworkplace.com.

McKinsey & Company. (2011). Unlocking the full potential of women at work. Women Matter Report. Retrieved from http://www.mckinsey.com/global-themes/women-matter.

McKinsey & Company. (2012). Women as a valuable asset. Retrieved from http://www.mckinsey.com/~/media/mckinsey%20offices/russia/pdfs/women_as_a_valuable%20asset_eng.ashx.

McKinsey & Company. (2013). Gender diversity in top management: Moving corporate cultures, moving boundaries. Women Matter Report. Retrieved from http://www.mckinsey.com/global-themes/women-matter.

Milligan, P.A., Levin, B., Chen, L. & Edkins, K. (2014). When women thrive, businesses drive. Mercer Consulting. Retrieved from http://www.mmc.com/content/dam/mmc-web/Files/Gender-Diversity-When-women-thrive-businesses-thrive-Mercer.pdf.

Naschberger, C., Quental, C. & Legrand, C. (2017). The leaky leadership pipeline in France. A study of career levers and barriers to foster women's leadership development. In C.M. Cunningham and H.M. Crandall (Eds.), *Gender, Communication, and the Leadership Gap*, Women and Leadership Book Series, Vol. 6, Forthcoming.

Naschberger, C., Quental, C. & Legrand C. (2012). Le parcours de carrière des femmes cadres: pourquoi est-il si compliqué et comment le faciliter? *Gestion: Revue Internationale de Gestion*, 37(3), 43-50.

Post, J.E. (2013). The United Nations Global Compact: A CSR milestone. *Business & Society*, 52(1), 53-63.

Ricart, J.E., Rodríguez, M.A. & Sánchez, P. (2005). Sustainability in the boardroom: An empirical examination of Dow Jones Sustainability World Index leaders. *Corporate Governance: The International Journal of Business in Society*, 5, 24–41.

RobecoSAM's. (2015). Corporate Sustainability Assessment Methodology. Retrieved from http://www.robecosam.com/images/DJSI_FAQ_2016.pdf and http://yearbook.robecosam.com/methodology.html.

Rose, C. (2007). Does female board representation influence firm performance? The Danish evidence. *Corporate Governance: An International Review*, 15, 404-13.

Sandberg, S. (2013). *Lean In: Women, Work and the Will to Lead*. New York: Knopf Doubleday Publishing Group.

Siemens Website. (2016). Family and career is not a contradiction. Retrieved from http://www.siemens.com/about/sustainability/en/core-topics/employees/references/family-and-career.htm.

Soares, R., Marquis, C. & Lee, M. (2011). *Gender and Corporate Social Responsibility. It's a Matter of Sustainability*. Catalyst. Retrieved from http://www.catalyst.org.

Teigen, M. (2012). Gender quotas for corporate boards in Norway. Innovative gender equality policy. In C. Fagan, M. Gonzalez Menendez & S. Gomez Anson (Eds.), *Women on Corporate Boards and in Top Management: European Trends and Policy* (pp. 70-90). Basingstoke: Palgrave Macmillan UK.

Terjesen, S., Sealy, R. & Singh, V. (2009). Women directors on corporate boards: A review and research agenda, *Corporate Governance: An International Review*, 17(3), 320-337.

The World Factbook. (2015). Country Comparison: Total Fertility Rate. Retrieved from https://www.cia.gov/library/publications/the-world-factbook/rankorder/2127rank.html.

Case study company documents

Protecting the Future. Annual Report 2014, 282 pages. Accessed January 2016.

Company Website. Accessed January 2016.

HR Factbook 2014, 39 pages. Accessed January 2016.

HR Factbook 2015, 39 pages. Accessed May 2016.

Our Sustainability Journey. Sustainability Report 2014, 118 pages. Accessed January 2016.

Encouraging Tomorrow. Sustainability Report 2015, 85 pages. Accessed May 2016.

Company Group Global Compact – Communication on Progress 2007/2008. Accessed May 2016.

Christine Naschberger holds a doctorate in human-resource management and was educated in Austria, Germany, and France. She is currently an Associate Professor at Audencia Business School, France. Her research focuses on diversity and inclusive practices in an organizational context. More specifically, she studies women's careers, work-life balance issues, disability in the workplace, generational issues, and LGBT inclusion.

cnaschberger@audencia.com

Madhumitha Ravikumar has a master's degree in education from the Technical University of Munich, Germany. Currently, she is working in the field of Corporate Governance with a leading Big 4 organization in Germany. Her professional interests focuses on sustainability development, women empowerment, and corporate governance. She is very passionate about working on a movement to change the position of women in the workforce.

madhu12290@gmail.com

Section 3

Country-Specific Considerations

9

Reaching the Bottom Billion through Inclusive Business
Lessons from Enterprises in Africa

Ijeoma Nwagwu
Lagos Business School, Nigeria

According to the United Nations Development Programme,

> Inclusive businesses are businesses that include poor people on the demand side as clients and customers and on the supply side as employees, producers and business owners at various points in the value chain. Inclusive businesses also work actively to benefit other socially and economically disadvantaged groups such as women, ethnic and religious minorities, and handicapped people. (UNDP, 2010)

Context

The challenges surrounding large numbers of people living in poverty across Africa[1] and other parts of the developing world brings antipoverty thinking and action squarely to the doorsteps of businesses. While most businesses would not have originally considered antipoverty action as core to their purpose, businesses are increasingly pioneering entrepreneurial solutions to meet the need for products

---

[1] Africa is the world's second largest and second most populous continent with 55 independent countries and five regions (Population Reference Bureau World Population Data sheet, 2015).

and services for people at the base of the pyramid (BoP) – the bottom billion.[2] These inclusive business models also advance understandings of corporate social responsibility (CSR) beyond simple philanthropy to a source of innovation and competitive advantage. As the illustrative examples in this chapter show, inclusive business models exemplify distinctive strategies around human-resource management and product innovation, which drive competition. Inclusive business models present an important avenue for creating shared value, redirecting businesses to look beyond the typical bottom line of financial profit to the social as well as economic and environmental benefits they bring to the society. In doing so, inclusive businesses contribute to the integration of the UN Global Compact (UNGC) principles into business practice and the advancement of the Sustainable Development Goals (SDGs). Specifically, inclusive business models directly address three of the SDGs: end poverty in all its forms everywhere (goal 1), promote sustained, inclusive, and sustainable economic growth, full and productive employment and decent work for all (goal 8), and reduce inequality (goal 10) (SDGs, 2015). In relation to the UNGC principles, inclusive businesses are framed around norms of human rights, labor, environmental protections, and anticorruption that inform the UNGC principles.

This chapter considers the meaning and implications of concepts such as "the bottom billion" and "bottom of the pyramid" (BoP) as the focal point for inclusive business models. It elaborates on the context of poverty in African countries and documents the experience of two companies serving the bottom billion while gaining competitive advantage and expanding institutional possibilities around CSR. Africa's bottom billion forms a significant percentage of its population, particularly in sub-Saharan Africa where over 40% of the population lives in poverty. The full range of possibilities for inclusive businesses to address poverty across Africa will be realized with the growth of businesses reflecting shared value models in their conception of product innovation, marketing, finance, social entrepreneurship, and so on. This chapter also indicates that the topic of inclusive business highly resonates with the six Principles of Responsible Management Education (PRME) – purpose, value, method, research, partnerships, and dialogue – and the respective role that management education could and should play in advancing the UNGC and SDGs.

---

2 Some scholars argue that this position detracts attention from the proper role of the state as provider of basic services such as health care, education, and infrastructure. It also draws attention away from the regulatory role of the state, which is to set limits on markets to defend the poor from exploitation. See Karnani, A. (2009). "The Bottom of the Pyramid Strategy for Reducing Poverty: A Failed Promise," UN Department of Economics and Social Affairs (DESA) Working Paper No. 80. In response, others make the point that inclusive business models serve complementary, not substituting, roles for government obligations and responsible business practices that respect human rights. Companies supporting the rights of people living in poverty by implementing inclusive business models are going beyond the minimum responsibility (Business Call to Action and UNGC, 2015).

Theoretical Framework

Traditionally, CSR was seen as "the firm's consideration of, and response to, issues beyond the narrow economic, technical, and legal requirements of the firm" (Davis, 1973, p. 312). Scholars (Ashley, 2009; Porter and Kramer, 2006) argue that traditional CSR programs were no longer working because they were so detached from the core business strategy, which made their justification and maintenance over the long run difficult. This is why an alternative approach – creating shared value (CSV) – was proposed by Porter and Kramer in 2006 and later expanded on in their famous 2011 article, "Creating Shared Value: How to reinvent capitalism and unleash a wave of innovation and growth" (Porter and Kramer, 2011). CSV can be defined as policies and operating practices that enhance the competitiveness of a company while simultaneously advancing the economic and social constitutions in which it operates.

The business practices associated with inclusive business models link with the idea of creating shared value to the extent that they offer market-based solutions to social problems. Inclusive business models frame the business-value chain to maximize social as well as economic benefit (RIB, Asia, 2015). For instance, when markets become open to the masses where they had been closed before, as in the case of Voltic Cool Pac Ghana – that is, "selling premium product in a commodity market" (Karamachandani *et al.*, 2011, p. 111) – economic value is generated while also creating social value (Porter, 2011).

The Bottom Billion

The bottom billion, which is here referred to also as the "base of the pyramid" (BoP) or "bottom of the pyramid" (Chikweche, 2013, p. 240) was hitherto considered neither a segment/market to be a focus of businesses globally nor a principal focus of management educators in the design of leading business models. The PRME provide a platform for business students to understand and address social, environmental, and economic concerns. The term bottom billion was coined by Paul Collier, professor of economics and public policy, in his book *The Bottom Billion: Why the Poorest Countries are Failing and What Can Be Done about It* (Collier, 2007). The concepts of the bottom billion and the BoP very similar and can be used interchangeably. The BoP is a socioeconomic designation for the 4.5 billion individuals, primarily living in developing countries, whose annual per capita income is below $3,000 (Hammond *et al.*, 2007).

By definition, the BoP segment largely lacks access to the formal market setup for the fulfillment of basic needs in their societies, such as food, energy, water, sanitation, health care, transportation, education, and housing (Hammond *et al.*, 2007; Kapoor and Goyal, 2013; Goyal *et al.*, 2014). The large numbers of people still lacking adequate nourishment across Africa are indicative of the widespread poverty across the region (Fig. 9.1). Across the continent, close to one in every four people or 23.9% of the population is estimated to be undernourished in 2014–16. There has been a slow pace of growth in fighting hunger and other conditions associated with poverty.

Table 9.1 *Undernourishment around the World, 1990–92 to 2014–16*
Number of undernourished and prevalence (%) of undernourishment

	1990–92 (in millions)	1990–92 (%)	2014–16 (in millions)	2014–16 (%)
World	**1,010.6**	**18.6**	**794.6**	**10.9**
Developed regions	**20.0**	**<5**	**14.7**	**<5**
Developing regions	**990.7**	**23.3**	**779.9**	**12.9**
Africa	**181.7**	**27.6**	**232.5**	**20.0**
Sub-Saharan Africa	175.7	33.2	220.0	23.2
Asia	**741.9**	**23.6**	**511.7**	**12.1**
Eastern Asia	295.4	23.2	145.1	9.6
Southeast Asia	137.5	30.6	60.5	9.6
Southern Asia	291.2	23.9	281.4	15.7
Latin America & Caribbean	**66.1**	**14.7**	**34.3**	**5.5**
Oceana	**1.0 million**	**15.7**	**1.4**	**14.4**

Source: Food and Agriculture Organization (FAO) of the UN, The State of Food Security in the World 2015, p. 8.

The major BoP markets are found in countries in South Asia, East Asia, "non-resource-rich" countries in Latin America, the Caribbean, and sub-Saharan Africa[3] (Hammond *et al.*, 2007). Alkire *et al.* (2015) provide criteria that identify the bottom billion. These criteria are the billion living in the poorest countries, the billion living in the poorest subnational regions, and the poorest billion according to the intensity of their deprivation. Collier (2008) further adds that these low-income countries have missed an unparalleled period of global growth. In addition, not only does the gulf exist between the bottom billion and the "fortunate billion" living in developed countries, but the gulf between the bottom billion and the middle 4 billion has widened (Collier, 2008).

The BoP across Africa

African countries make a major part of this BoP market segment and are thus described by Collier as the bottom billion. The BoP consumer is the dominant

---

3   Fifty-one countries in Africa identified as the poorest in the region (Population Reference Bureau World Population Datasheet, 2015).

consumer in Africa. The World Bank forecasts that the number of this consumer in the region would exponentially increase between 2005 and 2050 (Hammond *et al.*, 2007). By 2009, the distribution of extremely poor people (those who lived on less than $1.25 a day) across developing regions had changed significantly since 1981, when South Asia and sub-Saharan Africa had the highest shares. The World Bank claims that as of 2012 sub-Saharan Africa had a headcount ratio of 42.7% living in absolute poverty on less than $1.90 a day compared to 56.8% in 1990 (Fig. 9.1). Therefore, African countries are not as poor as they used to be, but most have not had significantly fast growth either.

Figure 9.1 **Sub-Saharan Africa Poverty Headcount Ratio**
Source: The World Bank (2016).

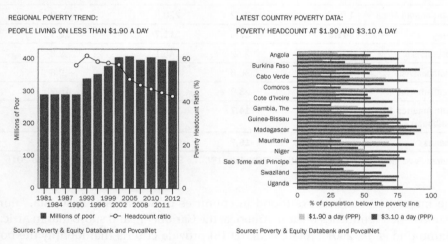

REGIONAL POVERTY TREND:

PEOPLE LIVING ON LESS THAN $1.90 A DAY

■ Millions of poor   –○– Headcount ratio

Source: Poverty & Equity Databank and PovcalNet

LATEST COUNTRY POVERTY DATA:

POVERTY HEADCOUNT AT $1.90 AND $3.10 A DAY

▨ $1.90 a day (PPP)   ■ $3.10 a day (PPP)

Source: Poverty & Equity Databank and PovcalNet

Inclusive Business as a Viable Option

The BoP has been used as a basis for describing a business strategy that focuses on meeting the segment's basic needs by including them in a company's value chain as consumers, producers, and entrepreneurs. This is often termed "inclusive business" (Hammond *et al.*, 2007). BoP business strategies involve shifts in the orientation of global and indigenous enterprises toward the underserved needs of the low-income population living across the rural and semi-urban locations of developing countries. (Goyal *et al.*, 2014). Nelson *et al.* (2009, p. 2) call inclusive business as "the new order for doing business" and describes the concept as business opportunities that involve the poor and unemployed local people in the business value chain.[4]

Gracia-DeLeone and Taj (2015) posit that evidence exists to prove that BoP can be a profitable venture. Chikweche (2013) posits that the BoP market is worth US$429 billion.[5] Gracia-DeLeone and Taj claim that companies that want to explore the BoP market can do so through the adoption of business models that create and revise products to fit the BoP needs and adapt their distribution methods to reach rural areas. Although it might be referred to as the bottom billion, this market segment desires quality products – at affordable prices. To deliver these affordable quality products, a different model, including production process and product design, must exist to ensure profitability (Gracia-DeLeone and Taj, 2015).[6]

These authors emphasize the critical nature of profits in ventures targeting the BoP, distinguishing them from social enterprises, the more mission-driven business entities geared to addressing social problems that disproportionately affect the poor.[7] The fundamental idea is derived from the observation that "business activities can contribute to the long-term goal of poverty alleviation by embedding

4 The BoP model flags contradictions where suppliers as BoP participants are at the receiving end of unequal bargains or as employees; they are subjected to suboptimal conditions. There is the further possibility that as customers, BoP participants are exposed to substandard goods or products that are outright bad for them. See Karnani, A. (2007). "Doing Well By Doing Good – Case Study 'Fair and Lovely' Whitening Cream," which highlights the divergence between private profits and public welfare in the case of marketing a health-threatening skin-whitening product formulated by Unilever for BoP markets in Africa and India.

5 The size of this market is disputed as scholars claim that this market is not as large and lucrative as it appears. *The Next 4 Billion*, a 2007 publication of the World Resources Institute and the World Bank, estimates the size of the BoP market to be a staggering $15 trillion a year. Karnani disputes this figure, positing that the BoP market is worth somewhere in the region of $0.36 trillion based on a poverty line of $1,000 at purchasing power parity (PPP) (which tallies with the commonly used $2/day) as opposed to the poverty cut-off level of $3,000 PPP used by the *Next 4 Billion* report. See Karnani, A. (2007). The Mirage of Marketing to the Bottom of the Pyramid. *California Management Review*, 49(4), 90-111.

6 Payaud (2014) posits that because the BoP market serves some of the poorest individuals on the planet, there are significant differences across marketing strategies directed at BoP consumers.

7 Inclusive businesses are also sometimes referred to as social enterprises – entrepreneurial initiatives seeking to build bridges between business and low-income populations for the benefit of both (SNV and WBCSD, 2008). Simanis and Duke (2014) assert that certain multinational companies in the past decades, preoccupied with social mission, have taken the challenging project of reaching the bottom billion with products or services and have ended up disillusioned by low consumer demands and obstacles such as bad roads that keep costs high and revenues low. Social enterprises in the inclusive business mold focus not only on integrating low-income earners in a business's value chain but also on solving particular social problems.

the neglected poor parts of the world population into efficient value chains and market structures, both as consumers and as producers or distributors" (Hahn, 2012, p. 51). Other literature sources suggest that the main difference between BoP initiatives and social enterprises is not related to profit-making (versus mission-serving) but rather to how the profits are owned and distributed: social enterprises reinvest profits to further strengthen social mission and/or scaling, rather than distribute them to shareholders.[8]

Research into the impact of BoP initiatives has reported some positive impacts economically for the business and socially for the local communities (Kolk *et al.*, 2013). Although not all studies reported positive impacts, the common assumption is that inclusive business is paying off for companies who choose it as a strategy. However, embedding inclusion in business models is not easy. There are hidden pitfalls, which are likely to hinder innovative BoP strategies. Lack of support from top management, focus on the wrong performance metrics, failure to recruit the right talent, employing old business models, and collaborating with the wrong organizations could easily lead to counterproductive results for a business. Further, Simanis and Duke (2014) posit that BoP consumers' resistance to new products because of reluctance to alter deeply ingrained mindsets and routines can be a pitfall to inclusive businesses. The lack of understanding of how to create a market based on the culture of the BoP can be another hurdle (Ahmed, 2013).

These pitfalls appear in sharp relief when doing business in sub-Saharan Africa where challenges such as lack of infrastructure and a strong informal economy could limit the execution of BoP strategies. In Africa's emerging economies, certain factors have to be taken into serious consideration, including focusing strategy based on the unique country and industry, planning operations management cognizant of external limitations, identifying local partnerships and ownership for finance and resources, developing and retaining the right talent, understanding the power of the communities, and engaging them as pertinent stakeholders (Mudida and Lago, 2015).

For instance, Gracia-DeLeone and Taj (2015) posit that since much of the BoP population is located in rural areas of developing countries where road networks are broken down, companies pursuing the BoP market must create innovative strategies to transfer products and services to the people. Such innovative strategies might include local distributors and distribution centers. Further, Ansari *et al.* (2012) assert that inclusive business initiatives should be evaluated on the basis of whether they advance capability transfer, diffusion, and retention by enhancing the social capital between a particular community and other, more resource-rich networks, and preserving the existing social capital in the community.

A profitable BoP market requires an understanding of BoP consumer behavior and best product creation and delivery methods (Simanis and Duke, 2014). This chapter presents illustrative examples of two businesses with such innovative

8 Social Enterprise UK (2011). Social Enterprise Explained.

inclusive business models in Africa. The examples are based on both primary (interviews, observations) and secondary research on the various companies.

Equity Bank Ltd's Shared Prosperity Model

Equity Bank Ltd is a leading inclusive bank in Africa by customer base, with over 9.2 million bank accounts. It hosts more than 50% of all bank accounts in Kenya and has operations across East Africa.[9] The bank evolved from a building society to a microfinance institution and then to a publicly traded commercial bank listed in the Nairobi Securities Exchange and cross-listed on the Uganda Securities Exchange. Equity Bank has been a leader in financial innovation influencing the agricultural sector in rural and remote regions of the country. It also played a leading role in championing agency banking in Kenya that continues to demystify banking by taking financial services to the doorsteps of citizens in Kenya, Rwanda, and Tanzania. The bank caters mainly to Kenyans in remote areas who are forced to travel long distances and spend huge amounts on transport in order to access a bank branch. In addition to the cost of transport, there are transaction costs relating to the loss of productive time.

The Central Bank of Kenya issued a law permitting commercial banks to contract third-party retail networks as agents to reduce the challenge of access to formal financial services. Equity Bank developed an agency-banking model that draws in BoP populations as commercial third-party agents in rural areas (bottom billion areas), providing access to financial services to the poor. The model equips the Equity Agents with the skills necessary to provide basic banking services according to standards set by the bank. The ease of access to financial services, which the agencies give the customers, is a major milestone in achieving financial inclusion in one of Africa's emerging economies. This model not only provides financial services to the unbanked in East Africa but also integrates them into the value chain of the bank as agents. Residents of the rural areas run agencies, thus leading to boosts in employment and income. For the bank, in addition to building markets through the innovative agency network, it reduces costs by having fewer branches to run to cover a large number of customers than would a traditional bank. Its network also forms the backbone of numerous international development-project partnerships, enabling the poor have access to health insurance, educational scholarships, primary health interventions, and agricultural aid.

---

9 Equity Bank has subsidiaries in Kenya, Uganda, South Sudan, Rwanda, and Tanzania. (http://ke.equitybankgrou.com/about-us/our history/our history)

Dufil Prima Foods' BoP Food and Retail Model

Dufil Prima Foods Plc is a subsidiary of the Indonesian company Tolaram Group. Dufil[10] entered the Nigerian culinary market more than 16 years ago and has made quite an impact. The company's most popular brand and product, Indomie Instant Noodles has a very high category penetration (60%), with a market size of 250,000 tons worth $600 million as of 2012, and it continues to be the dominant noodle brand in the country.

The company's BoP strategy resulted in innovations like producing the instant noodles in various local flavors and seasonings. Other innovations to serve the poor include the Hungry Man Pack and Family Pack Indomie instant noodles, which give the lowest of income earners the advantage of having a good meal for as low as 45 to 55 Naira ($0.23 to $0.28). This BoP strategy has indeed paid off, and the company continues to be profitable and enjoy the loyalty of its consumers.

Dufil Prima Foods Plc also integrates microbusinesses into its value chain in the form of distributors and retailers. The product is sold in corner shops in urban areas and in most kiosks and stores in rural areas. There, customers buy Indomie meals in minutes at prices affordable to the bottom billion. These local food spots not only provide nutritious meals for the poorer population but also serve as a lucrative business and means of employment for many distributors and retailers who would otherwise be without a means of livelihood. The employees in Dufil factories benefit from free meal programs, training/up-skilling opportunities, and a working environment that observes the highest standards in industrial hygiene and protection. The company operates three noodle factories across Nigeria, which are pioneers in the movement toward clean energy in the country. Dufil factories are predominantly gas-powered, in contrast to the ubiquitous use of highly polluting diesel generators, which are standard in energy-poor industry settings across the country. The company also engages in large-scale philanthropy in the educational and health sectors in poor urban and rural areas.

Using the UNGC framework, Dufil voluntarily reports and tracks (through its parent company the Tolaram Group) conditions relating to labor, human rights, and anticorruption in its factories. It has taken the further step of systematically analyzing the social and economic impacts of its business on the national economy and society, a process that holds interesting possibilities for addressing poverty. Dufil is focused on broadening its engagement with stakeholders and improving its already considerable impacts on livelihoods (labor rights, access to training, earnings and wages, community economic development), empowerment, health, and wellbeing.

10 De United Foods Industries Limited (Dufil) Noodle Division started operations in 1996. It is based in Nigeria, but its market is the West Africa region (http://www.dufil.com/about-companies.html).

Conclusion

The examples of Equity Bank Ltd and Dufil Prima Foods are but two illustrative cases emerging out of African countries, demonstrating that inclusive business models can be worthwhile ventures with significant benefits for addressing the multidimensional limitations of poverty. These benefits include value for both the business in terms of driving innovation, building markets, ensuring employee commitment, and strengthening supply chains, and for the poor in the form of increased access to essential goods and services, sustainable earnings, empowerment, and higher productivity.

In terms of management practice, these inclusive business models point the way to an expanded understanding of CSR as a shared value proposition, beyond philanthropy, in which business growth is aided by opportunities of earning and consumption it creates in broader society. Our understanding of the real impact these companies are making on the SDGs relating to poverty, inequality, and sustainable growth will become clearer as measuring socioeconomic impacts, corporate governance, and stakeholder engagement become standard practice in these companies operating locally in a global context. Therefore, PRME-based management education could help prepare business owners and managers in properly embedding inclusive business models into their organizations.

The SDGs offer a conceptual framework for businesses to focus their efforts on the most urgent development issues – stimulating whole new ideas for new businesses, products, and services. Besides advancing the SDGs related to reducing poverty and hunger, Dufil's business model, like that of Equity Bank, creates opportunities for realizing goal 8 (promote sustained, inclusive, and sustainable economic growth, full and productive employment, and decent work for all).

Noting the potential for inclusive businesses to address societal needs and drive developmental outcomes, Kofi Annan, former secretary-general of the United Nations and chief architect of the UNGC, stated: "It is the absence of broad-based business activity, not its presence, that condemns much of humanity to suffering. Indeed what is utopian is the notion that poverty can be overcome without the engagement of business" (Business Contribution to the Millennium Development Goals Conference, 2005).

References

Ahmed, F.E. (2013). The market at the bottom of the pyramid: Understanding the culture of poverty. *Perspectives on Global Development and Technology*, 12, 489-513.

Alkire, S., Roche, J.M., Seth, S., & Sumner, A. (2015). Identifying the poorest people and groups: Strategies using global multidimensional poverty index. *Journal of International Development*, 27(3), 362-387.

Ansari, S., Munir, K., & Gregg, T. (2012). Imapct at the "bottom of the pyramid": The role of social capital in capability development and community empowerment. *Journal of Management Studies*, 49(4), 813-842.

Ashley, C. (2009). Harnessing core business development impact: Evolving ideas and issues for action: Overseas Development Institute, 1-8.

Business Call to Action & United Nations Global Compact. (2015). *Implementing inclusive business models: How businesses can work with low-income communities: Inclusive business primer*. Retrieved January 9, 2017, from UN Global Compact: https://www.unglobalcompact.org/docs/issues_doc/human_rights/InclusiveBusinessPrimer.pdf

Chikweche, T. (2013). Revisiting the business environment at the bottom of the pyramid (BoP) - From theoretical considerations to practical realities. *Journal of Global Marketing*, 26, 239-257.

Collier, P. (2008). Global policies for the bottom billion. A progressive agenda for global action. London: Policy Network, 141-149.

Collier, P. (2007). *The Bottom Billion: Why the Poorest Countries Are Failing and What Can Be Done About It*. Oxford: Oxford University Press.

Davis, K. (1973). The case for and against business assumption of social responsibilities. *The Academy of Management Journal*, 16(2), 312-322.

Food and Agriculture Organization (FAO), International Fund for Agricultural Development (IFAD), and World Food Programme (WFP). (2015). The State of Food Insecurity in the World 2015. Meeting the 2015 international hunger targets: taking stock of uneven progress. Rome, FAO. Retrieved January 9, 2017, from FAO: https://www.google.com.ng/url?sa=t&rct=j&q=&esrc=s&source=web&cd=1&cad=rja&uact=8&ved=0ahU KEwiM3Niyg7HRAhWL1xoKHbVmBzoQFggbMAA&url=http%3A%2F%2Fwww.fao. org%2F3%2Fa-i4646e.pdf&usg=AFQjCNG5gCNRnzVVhdz9Nm5KI9rql7B23g&sig2=E K2W4-WozCIqlB-poMw-Pw

Goyal, S., Bruno, S. Sergi, Kapoor, A. (2014). Understanding the key characteristics of an embedded business model for the base of the pyramid markets. *Economics and Sociology*, 7(4), 26-40.

Goyal, S., Esposito, M., Kapoor, A., Jaiswal, M.P., Sergi, B.S. (2014). Linking up: inclusive business models for access to energy solutions at base of the pyramid in India. *International Journal of Business and Globalisation*, 12(4), 413–438.

Gracia-DeLeone, S., & Taj, S. (2015). A business model designed to tap into the bottom of the pyramid. *International Journal of Business, Marketing, and Decision Science*, 8(1), 136-149.

Hahn, R. (2012). Inclusive business, human rights and the dignity of the poor: a glance beyond economic impacts of adapted business models. *Business Ethics: A European Review*, 21(1), 47-63.

Hammond, A., Kramer, W., Katz, R., Tran, J., & Walker, C. (2007). *The Next 4 Billion: Market Size and Business Strategy at the Base of the Pyramid*. Washington, D.C.: World Resources Institute.

Kapoor, A., Goyal, S (2013). Inclusive healthcare at base of the pyramid (BoP) in India. *Int. J. Trade and Global Markets*, 6(1), 22-39.

Karamchandani, A., Kubzansky, M., & Lalwani, N. (2011). Is the bottom of the pyramid really for you? *Harvard Business Review*, 89(3), 107-111.

Karnani, A., (2009). The bottom of the pyramid strategy for reducing poverty: A failed promise. Department of Economics and Social Affairs DESA Working Paper No 80. New York.

Karnani, A. (2007a). Doing well by doing good—Case study: "Fair & Lovely whitening cream." *Strategic Management Journal*, 28(13), 1351-1357.

Karnani, A. (2007b). The mirage of marketing to the bottom of the pyramid: How the private sector can help alleviate poverty. *California management review*, 49(4), 90-111.

Kolk, A., Rivera-Santos, M. and Rufín, C. (2013). Reviewing a decade of research on the "base/ bottom of the pyramid" (BoP) concept. *Business & Society*, 53(3), 338-377.

Mudida, R., Lago, A. (2015). Five pillars for doing business in Africa: A roadmap to opportunities. *IESE Insight*, 24, 15-23.

Nelson, J., Ishikawa, E., & Geaneotes, A. (2009). *Developing Inclusive Business Models: A Review of Coca-Cola's Maual Distribution Centers in Ethiopia and Tanzania*. Cambridge: Harvard Kennedy School and International Finance Corporation.

Payaud, M.A. (2014). Marketing strategies at the bottom of the pyramid: Examples from Nestle, Danone, and Procter & Gamble. *Global Business and Organizational Excellence*, 33(2), 51-63.

Population Reference Bureau. (2015). 2015 World Population Data Sheet with a special focus on women's empowerment. Retrieved from http://www.prb.org/pdf15/2015-world-population-data-sheet_eng.pdf.

Porter, M.E., & Kramer, M.R. (2006). Strategy & society: The link between competitive advantage and corporate social responsibility. *Harvard Business Review*, 85, 78-92.

Porter, M.E., & Kramer, M.R. (2011). Creating shared value: How to reinvent capitalism – and unleash a wave of innovation and growth. *Harvard Business Review*, 89(1/2), 62-77.

Responsible and Inclusive Business (RIB) Asia. (2015). Creating shared value through inclusive business strategies (pp. 1-31). RIB Asia.

Simanis, E., & Duke, D. (2014). Profits at the bottom of the pyramid: A tool for assessing your opportunities. *Harvard Business Review*, October 2014, 87-93.

Stichting Nederlandse Vrijwilligers (SNV) and World Business Council for Sustainable Development (WBCSD). (2008). Inclusive business: Profitable business for successful development Geneva: WBCSD and SNV.

Social Enterprise UK. (2011). Social Enterprise Explained. Retrieved from http://www. socialenterprise.org.uk/uploads/editor/files/Publications/Social_Enterprise_ Explained.pdf.

Sustainable Development Goals. (2015). Sustainable Development Goals. Sustainable Development Knowledge Platform. Sustainabledevelopment.un.org. Retrieved from http:// sustainabledevelopment.un.org/?menu=1300.

The World Bank. (2016). Sub-Saharan Africa [Latest Country Poverty Data: Poverty Head Count at $1.90 and $3.10 a day] based on data set released 2016-10-18 and accessed 2016-11-15 at http://povertydata.worldbank.org/poverty/region/SSA.

Ijeoma Nwagwu is Center Manager at the First Bank Sustainability Centre of Lagos Business School. She earned her doctorate in law (S.J.D) and Master's in Law (L.L.M) degrees from Harvard Law School. She is a researcher, lecturer, and writer and currently teaches corporate social responsibility, sustainability strategy, and social entrepreneurship at Lagos Business School.

inwagwu@lbs.edu.ng

10
The Global Sanitation Crisis: A Role for Business

Diane M. Kellogg
Bentley University, USA

Talking about Toilets

About two-thirds of the 7.4 billion people living on the planet take household toilets for granted. The other third, 2.4 billion people, do not have access to safe sanitation.[1] This chapter attempts to bring this reality into the light of day, with the intention of engaging business and management education in the challenging work of providing safe sanitation. It requires talking about toilets.

The depth and breadth of the sanitation crisis has been acknowledged by the United Nations and the Sustainable Development Goals (SDGs). Goal 6 is "Ensure access to water and sanitation for all." Millions of people live off-grid – no water pipes and no sewer pipes. Clean water and clean sanitation go hand in hand; however, this chapter focuses on toilets and the millions of people among the urban and rural poor who are forced to resort to makeshift solutions.

Off-grid toilets do exist; however, private enterprise has not yet succeeded in developing sustainable business models, reliable supply chains, or financial-service products that appeal to the poor. To encourage managers and aspiring managers to thoughtfully engage with the topic of toilets, this chapter poses the question, "How can business and management education address the need for household toilets for the urban poor?"

---

1 http://www.gatesfoundation.org/What-We-Do/Global-Development/Water-Sanitation-and-Hygiene

The chapter summarizes the current reality and consequences for public health and then analyzes the root causes of the sanitation problem, especially as experienced by the urban poor. It then looks at business opportunities that could help address the problem and implications for the curriculum for business and management education.

Current Reality and Consequences for Public Health

Of the 2.4 billion people who do not have access to safe sanitation, 1.1 billion rely on open defecation. Population growth has outstripped the capacity of sewage-treatment plants, which must stop accepting sewage as soon as they reach their daily capacity. "Suck truck" drivers are on their own to find a place to dump untreated sewage. In Ghana, the Metropolitan District of the city of Accra complains that the federal government has not provided enough legal sites for dumping; the federal government complains that the Metropolitan District is not fining drivers who dump raw sewage into the ocean.

Septic tanks offer a sanitary solution that can be good for the environment if the tank is emptied often enough, is treated properly, and if groundwater conditions are suitable. However, in many countries with inadequate infrastructures, untreated sewage is dumped illegally into the environment. Dumping large amounts of untreated waste into a single location makes this practice even more dangerous to the environment than open defecation.

When waste is left on the surface of the land, natural decomposition processes take over. Evaporation dries it out, taking away the smell, and macro- and micro-organisms that have evolved to thrive on excrement do their work. (The smell lasts long enough to attract macro-organisms and the micro-organisms live in the soil and air in the first place.) Pathogens die off as liquids are filtered through the earth. Open defecation is not an unsafe solution if the population density is low enough and the water table is not close enough to the surface to be at risk. However, the risk of harassment and rape to women and girls out at night is a very real danger that cannot be dismissed. Most countries want to end open defecation completely, and the community-led total sanitation (CLTS) movement is gaining momentum. CLTS refers to efforts to achieve sustained behavior change that will lead to the complete abandonment of open defecation practices.

As agrarian living gave way to urbanization, societies developed manmade sanitation solutions, such as flush toilets and sewer pipes leading to sewage treatment plants. However, sometimes infrastructure did not stay ahead of the curve, especially on the outskirts of cities where people created informal settlements. Figure 10.1 shows rooftops of tin, thatch, and plywood; closely packed makeshift housing; and foot paths instead of the roads that would be necessary for trucks to access septic tanks for household toilets.

Figure 10.1 **Aerial view of a crowded, informal settlement**
Source: Shutterstock.

Some see public facilities as the most practical solution in crowded areas, though they can be fraught with problems. The smell can be overwhelming, and septic tanks overflow if owners expecting to maximize their profits call the "suck truck" infrequently. Residents who cannot afford to pay for public toilets (and some who can) preserve their dignity by resorting to buckets or plastic bags used in the privacy of their own home. The bags become "flying toilets." Neighbors cooperate with each other to toss bags and empty buckets in agreed upon areas. People do the best they can.

Disease is the consequence of inadequate sanitation. Sarkodie (2014) highlights that the incidents of cholera in Accra, Ghana, in 2014 were most prevalent in the densely populated areas. He points out that diarrhea, caused by exposure to untreated waste, unsafe drinking water, inadequate sanitation, and poor hygiene, kills nearly 2 million people worldwide each year, and 1.5 million of those are children.

The whole population suffers if water supplies and the environment become polluted. Disease takes a toll on productivity, and there are financial costs, too. Polluted water, loss of land for agriculture and increasing need for health care all place demands on household budgets. At the local, state, and federal government levels, tax revenues go toward remedial expenses, such as cleaning up areas where flying toilets accumulate, instead of investments in prevention.

Root Causes of the Sanitation Crisis

Some of the failures contributing to the sanitation crisis include:

- **A failure of urban planning.** When people began squatting on land on the outskirts of cities where services and infrastructure did not extend (no water pipes, no sewer pipes, no schools, no storm drains, and no hospitals) governments did not respond quickly enough with alternatives. Urban-planning processes and zoning laws were nonexistent, inadequate, or unenforced.

- **A failure of law enforcement.** Governments restrict building on floodplains and in dry river beds; yet squatters find open land during the dry season and establish a home. Compassion sometimes guides inaction, but in the long run, nature takes back the land it needs for water management, and people live in swampy conditions during the rainy season. Since governments don't provide sewers or even roads that suck trucks need to access septic tanks, governments are not in a good position to enforce laws requiring homeowners and landlords to provide toilets.

  A high percentage of urban poor residents are renters who cannot be expected to invest in a toilet for a home they don't own. Landlords – both live-in and absentee – are often just as poor as their tenants. Without some legal protection, people who may have built homes as squatters are unwilling to invest in household toilets since they don't have clear title to the land. Water and Sanitation for the Urban Poor produced an informative report on land tenure and tenancy issues that impact sanitation progress (WSUP 2013).

- **A failure of market-based approaches.** The private sector succeeds when entrepreneurs are motivated to design, build, and sell products that people want, need, and can afford. The urban poor may want toilets, but their limited incomes go to higher priority items: food, shelter, education, and health care. They are not buying toilets. Reliance on "pure" free-market thinking will get the same results: no toilets for the poor. Meanwhile, businesses selling trips to outer space or smaller, more powerful computers thrive.

- **A failure of the financial-services industry, including microfinance**. The financial-services industry offers credit to the creditworthy and balks at giving loans to high-risk customers or offers them loans with higher interest rates. If a middle-class family needs a refrigerator and cannot afford the purchase price, it can use a credit card and pay over time. The poor do not have such instant access to capital. Microfinance has been touted as the key to economic development, yet success has been limited to cases where the loan enables the purchase of a "productive asset" – an asset that generates income. Household toilets do not generate income, and families who are not paying for public toilets in the first place will not even be saving money if they own a household toilet.

- **The inability to shift momentum away from established practices.** The solution of mixing excrement with water so it can be flushed out of sight became the norm and has momentum. Cities still require sewer pipes even though safe, off-grid alternatives are now available, cost-effective, and environmentally friendly. City populations have grown beyond the capacity of sewage- and water-treatment plants, outdated technology is in need of repair or replacement, and urban planning has not stayed ahead of population growth. Still, the momentum of history favors the "flush and forget" approach.

Shared Responsibility

Regardless of the root causes, responsibility for achieving SDG6 needs to be shared among a number of actors and organizations. The Sustainable Sanitation Alliance (SuSanA)[2], the brainchild of Arno Rosemarin of the Stockholm Environmental Institute (SEI) and Christine Werner of the Germany Agency for Technical Cooperation (GTZ), now has over 7,000 members. "The purpose of creating SuSanA in 2007 was to bring together organizations and individuals to advise the UN prior to the UN Year of Sanitation in 2008," said Rosemarin. "It wasn't meant to last longer than a year or two but SuSanA self-ignited once we established the 12 working groups."[3]

The SuSanA secretariat concluded that a new approach was needed for the 2016 symposium held in Kampala, Uganda. The three-day gathering explored two key questions: what are the broader systems that impact sanitation and how can we, as a community of practice, impact those broader systems? Patrick Moriarty, CEO of IRC (originally International Water and Sanitation Center) summarized the insights of the gathering of sanitation professionals with "Our job will not be finished until we have the full engagement of government and the private sector" (Moriarty, 2016). NGOs, foundations, and sanitation specialists might be valuable, but they are not going to succeed on their own.

Achieving the full engagement of governments has been challenging. Sanitation is one of many priorities competing for a place in tight budgets. Sanitation consultants are discouraged, yet realistic about the role government must play. Marijn Zandee, a freelance sanitation consultant based in Kathmandu, Nepal, has said, "Governments need to convince people, through public campaigns and enforced regulations, that their life is not complete without proper sanitation. Then they need to set and enforce sanitation standards."[4]

---

2 http://www.susana.org/en
3 E-mail correspondence between Rosemarin and the author, July 2016.
4 E-mail correspondence between Zandee and the author, July 2016.

Achieving the full engagement of the private sector is equally challenging. The Stone Family Foundation (THESFF), a UK charitable trust, is keenly focused on market-based solutions because, as stated on the foundation's website, "Solutions based on free products and services cannot be sustained: funds will inevitably dry up long before all needs are met. In comparison, market based solutions that create a revenue stream have the potential to become truly sustainable."

While this chapter focuses on the role of the private sector, experience suggests that individuals, governments, and philanthropic foundations are needed to support private-sector engagement.

Engaging the Private Sector in Selling Off-Grid Toilets

An excellent discussion of the topic is found in "Private sector engagement in sanitation and hygiene: Exploring roles across the sanitation chain" (Caplan, 2016). It summarizes a month-long, online discussion available to thousands of sanitation professionals and notes that the whole supply chain for sanitation represents a long list of untapped business opportunities.

Off-grid toilets also represent a wealth of "untapped opportunity." Ecological sanitation (eco-san) alternatives have been around for a long time though no private companies have successfully scaled up and marketed to the poor. In 2011 the Bill and Melinda Gates Foundation (BMGF) issued a "Reinvent the Toilet Challenge" to encourage even more innovation and new ideas. The foundation interviewed leaders of the eco-san movement extensively and proposed criteria for acceptable toilets, including "no connection to water, sewer or electricity required" and "removes germs from human waste and recovers valuable resources (energy, clean water, nutrients)" (BMGF, 2011). The foundation funded a number of new ideas. However, as of 2016, success in bringing any of these products to scale could not yet be reported.

Several companies have taken up the challenge of turning human waste into something that has market value ("waste-to-value" solutions), such as energy, fertilizer, or briquettes for cook stoves. Classified as "container-based" solutions, each toilet has an easily removed container that collects the human waste, which companies periodically pick up. As of this writing, these enterprises are still somewhat dependent on grants and foundations, though each aspires to build a profitable business.

Several toilet companies produce an off-grid, on-site waste-processing unit, which is a specially designed box or tube that first separates liquids and solids and then provides a hospitable environment for aerobic organisms to eat the dried solids. All use naturally occurring aerobic bacteria; some add a specially formulated bacteria packet to seed the system and some seed with larger fecal-eating organisms such as black soldier flies or worms. The term "tiger toilet" is used when tiger worms are seeded to promote faster decomposition. Each of these companies has its own proprietary design for the digester or vermi-composting unit.

Any company formed to sell off-grid toilets to the poor faces the same problem. The very customers who need off-grid toilets find it difficult to pay for a household toilet. They have higher priorities and little to no disposable income that would enable them to buy more than basic necessities.

Redefining the Customer as "Society"

The question can be asked: are businesses targeting the right customer? Profit-making businesses will – and must – gravitate toward customers who can and will pay for a product. If the poor cannot pay, perhaps businesses aren't selling to the right customer.

Since whole communities are at risk if we continue to tolerate open defecation and the illegal dumping of untreated waste, perhaps the community is the right customer. Could governments not step in and provide off-grid toilets for off-grid settlements to protect the community as a whole? Other possible "customers" are philanthropists and foundations. The Stone Family Foundation adamantly supports market-based approaches yet acknowledges that "the very poor may never be able to afford to pay for services – and here philanthropy will always play a role" (THESFF, 2016).

Redefining the customer as "society" acknowledges that the sanitation crisis is global and makes it possible for business to play a role in the sanitation crisis. Governments, foundations, and philanthropists can (and do) put pressure on companies to sell at reasonable prices, so price gouging isn't likely, yet profits will add up if companies can grow based on large purchases.

For example, Ecoloo Africa is growing its business by selling Ecoloo Economy (a digester-based toilet) to foundations and governments who are replacing pit latrines in Nairobi's urban poor schools with more hygienic toilets. The company has found a way to benefit the poor and are still looking for a way to sell its household toilet to the poor.

Business Opportunities

As long as affordability issues persist, it may continue to be impractical to scale up a toilet business. The lack of access to upfront capital necessary for buying an off-grid toilet seems to be a primary, if not *the* primary, roadblock standing between the urban poor and household toilets. Given that, the following business opportunities seem most promising.

- **Venture capital investments.** Toilet companies have the option of seeking venture-capital money to enable them to finance sales on credit to customers who can't afford the upfront capital. "Social investors" can be satisfied with modest profits when they are supporting social causes or underserved populations.

- **Toilet loans.** Banks in Africa quote interest rates by the month, making rates sound reasonable. For example, a simple interest 3% loan sounds better than a 36% per annum loan. While this seems outrageous to Westerners, banks are protecting their assets from inflation. In 2014, Ghana's inflation rate was 29%. "Sanitation loans" are available in Ghana, but in interviews conducted by the author in 2016, banks report they have a hard time finding customers. The option of requiring buyers to save a certain percentage before being granted a toilet loan can be built in to the business model. Improve International (2015) compiled a list of case studies about sanitation loans that suggests some business models that have and haven't worked.

- **Pay-as-you-go (PAYG) household toilets.** Solar power can be turned off via a cell-phone chip if owners who have purchased a home solar unit on credit fail to make payments. Such a chip could be installed that would lock and unlock the door of the toilet room as loan payments are made using mobile money networks (MMNs), with the lock being received when the final payment is made. The risk of forced entry makes this solution questionable, and the lock will increase the price.

- **Cross-subsidies.** New ideas and new thinkers are needed, yet trying some of the old ideas in the sanitation space could also work. First-class seats subsidize economy seats on airplanes, and neither the first-class nor the economy passengers are complaining: natural market forces are at work. Sanitation companies that have a range of products could redefine themselves as social enterprises and make their profits on sales to the middle class to enable them to be sustainable while charging affordable prices for products for off-grid customers.

- **Public-private partnerships.** For input to this chapter, the author crowdsourced two questions with sanitation consultants who are active on the SuSanA Forum: what is the role of business? What is the role of government? There was a consensus about the importance of both, as already discussed. In his Impatient Optimists blog, Jan-Willem Rosenboom, BMGF Senior Program Officer of Demand-led Sanitation, calls for the support of both government and business (Rosenboom, 2011).

  This speaks to the importance of the private sector not trying to "go it alone," but working to find synergies with local, regional, and federal governments in marketing off-grid toilets to the poor. The need for PPPs speaks to the importance of the last SDG. Goal 17 calls for the strengthening of global partnerships in working toward all the SDGs.

- **Radically new business models.** Could business interests find a way to radically change the sanitation industry, making sanitation accessible to the poor? Hopefully a new generation of students and problem-solvers can come up with sustainable business models.

Potential Business and Management Education Curriculum

The UN Global Compact challenges organizations across the globe to support the SDGs. The Principles for Responsible Management Education (PRME) encourage universities to educate students about each of the SDGs. Sanitation cuts across many disciplines including both liberal arts and sciences courses and business courses. Courses in which the topic of sanitation could be incorporated to challenge the next generation of leaders in the business world to think about the sanitation crisis are suggested below. One compelling question is proposed for each area of study.

- **Entrepreneurship**
  Upon visiting an urban slum in Ghana in 2013, a successful "serial entrepreneur" noted that less than 1% of the population drinks cranberry juice once a week, yet the industry is extremely profitable. In contrast, 100% of the population uses a toilet every day of the week, and more than once a day. If 2.4 billion people do not have a toilet? Now that's a business opportunity. Cheryl Hicks, the executive director of the Toilet Board Coalition and author of the article "Toilets for 2.4 Billion—the Business Opportunity of the Decade," agrees (Hicks, 2015). *What products and business models would enable entrepreneurs to start profitable businesses in the sanitation industry?*

- **Global Health**
  According to the Centers for Disease Control and Prevention (CDC), diarrhea kills more children every day than AIDS, malaria, and measles combined[5]. Further, every dollar spent on preventing diarrhea yields a return of $25.50 (CDC, 2013). Instead of spending money on treating preventable diseases, money could be spent on sanitation to eliminate the root cause of many preventable diseases. Investments in sanitation will mean less money needed for environmental remediation and medical care. *What would motivate governments to make better investments in sanitation to prevent disease?*

- **Marketing to the BoP**
  Taken as a whole, the poor represent a great deal of buying power. Some argue that businesses should be targeting that market with relevant products and

5 http://www.cdc.gov/healthywater/pdf/global/programs/globaldiarrhea508c.pdf

services. Others argue that businesses should start by employing the poor, so that they have more disposable income in the first place. In "The Wealth of the Poor" the authors assert that "Marketing innovative solutions for the BoP is not about selling cheap products or reducing the size of packaging. It is about caring enough about customers to ensure that all of them get all the benefits that these products claim to offer" (Kayser, 2015). *What conditions would motivate businesses to take the risk of marketing products to the BoP?*

- **Business Ethics**
  Should businesses serve the poor, even if it is not as profitable? Should businesses employ the poor, even if they have to spend more on education and/ or training? Is sanitation a basic human right? Should government accept responsibility for health, education, and sanitation? *What kind of a society do we want to create?*

- **Organization Behavior and Change**
  Changing the habits of communities that have long practiced open defecation is a challenge. In India, the government installed latrines in the yards of thousands of families only to find that they were being used for storage or other purposes. People did not like the idea of being closed in a tiny box, where the smell was so repulsive. Many cultures of the world eat only with the right hand, and the left hand is reserved for hygiene purposes: handwashing requires water, and taking water "to the bush" is inconvenient and impractical if water is scarce and reserved for drinking and cooking. November 19 has been World Toilet Day since 2001, and Global Handwashing Day is always on October 15. *What would it take to change social and cultural habits to eliminate open defecation and promote hand-washing?*

- **Public Policy**
  What priority does sanitation have in the budgeting processes of federal, state, and local governments? How do budget figures for education and health care compare to sanitation spending? Is sanitation treated as an investment in the future, taking into account population growth? *How can citizens influence government to give higher priority to sanitation for the poor?*

- **Finance**
  How can the banking industry address the need for capital that is so crucial to economic development at the BoP? How can banks in the developing world cope with inflation while attempting to provide affordable loans to the population? What role does society play in assuring that the poor do not get boxed out of prosperity? *What roles can the banking industry play in alleviating poverty?*

Concluding Comment

Sanitation deserves attention and investment. The health of the population and the health of the planet are at stake. Government alone has not been able to provide adequate sanitation for growing populations, and the involvement of private enterprise appears to be crucial. New business models and new partnerships are needed to achieve "water and sanitation for all." The call for better approaches to sustainable sanitation places responsibility on business and management education to encourage more talk about the issues.

Bibliography and Key Resources on Sanitation

Caplan, Ken. Private sector engagement in sanitation and hygiene: Exploring roles across the sanitation chain.Susana.org. Retrieved from http://www.susana.org/en/resources/library/details/2405.

Hicks, C. (2015, November 19). Toilets for the 2.4 billion – the business opportunity of the decade. *Triple Pundit: People, Planet, Profit.*

Improve International. (2015, December). Resources on Microfinance for Water & Sanitation. Retrieved from https://improveinternational.files.wordpress.com/2015/12/resources-on-microfinance-for-water-sanitation-12-16-15.pdfn.

Kayser, O.& Budinich, V. (2015, February). Scaling up business solutions to social problems. Retrieved from http://community.businessfightspoverty.org/profiles/blogs/olivier-kayser-and-valeria-budinich-the-wealth-of-the-poor.

Moriarty, P. (2016, June). Keynote Address. SuSanA Conference. Kampala, Uganda.

Rosenboom, J.W. (2012, November 17). Funding a safe way to poop. *Impatient Optimists.* Retrieved from http://www.impatientoptimists.org/Posts/2011/11/Funding-A-Safe-Way-to-Poop#.V5YMhfkrLX4.

Sarkodie, Badu. (2014). Addressing the cholera epidemic. UER Health Training Center. Bolgotanga, Ghana. Retrieved from http://www.slideshare.net/GeorgeAkowuah/cholera-update-ddhs-group-agm-05-sep2014-dr-sarkodie.

Toilet Board Coalition (TBC). http://toiletboard.org/.

WHO/UNICEF. (2008). Joint Monitoring Programme for Water Supply and Sanitation. Retrieved from http://www.who.int/mediacentre/news/releases/2008/pr23/en.

World Toilet Organization (WTO). http://worldtoilet.org/media/resource-portal.

Water and Sanitation for the Urban Poor (WSUP). (2013, February). Dealing with land tenure and tenancy challenges in water and sanitation services delivery. Retrieved from http://www.bpdws.org/web/d/DOC_353.pdf?statsHandlerDone=1 TB#006.

Diane M. Kellogg, Associate Professor of Management, founded The Ghana Project at Bentley University in 2006 to challenge students to consider how business could address problems in the developing world. As a Managing Partner of Kellogg Consultants, she is a strategic management and marketing consultant supporting social enterprises related to sanitation, solar energy, and poverty alleviation.

dkellogg@kelloggconsultants.com

11

Gender, Poverty and Leadership
The Case of the Chibok Girls

Roni Ajao
MRL Public Sector Consultants Ltd, UK

Nikos Bozionelos
EM Lyon Business School, France

Camilla Quental
Audencia Business School, France

In the Quiet of Twilight

This chapter focuses on the kidnapping of nearly 300 girls in Chibok, Nigeria, in April 2014. The case involves issues including human rights, gender equality, governance, and leadership. The analysis shows that these subjects are interconnected and issues that on the surface appear unidimensional are, in fact, caused by interactions of many factors. The case indicates the profound role of gender bias, the role that businesses can play in areas plagued by armed conflict, and the importance in management education of encouraging critical thinking and the development of the ability to investigate and uncover the root causes of problems, especially those that have connections with the wider society.

The case of the Chibok girls could appear to be simply an act by an illegal or terrorist group. However, its actual causes and outcomes (that are still in progress) have much more to do with poverty, cultural mentality about gender, leadership, and governance. With reference to the principles of the UN Global Compact (UNGC), the case suggests that education can assist at every level, analyzing, for example, how leaders can and should act in crisis situations, governance issues, and societal/stakeholders' views about gender and diversity more generally. It also highlights the importance that businesses can play on these fronts.

What follows is the description of the event, which made shocking headlines around the world more than two years ago. It continues to do so. The story re-emerged following the discovery of one of the girls on May 18, 2016 (BBC, 2016) and the recent release of a further 21 girls (BBC, 2016). The plight of the 197 remaining kidnapped girls, however, remains for the most part unresolved.

The Case

The kidnapping took place in the quiet of twilight on April 14, 2014 from a secondary school in Chibok, in the state of Borno, in northeastern Nigeria. On that evening, members of Boko Haram, an extremist group based in northeastern Nigeria, arrived at the school premises pretending to be soldiers with the mission to protect the girls (Amnesty International, 2015). The girls, aged 16 to 18, were at the school to take their final West African School Certificate examinations but instead were herded into vehicles at gunpoint. The intruders did not discriminate between Christians and Muslims. During the kidnapping some girls escaped by putting their lives at risk, such as hanging on to tree branches when the trucks slowed down or simply jumping from the truck. Official reports about the number of missing girls varied and contradicted each other, sometimes being retracted a few hours after their release. The most reliable estimate brings the number of abducted girls to 276 (Usman, 2014), and the number of girls left in captivity after those who escaped to 219 (BBC, 2016).

False hopes in the recovery of the girls were raised in October 2014 when an apparent agreement between the Nigerian government and the abductors was claimed. However, this did not prove fruitful. Today, more than two and a half years after the event, the fate of these girls remains unknown and uncertain. Reports that trickled out from the abductors themselves, along with the single girl who was recovered two years later (see below) indicate that the captured girls were forced to convert into Islam and then were sold as wives mostly to members of the group (LaFranchi, 2014; BBC, 2016) . Some of them have systematically been turned into terrorists (Searcey, 2016; BBC, 2014a). The girl who escaped in May 2016 was rescued by an army-backed vigilante group who found her wandering with her baby, fathered by her "husband," a Boko Haram member (BBC, 2016).

Immense criticisms were made against the government at the time relating to the lack of a sense of urgency and of readiness, as well as inadequate efforts in the rescue operation and ineffective and inefficient management overall. The mass kidnapping resulted in unprecedented worldwide attention leading to a viral social media campaign (#BringBackOurGirls) demanding the release of the girls that was backed by well-known personalities including the U.S. first lady Michelle Obama and the then-U.K. prime minister David Cameron. On January 14, 2016, 652 days since the kidnapping, the newly elected Nigerian president, Muhammadu Buhari, and his administration ordered a new investigation (Newsweek, 2016). A further ray of hope emerged on the 13th October, 2016 when 21 of the kidnapped girls were freed by Boko Haram following intense negotiations by the 'new' Nigerian government and the International Red Cross (BBC, 2016). Discussions with Boko Haram are continuing to secure the release of the remaining girls.

This case is not unique: in certain parts of the world abductions of young females to deprive them of education are not rare. Boko Haram praises itself as an organization that safeguards and promotes traditional Islamic education, including the idea that women should not be educated. In fact, the name of the organization means "Western education is sinful."

What makes this case particularly important is the intricately interconnected issues relating to gender (in)equality, education, poverty, leadership, and governance. Nearly three weeks following the kidnapping, under the previous Nigerian administration, officials within the Nigerian government came forward with conflicting statements (BBC, 2014b). Some officials denied the abduction; others gave contradictory statements with regard to the total number of girls kidnapped; some even proclaimed the girls had been rescued. Amid these uncoordinated and inconsistent public relations exercises that magnified the confusion and lamentation of the parents, a video was released on May 5, 2014 by Boko Haram itself claiming responsibility for the kidnappings (BBC, 2014a). Moreover, the Nigerian army officially acknowledged that it had been given a four-hour notice about the imminent kidnapping but had failed to mobilize its resources (ABC News, 2014).

The kidnapping of the Chibok girls – from the event itself to the way it has been handled – is fundamentally at odds with the UNGC Principles on Human Rights and Labour[1]. The case can, therefore, serve as a vehicle for more attention to issues of women's and girls' rights from the international community, for action from multinational corporations who operate in the region, and also for educational initiatives in leadership.

The Context of Nigeria and How It Relates to the Case

Nigeria is a diverse and complex nation. Popularly referred to as the Giant of Africa, it is the continent's largest economy, with a variety and abundance of natural resources including oil (Shendy *et al.*, 2015). However, like many African and developing nations, Nigeria faces extreme poverty in parts of the population. What makes the situation especially difficult is that Nigeria's estimated population of 170 million is divided into six geo-political zones (Shendy *et al.*, 2015) and comprises

---

1 https://www.unglobalcompact.org/what-is-gc/mission/principles

well over 250 ethnic groups (CIA, 2016). Despite Nigeria's ethnic multiplicity, the country is arbitrarily divided on religious grounds. Islam dominates the northern part of the country, with approximately 50% of the population, whereas Christianity is the main religion of the south, with approximately 40% of the population. The remaining 10% is composed of local traditional religions.

The northern states of Nigeria have higher rates of poverty and illiteracy. For example, in Borno, the home state of the kidnapped Chibok girls, two-thirds of the population is illiterate (Amnesty International, 2015). This leads to perceptions of inequity with consequent blaming of other parts of Nigeria for the situation. In particular, a widespread view in Borno is that the wealthy Christian elite are responsible for the impoverishment of Muslim communities by means of influencing decisions about development and resource allocations in their favor (Agbiboa, 2013).

Such circumstances gives rise to groups like Boko Haram. The idea, emanating from beliefs as those illustrated above, is that anything "Western," including concepts of equality and education for both genders, weakens the Muslim religion and is a cause of poverty. Education is perceived as a way of converting Muslims to Christians and as a form of southern wealthy elite domination over the north (Agbiboa, 2013).

Integrating the UNGC

The case of the kidnapping of the Chibok girls calls our attention to the importance of integrating the principles of the UNGC into management practices, especially leadership and decision-making. Of the ten principles, six are most relevant to this case:

- Principle 1: *Businesses should support and respect the protection of internationally proclaimed human rights*

- Principle 2: *make sure that they are not complicit in human rights abuses*

- Principle 4: *the elimination of all forms of forced and compulsory labour*

- Principle 5: *the effective abolition of child labour*

- Principle 6: *the elimination of discrimination in respect of employment and occupation*

- Principle 10: *Businesses should work against corruption in all its forms*

What role can businesses play in implementing these principles?

In fact, by adhering to these principles, businesses can do much to prevent and defuse the threat of terrorist groups such as Boko Haram.

First, businesses can create local job opportunities for young people. In Nigeria and in neighboring countries such as Cameroon, Chad, and Niger, a lack of opportunities makes young people more vulnerable and consequently more inclined to join insurgent groups (Onuoha, 2014). Recent empirical research shows that offering employment opportunities to young people in fragile (poor and undergoing civil war) states reduces the risk of their engaging in illegal activities and of joining military groups (Blattman and Annan, 2016). Thus, creating jobs for young people, especially in the north of Nigeria, would help to dry up the terrorist groups' recruiting base.

Second, support regional counter-extremism programs. We know from scientific research that by starting and enacting some counterterrorism measures, businesses can create a feeling of security in the community (Howie, 2009). Such operations should be framed in Arabic, Hausa, and Kanuri languages, respecting traditions and culture, in order to deflate Boko Haram's ideology, narratives, and messages, and thus making local recruitment difficult for terrorist groups (Onuoha, 2014).

Third, cut off the terrorist funding stream. Some businesses, such as Kidnapping for Ransom (K4R), constitute a significant source of revenue for terrorist and criminal groups operating in this region (Onuoha, 2014). Banks and oil companies operating in Nigeria and neighboring countries should not, directly nor indirectly, bolster the operational capabilities of terrorist groups.

Fourth, fight against corruption, which represents a very insidious problem for companies doing business in the region. Practical advice given by Shapiro (2014) is for companies to obtain legal, accounting, consulting, and brokerage advice from reputable global service providers with a local presence.

Fifth, support public-private partnerships that are an emerging form of business development in Nigeria, offering the potential to meet social demands in many areas such as infrastructure, health care, energy, education, agriculture, and even the film industry (dubbed "Nollywood") (Shapiro, 2014). For example, the World Bank is financing research into chemical engineering, crop science, and control of infectious diseases. Businesses can thus be part of these public-private partnerships that can lead to substantial benefits for the local population, hence reducing the extent of support and membership in extremist groups.

Finally, hire and/or promote local women in positions of visibility. This will not only provide women gainful employment, but also contribute toward changing the stereotype of women in the local population.

Gender, Education, and Poverty

The high degree of gender inequality in education in northern Nigeria places the majority of girls at a severe disadvantage. For example, less than half of young girls (starting from the age of six) living in northern Nigeria are currently enrolled in school (Nmadu *et al.*, 2015).

Notwithstanding the progress that has been made in past decades (e.g., the gender gap between men and women in career outcomes seems to narrow, Baruch and Bozionelos, 2011), the issue of girls' and women's disadvantage is far from resolved, especially in developing countries. A profound illustration is the case of the Taliban's assassination attempt on Malala Yusafzai, the laureate of the 2014 Nobel Peace Prize for her advocacy for women's right to education. The UN 2015 International Women's Day focused on the role of governments in addressing the existing gaps in gender equality[2]. Numerous organizations, such as the European Parliament through its Committee on Women's Rights and Gender Equality, also emphasize the need for empowerment of women and girls through education (European Parliament Committees, 2016).

The Tenet of Education

Over the years, scholars have stressed the role of education as a fundamental human right and an essential means for achieving equality, progress, and peace (Alabi and Alabi, 2014). It is proven beyond doubt that educating girls is solidly linked to poverty reduction and economic growth. For example, a recent multinational study that included mostly developing countries, some with predominantly Muslim populations such as Malaysia and Indonesia, found that the female primary-school enrollment rate is related to annual per capita income growth (Oztunc *et al.*, 2015). This is because uneducated girls slip into the margins of society, ending up less skilled with fewer choices and unable to contribute substantially to economic and also social and political development of their communities (Nmadu *et al.*, 2015). The benefits of educating young females, however, go beyond sheer growth and income figures, as for example, relates to reductions in infant mortality in developing countries (Schell *et al.*, 2007). Therefore, educating girls should be imperative for every society, and especially for those lagging behind in economic development.

Despite this and all available evidence for the critical role of girls' education in nations' welfare, a wide gap remains in gender enrollments in primary and secondary education in sub-Saharan Africa (Abdulkareem, 2015). Nigeria is a case in point. While Nigeria is the largest economy in Africa, it invests less in education than many other African countries[3]. Unfortunately, Nigeria is currently confronting economic, social, educational, and political challenges that further leave education in crisis (The Guardian, 2014). Relevant statistics indicate a lack of

2 http://www.unwomen.org/en/news/in-focus/international-womens-day/2015
3 http://www.aworldatschool.org/country/nigeria

education nationwide. For example, Nigeria has the highest proportion of children out of school in Africa (The Guardian, 2014), with the greatest need for assistance predominately identified in the north (Liman *et al.*, 2011). Less than a quarter of women in the north of the country are literate or have attended some form of education (Liman *et al.*, 2011). Recently, the UN Educational, Scientific and Cultural Organisation (UNESCO) suggested two main indicators of good practice in a country's education expenditures: government spending of at least 6% of gross domestic product (GDP) and spending of approximately 20% of the total budget on education (UNESCO, 2012). As of 2015, Nigeria spent only 1.5% and 6% respectively (The Guardian, 2016b). Nonetheless, education, including at primary- and secondary-school levels, constitutes a major priority for the new Nigerian government, as it understands it to be a key instrument for national development to achieve social, economic, and political revival (Alabi and Alabi, 2014).

Education, Governance, and Leadership

Leadership involves decisions about priorities, especially in situations where there are competing uses for scarce resources. As such, decisions on education can be considered political decisions. While this argument generates discomfort among some researchers and educators, a strong relationship exists between education and politics (Alabi and Alabi, 2015; Liman *et al.*, 2011).

An illustration is provided by the apparently poor decisions and actions taken in the rescue of the Chibok girls. The political division between the north and the south of Nigeria; gender inequality, which is more of a challenge in the north (Liman *et al.*, 2011); poor leadership; and inept decision-making contributed to the mismanagement of the Chibok Girls case. The question that remains on the lips of many is: "What has happened to the girls?" Indeed, regional disparity in income is likely to lead to rivalry and contempt between regions of a country (Felice and Vecchi, 2015). Furthermore, empirical evidence suggests that disharmony and lack of meaningful social ties between the various stakeholders reduces the effectiveness of leadership (Sanders, 2010).

Some would argue that the kidnappings may have been "legitimized" in the minds of many people and contributed to the delayed and largely erroneous action of the then government. As a consequence of that "legitimization," certain key Nigerian officials may have assigned the event low importance, which led to inaction or delay in the response to the incident. In addition, the "rivalry" between the various political groups probably hindered coordination between officials.

One the one hand, it is encouraging that, despite the endemic problems of inequality in education, young girls and women make the decision to pursue an education amid sectarian violence as in the case of the Chibok girls. On the other hand, however, events such as the Chibok abduction do cause intensification of the problem, by means of deterring children, especially girls, from attending school (The Guardian, 2016a).

Another element in the original handling of the case by the government was the unwillingness to accept help from abroad, especially from wealthy, technologically advanced nations, who offered such assistance. Since then, a committee composed of the new Nigerian government (elected in 2015) and members of the international community has been established to commence redevelopment of the north of the country, among other regions. Other initiatives to rebuild the region include the North East Marshall Plan (NEMAP), which is in line with the UNGC initiative that involves companies as partners in sustainable development and demonstrates the potential of multinational companies who operate in the region to help. At the time of writing this chapter, the intensity of the activities of such extremist groups in the northeastern parts of Nigeria has been significantly quelled as the new administration has made immense efforts to quash the activities of Boko Haram through joint military forces with neighboring countries such as Chad, Cameroon, and Niger.

Concluding Remarks

Gender ideology, poverty, and the quality of leadership (as reflected in coordination, readiness, and decision-making) are issues that will remain under scrutiny in Nigeria for many years to come. Girls and women in some societies still face severe discrimination and many dangers in their quest to exercise their basic right to an education (Omwami, 2015). As noted above, gender equality is a way to solve many problems facing society today including reduction of poverty.

Taking a closer look, a "silver lining" to the kidnapping of the Chibok girls might be the laudable efforts by the new Nigerian administration to work toward education and gender equality, including making the education of girls a top priority. For instance, in Niger, located in the north-central part of Nigeria, under the leadership of the new governor, a comprehensive educational-transformation program known as TENS (Transforming Education in Niger State) is being implemented (Nigerian Ministry of Education, Science and Technology, 2016; Transforming Education in the Niger State, 2016). The program will involve obtaining up-to-date statistics on the number of girls in school and implementing special measures to facilitate access to schools and to encourage girls to attend. The aim is also to ensure that girls are educated in a safe and stimulating environment. TENS endeavours to bring parents, community leaders, religious leaders, businesses, and civil societies together and make them realize and internalize the importance of education – especially education of the girl child – to assuage fear and reluctance.

The Chibok girls case can be an excellent resource in management/leadership development. It illustrates that single events may contain great complexity due to multiple root causes along with the presence of actors with conflicting motives.

It also shows that in cases like this, routine decision-making based on learned formulas may not be the best option. Critical analysis and reflection characterize a preferable approach during and in the aftermath of such events. The case also illustrates the importance of strong decisive leadership, something that was clearly missing. Furthermore, the case highlights the potential value of preventive strategies in eliminating or minimizing the negative effects of such situations, along with the importance of realizing the limitations of one's resources and accepting or requesting assistance from other parties.

Finally, the Chibok girls case has lessons both for Nigeria and for neighboring and other countries that face similar challenges. The international community can prime multinationals to invest in the afflicted parts of the world, so jobs are created and extremist organizations have reduced options for recruits. This should be coupled with collaboration between legitimate governments and the international community so the former can respond to crises effectively. Finally, improvement in education opportunities for all and especially for girls and women should be seen as an overarching measure. In this respect, wives of political leaders such as state governors can undertake social initiatives to promote the importance of women in society. These programs can help to reduce discrimination against women due to religious bias, the traditional roles of women, and cultural beliefs. Education has the power to remove prejudice and improve key factors that relate to the economy and quality of life. In the words of Kofi Annan, the former UN secretary-general, "Educating the girl child is a social development policy that works and a long term investment that yields an exceptionally high return."

References

ABC News. (2014, May 9). Nigeria had 4-hour warning on school raid, Amnesty International says. ABC News. Retrieved from http://abcnews.go.com/International/nigeria-hour-warning-school-raid-amnesty-international/story?id=23652165.

Abdulkareem, A.K. (2015). Girl-child education in Nigeria, policy issues and challenges. Working paper: University of Ilorin, Ilorin, Nigeria. doi: 10.13140/RG.2.1.2022.1280

Agbiboa, D. (2013). Why Boko Haram exists: the relative deprivation perspective. *African Conflict and Peace building Review*, 3(1), 144-157.

Alabi, T. and O.S. Alabi. (2014). Female education: A sociological analysis of the girl-child education in Nigeria. *International Journal of Educational Policy and Research and Review*, 1(1), 6-13.

Amnesty International. (2015, April 4). Nigeria: "Our job is to shoot, slaughter and kill": Boko Haram's reign of terror in north-east Nigeria. Retrieved from https://www.amnesty.org/en/documents/afr44/1360/2015/en.

Baruch, Y., & Bozionelos, N. (2010). Career issues. In S. Zedeck (Ed.), *APA Handbook of Industrial and Organizational Psychology, Vol. 2: Selecting & Developing Members of the Organization* (pp. 67-113), Washington, D.C.: American Psychological Association.

BBC. (2014a, June 29). Chibok girls forced to join Nigeria's Boko Haram. BBC News. Retrieved from http://www.bbc.com/news/world-africa-33259003.

BBC. (2014b, May 5.) Boko Haram admits abducting Nigeria girls from Chibok. BBC News. Retrieved from http://www.virginislandsnewsonline.com/en/news/boko-haram-admits-abducting-nigeria-girls-from-chibok.

BBC. (2016, May 18.) Chibok girls: Kidnapped schoolgirl found in Nigeria. BBC News. Retrieved from http://www.bbc.com/news/world-africa-36321249.

BBC. (2016, October 15) How did Nigeria secure the 21 Chibok girls release from Boko Haram. BBC News Retrieved from http://www.bbc.co.uk/news/world-africa-37667915

Blattman, C., & Annan, J. (2016). Can employment reduce lawlessness and rebellion? A field experiment with high-risk men in a fragile state. *American Political Science Review,* 110(1), 1-17.

Central Intelligence Agency. (2016). The World Factbook: Africa: Nigeria. Retrieved from https://www.cia.gov/library/publications/the-world-factbook/geos/ni.html.

European Parliament Committees. (2016). Women's Rights and Gender Equality. Retrieved from http://www.europarl.europa.eu/committees/en/femm/home.html.

Felice, E., & Vecchi, G. (2015). Italy's modern economic growth, 1861-2011. *Enterprise and Society,* 16(2), 225-248.

Howie, L. (2009). A role for business in the war on terror. *Disaster Prevention and Management,* 18(2), 100-107.

The Guardian. (2012, April 24). School attendance falls in northern Nigeria after Boko Haram attacks. Retrieved from http://www.theguardian.com/global-development/2012/apr/24/school-attendance-northern-nigeria-boko-haram.

The Guardian. (2014, May 15). Nigeria's girls and the struggle for an education in the line of fire. Retrieved from http://www.theguardian.com/global-development/poverty-matters/2014/may/15/nigeria-girls-education-boko-haram.

Kilgour, M.A. (2013). The global compact and gender inequality: A work in progress. *Business and Society,* 52(1), 105-134.

LaFranchi, H. (2014). What role for US in efforts to rescue Nigeria's kidnapped girls? *The Christian Science Monitor.* Retrieved from http://www.csmonitor.com/USA/Foreign-Policy/2014/0505/What-role-for-US-in-efforts-to-rescue-Nigeria-s-kidnapped-girls-video.

Liman, M.A., Asraf, R.M., & Tajudeen, A. (2011). Girl-child education in northern Nigeria: Problems, challenges, and solutions. *Interdisciplinary Journal of Contemporary Research in Business,* 2(12), 851-859.

Newsweek. (2016, January 14). Fresh probe launched into Chibok girls kidnapping. Retrieved from http://europe.newsweek.com/boko-haram-bring-back-our-girls-chibok-415883?rm=eu.

Nigerian Ministry of Education, Science and Technology. (2016). Transforming Education in the Niger State. Retrieved from http://tens-niger.com.

Nmadu, J.N., Yisa, E.S., Simpa, J.O, & Sallawu, H. (2015). Poverty reduction in Nigeria: Lessons from small scale farmers of Niger and Kogi states. *British Journal of Economics, Management & Trade,* 5(1), 124-134.

Omwami, E.M. (2015). Intergenerational comparison of education attainment and implications for empowerment of women in rural Kenya. *Gender Place and Culture,* 22(8), 1106-1123.

Onuoha, F.C. (2014). *A Danger Not to Nigeria Alone – Boko Haram's Transnational Reach and Regional Responses.* Abuja, Nigeria: Friedrich-Ebert-Stiftung.

Oztunc, H., Oo, Z.C., & Serin, Z.V. (2015). Effects of female education on economic growth: A cross-country empirical study. *Educational Sciences: Theory and Practice,* 15(2), 349-357.

Sanders, P. (2010). Managing under duress: Ethical leadership, social capital and the civilian administration of the British Channel Islands during the Nazi Occupation, 1940–1945. *Journal of Business Ethics,* 93(S1), 113-129.

Schell, C.O., Reilly, M., Rosling, H., Peterson, S., & Ekstrom, A.M. (2007). Socioeconomic determinants of infant mortality: A worldwide study of 152 low-, middle-, and high-income countries. *Scandinavian Journal of Public Health,* 35(3), 288-297.

Searcey, D. (2016, April 7). Boko Harman turns female captives into terrorists. *The New York Times.* Retrieved from http://www.nytimes.com/2016/04/08/world/africa/boko-haram-suicide-bombers.html?_r=2.

Shapiro, D. (2014). Doing business in Nigeria. *Journal of Corporate Accounting and Finance,* 25(4), 3-6.

Shendy, Riham M.E., Kaplan, Z.A., Mousley, P. (2015). Towards better infrastructure: Conditions, constraints, and opportunities in financing private-public partnerships – evidence from Cameroon, Cote d'Ivoire, Ghana, Kenya, Nigeria and Senegal. Washington, D.C.: World Bank Group.

Theirworld (2017). Countries and Regions: Nigeria. Accessed from http://theirworld.org/places/nigeria

UNESCO. (2012). Education for sustainable development in action: Good practices No 4. Paris: UNESCO.

United Nations Global Impact. (2016). The ten principles of the UN Global Compact. Accessed from https://www.unglobalcompact.org/what-is-gc/mission/principles

United Nations Women (2015). International women's day 2015. Accessed from http://www.unwomen.org/en/news/in-focus/international-womens-day/2015

Usman, T. (2014, May 2). Kidnapped Girls: Jonathan sets up presidential committee. *Premium Times.* Retrieved from http://www.premiumtimesng.com/news/160029-breaking-kidnapped-girls-jonathan-sets-presidential-committee.html.

Roni Ajao is an international consultant working at the helm of governments. In Nigeria, she has worked under the presidency – Bureau of Public Sector Reforms, and as the Special Technical Adviser to Ministers under the United Nations. She has also undertaken assignments relating to the opportunities and challenges faced by African governments. She received her doctorate from Durham University (UK) and a master's degree in Consulting and Coaching for Change from HEC Paris. Her research interests include leadership, public-sector reforms, and education, with a focus on Africa.

roni.ajao@mrl.uk.com

Nikos Bozionelos is Professor of International Human Resource Management in EM Lyon Business School (France). He received his PhD from the University of Strathclyde (UK). His work has attracted in excess of 3000 citations worldwide. His research interests include employability, careers, and international and cross-cultural management. He is Senior Editor for *Asia Pacific Journal of Management* and an active member of the Careers Division of the Academy of Management.

bozionelos@em-lyon.com

Camilla Quental is Assistant Professor in Management and Human Resources at Audencia Business School (Nantes, France). Her research involves gender and diversity in organizations, women's careers, and professional identity. She received a master's degree from Sciences Po Paris and a doctorate in management from HEC Paris. She has been a member of the UN PRME Working Group on Gender Equality since 2011 and a coordinator for the management discipline for the working group's global repository.

cquental@audencia.com

12

Ecosystem Restoration in the Limestone Mines in Odisha, India

Meenakshi Kakkar
Sustainability Resources Ltd., Canada

Lisa M. Fox, Executive Director
Sustainability Resources Ltd., Canada

Introduction

The Purnapani Ecosystem Restoration Program, carried out in the limestone mines in Odisha, India demonstrates how the Principles of Responsible Management Education (PRME) of the United Nations Global Compact (UNGC) can provide an engagement framework for institutions of higher learning to embed corporate sustainability in education, research, and campus practices. India's largest government-owned steel company, the Steel Authority of India Ltd (SAIL), partnered with the Centre of Environmental Management of Degraded Ecosystems (CEMDE), a Centre of Excellence at the University of Delhi, and the Department of Biotechnology of the Government of India to reclaim an area degraded by mining activities and converted it into a successful example that promotes research and facilitates dialogue around corporate sustainability with fellow educators and knowledge networks.

This case study examines the implementation of the six PRME, namely purpose, value, method, research, partnership, and dialogue in a multi-stakeholder setting and showcases how interested parties can develop solutions that meet social, environmental, and business needs.

Project Setting

SAIL is the largest steel-making company in India. The company also has the distinction of having the country's second largest mining network. The mines of SAIL started their operations as captive sources of raw materials for its integrated steel plants so as to achieve self-sufficiency in quality iron and flux ores. Purnapani mines of SAIL are located in Sundergarh district near its Rourkela Steel Plant in Odisha, and were one of the key SAIL mines that started operations in the 1960s to supply quality dolomite and flux to the steel plants. Geographically, the area consists of widely dissimilar tracts of expansive and fairly open country, dotted with isolated peaks, inaccessible forests, river valleys, and mountainous terrain. The forests in this region are of northern tropical dry-evergreen deciduous type. The climate is characterized by extremely hot summers and cool winters. The area is mostly studded with rich mineral deposits, like iron ore, manganese, limestone, and so on.

The district has a large tribal population. Nearly 50% of the rural population consists of tribal people represented by 40 ethnic tribal communities. Some of the major tribes are Oraon, Munda, Kharia, Kisan, Bhuiyan, and Gond. They are farmers and food gatherers by profession. More than 50% of the people earn their livelihoods from agriculture and allied sectors. Different social groups live together in the same villages and interact on different social, ceremonial worship, and festive occasions.

The advent of mining in the region by a major steel company brought new employment opportunities for the local communities. The mine is located in a remote place and was initially devoid of the many advantages that a town or a city may provide. SAIL management has endeavoured to provide facilities and amenities needed to support the people working in the mines. Employees enjoyed the conveniences of residential quarters, schools, hospitals, banks, post offices, market complexes, playgrounds, stadium, community centres, clubs, and so forth. As the mining reserves neared exhaustion and mine closure advanced in the 1990s, the area provided opportunities to scientifically reclaim the area for productive use. It also provided an opportunity for the company to address the social dimension of improving the quality of life of people by integrating them into the company's vision for productive use of the area.

At all SAIL mines including Purnapani, ecosystem restoration of degraded areas is a priority, and the company personnel like to keep abreast of new developments in this field. During one such series of interactions with the Centre for Environmental Management of Degraded Ecosystems (CEMDE) at the University of Delhi, the idea for the ecosystem restoration of mined-out areas was sown.

The CEMDE approached Steel Authority of India Ltd and the Department of Biotechnology of the Government of India in 2005 to initiate ecosystem restoration of mined-out degraded areas at SAIL mines using biotechnological interventions.

The program was conceived under the leadership of C.R. Babu, a professor emeritus of CEMDE and former pro vice chancellor at the University of Delhi, and he led the team to restore the barren landscapes to a pristine state over a span of ten years. Babu is a well-respected scientist known globally for his groundbreaking research in conservation and sustainable utilization of biodiversity, ecosystem dynamics, function and ecological restoration of mined areas and degraded ecosystems (Dalei, 2014).

One of this chapter's authors, Meenakshi Kakkar, served as general manager of environment management and sustainability development at the SAIL corporate headquarters in New Delhi and is a well-known international environment expert with a specialization in sustainability, impact assessment, and biodiversity conservation. She conceptualized the project and brought together a multidisciplinary team of university researchers and SAIL employees to restore the mining site and empower and improve the livelihoods of local people for more than a decade.

With Babu, Kakkar steered the first site visits to SAIL mines in 2005. The teams traveled to the SAIL iron ore and flux mines in the eastern region, namely Purnapani, Bolani, Barsua Kalta, and so on, to assess the site conditions and work out a detailed plan of action for the Ecosystem Restoration Program. The project was granted company approvals in 2005–2006. The Purnapani mine was selected as a suitable site to test the efficacy of the biotechnology approach for ecosystem restoration on a large scale covering about 250 acres.

Figure 12.1 **Punapani limestone mine – the degraded site in 2005**

Pre-Ecosystem Restoration Setting

The project area comprises 250 acres of a barren mined-out limestone site and 200 acres of deep water voids that were remnants of Purnapani limestone mines in the state of Odisha, India (see Fig. 12.1). Purnapani is a valley surrounded by low-lying hill ranges belonging to the Gangpur sequence of rocks adjacent to the Singbhum region.

Prior to taking up ecosystem restoration at this site, the mined-out area was a degraded patchwork of overburden dumps (OBD) infested with weeds, cut mining benches bereft of soil cover, and water voids 30 to 70 meters deep with negligible signs of biological activity. The OBDs were infested with invasive weeds such as *Chromolaena odorata, Hyptis, Parthenium, Lantana camara,* and so on. The above-ground biodiversity harbored small patches of common grasses such as *Cynodon dactylon* and *Dicanthium annulatum.*

Initial site assessments showed that the ecological degradation had taken place on multiple levels. The surrounding forests also showed signs of extensive denudation. Some of the hills, however, were wooded in the upper slopes and on the hilltops. The valley also includes rain-fed fields and a township in the near vicinity.

Stakeholder Engagement

Any successful ecosystem-restoration program should take into consideration the interest of the local communities. Mining sites in India generally are in forested areas which are also home to the tribal people, many of whom are dependent on the forests for their sustenance. Diversion of forests for mining, exploitation of forests and other natural resources beyond their carrying capacity and the migration of communities to industrial locations shifts the dependence on these resources and common goods in a dramatic manner (Pradesh, 2011). Community dependence on forests is evidenced in homes made with the help of mud, wood, bamboo, leaves, straw, rope, and handmade fire-baked tiles. Locals weave rope from grasses and collect roots, shoots, leaves, flowers, fruits, seeds, mushrooms, and the like from the forest in different seasons for sustenance and trade.

Detailed socioeconomic surveys were carried out in the neighboring villages to study the general social background of the area. Information regarding dependence on the forests and the environment was collected over four seasons. The local community was engaged to identify the characteristics of ecosystems they wished to be restored at the project site. This helped the teams to understand the importance of plants and animals in the daily life of local communities, the health of the natural resources, and the carrying capacity of the area and it also helped elicit community preferences and involve community members as decision-makers in the restoration program.

The local communities expressed a desire to have the area reclaimed to meet their needs. Consultation with local people highlighted the community's need for fodder plants and vegetation that would yield non-timber forest products and wood. The locals also expressed the desire to have fruit-bearing trees. Consequently, the area was designed to be developed into a mosaic of forest communities, interspersed with grasslands, bamboo thickets, orchards, and pisciculture.

Challenge

The challenge before the team was to develop a restoration plan that slowed ecological degradation and to develop sustainable use of mined-out areas.

In order to restore ecological function and empower the local communities, the team identified five tools:

- Applying scientific understanding of the signs of degradation

- Defining indicators of ecological health

- Using biotechnology to arrest ecosystem decline and begin recovery

- Involving local communities in identifying avenues for sustainable economic development through collaborative research and knowledge-sharing

- Educating mine operators and managers, company personnel, and other stakeholders about the benefits of ecosystem restoration and triple-bottom-line security.

Approach

Once thje goals and approach were defined, the team moved the project through three stages:

1. A site assessment, including studies on above- and below-ground biodiversity, geochemical studies, identification of useful vegetative indicator species and mapping, monitoring of numerous microclimates and investigation into plant-microbe interactions. This understanding guided the selection and implementation of microbial strains chosen to amend soil and water and foster restoration of desired species.

2. Development of microbial approaches for restoration, field trials, and broad implementation followed by monitoring using indicator species.

3. A study of the socioeconomic setting of the project including assessment of dependence of local populations on natural resources.

Outcomes

University researchers, mine managers, ecosystem specialists, biodiversity experts, microbial technologists, restoration ecologists, geologists, biotechnologists, government officials, and environment professionals from three organizations joined hands for this innovative collaborative program of action to restore ecological health of this degraded ecosystem into an asset providing sustainable livelihood opportunities for the local communities.

- The scientists focused on the phased ecological restoration using seed inoculation microbial biotechnology and use of plant species that grow in nutritionally poor habitats and are able to coexist and give way to other species in order to hasten restoration of degraded ecosystems. The ecosystem program followed the objective of assisted ecosystem restoration. Programs were designed to initiate grass cover, arrest soil erosion, stabilize slopes, rear forest communities, collect seeds and propagules from native forests, and hasten return to pre-mining ecosystem baselines.

- In the initial stages, the area was divided into zones. On the cut mining benches, which were bereft of any soil cover, 15 species of grasses were introduced. To prevent erosion, 300 clumps of *Dendrocalamus* bamboo thickets were planted on slopes. Communities of bamboo, *Dalbergia* (timber trees), started flourishing on the slopes with proper care and supervision.

- In 2005–06, 25 grass species were planted to provide ground cover along with legumes such as *Desmodium Trifolium, Indigofera, Atylosia,* and *Crotolaria albida.* Grass cover provided a rich source of biomass and integrity to the soils. The grass cover, ranging from 50% to 95%, established itself over 200 acres of OBDs, benches, and slopes over the following two years. Luxuriant fodder-giving grassland was available to the communities as a result of these scientific interventions.

- The team established 15 fruit-yielding tree orchards on the site using common native fruits. To enhance the growth of fruit-yielding species on the OBD, forest soil and farmyard manure were added to the mango, jamun, bel, litchi, citrus, and mulberry fruit trees. The orchards are a source of much interest to the local communities.

- Forest cover was initiated at the site after extensive ecological surveys in nearby forests yielding propagules for use in nursery development. About 10,000 saplings of 50 species collected from the forest floor were planted.

The area harbors deep voids. Some of these voids are devoid of water, and others contain water up to a depth of 30 to 70 m. Water voids did not support biological life. The reservoir was fed with fish populations which grew vigorously. The fish growth rate is high due to the large amount of organic matter in the reservoir supported by the grassland developed on the OBDs.

In a span of seven to ten years, the degraded, mined-out landscape was restored into a fully functional tropical forest ecosystem having diverse plant communities with biodiversity value (in terms of species diversity, canopy height and stratification, and abundance of species). The restored ecosystem is close to that of adjacent hill forest ecosystems, and the forest cover has increased due to the ecological restoration of the mined-out site. In terms of characteristics of the restored site:

- The soil chemical characteristics are similar to those of the adjacent hill forest ecosystem, but the below-ground biodiversity is much richer in restored sites as compared to the natural forest ecosystem.

- The below-ground biodiversity data suggest nutrient enrichment and establishment of nutrient cycling at the restored site. This is also evident by the absence of toxic trace metals in surface and ground waters due to their immobilization, absence of soil erosion, and enhanced recharging of ground water made evident by an increase in the water table.

- The 200-acre-deep water body has been restored to a biologically productive ecosystem that produces nutritive fish. Each fish weighs about 10 kg on average.

There are trends in below-ground biodiversity that follow the successional trends in above-ground biodiversity. For example, the bacterial community before restoration was predominantly composed of detoxifying bacteria; after the restoration, plant growth promoting bacterial community has dominated. The restored site has a much richer and diversified community consisting of bacterial, fungal, and micro arthropod species than in the nearby hill forest ecosystem. Figure 12.2 illustrates the mined-out area at Purnapani seven years after restoration.

The project has successfully restored the area to a fully functional, thriving forest ecosystem with 150 forest-tree species, a grassland to support soil development and reduce erosion, and a successfully transformed 200-acre end-pit lake to a biologically productive lake that supports local communities with food fisheries. Soil function and biodiversity have been restored and metal contaminants removed.

Importantly, because of the involvement of local communities, the area now provides sustainable livelihoods to local residents. As a part of the project, a study carried out by the socioeconomic team explored the intertemporal sustainability of livelihoods of the forest-dependent communities. The study covered 312 households in the Purnapani area and showed that sustainability of livelihoods increased marginally during the post-mining period due to the initiation of ecological restoration in the mine-spoiled area (Dalei, 2014).

An orchard with more than 20 native fruit species now provides harvestable fruit, and the restoration also provided host plants for tussar silkworm culture. About six different forest communities such as *Albizia procera, Adina, Dalbergia, Acacia, Anogeissus,* and *Terminalia* have been developed on the OBDs. These communities have developed closed canopies that have heights ranging from 45 to 60 m. Lac culture, pisciculture, forest produce, food collection, sericulture, and apiary are being practiced with much success at the restored sites (see Fig. 12.3).

Figure 12.2 **The mine as it appeared seven years after restoration**

Figure 12.3 **Seeing "the leaves from the trees" – healthy trees in the forest community in the restored ecosystem**

Stakeholder Impact

Many restoration projects focus only on scientific parameters to define the goals of restoration where success is measured by the survival rate of plants. This study proves that ecosystem restoration is more than growing plants in a barren landscape; it needs to involve society to be truly successful.

The success of this project lies in its multipronged approach that dovetailed local community needs such as livelihood dependence on natural resources into the research and restoration program. During the site visits, the project staff personally interacted with communities and shared their food and festivities and learned to understand their dependence on the bounties of nature. Chapter coauthor Kakkar has spent many seasons in their midst to understand how plants and culture and daily lives are entwined.

This study proved significant in providing a method to integrate society into ecological restoration and making it more inclusive. The diverse needs of the community, its preferences, and a restoration plan keeping in mind the long-term needs and usefulness to the local communities were duly understood.

The pre-restoration scenario at the mining location exhibited limited understanding among the employees of the company of the linkages between mining, ecological restoration, and conservation in a degraded mining location. Collaboration among ecosystem-restoration researchers, students of the University of Delhi, mining personnel, and environment professionals was established and nurtured through this program. Heightened awareness among the employees about the need to protect the natural resources has led to effectively secure necessary improvements in the program.

PRME Principles and Their Relevance to the Ecosystem Restoration Study

The project fits very well with PRME 1, purpose ("We will develop the capabilities of students to be future generators of sustainable value for business and society at large and to work for an inclusive and sustainable global economy"). The project provided an opportunity to the university researchers and students to interact with businesses and corporations in the community.

Many business schools and universities in Canada and India have used the outcomes of this project in their business curriculum to showcase PRME 2, values ("We will incorporate into our academic activities and curricula the values of global social responsibility as portrayed in international initiatives such as the United Nations Global Compact"). As a guest faculty member at the University of Calgary's Corporate Social Responsibility course, Kakkar has been leading discussions on this project with much interest among the students. Many students in Canada want to plan a field trip to the Purnapani site to see the transformation.

Principle 3 elaborates on method ("to create educational frameworks, materials, processes and environments that enable effective learning experiences for responsible leadership"). Indeed, the Purnapani template and educational framework has been used by university researchers and students to duplicate these efforts in different geographic settings with much success. Students are learning to use this experience to their benefit as well as to that of the organizations they serve. Many students of the University of Delhi who are pursuing a career in forestry and social science are incorporating this learning in their forestry and community-development plans.

In line with Principle 4, research, ("We will engage in conceptual and empirical research that advances our understanding about the role, dynamics, and impact of corporations in the creation of sustainable social, environmental and economic value"), the project involved students, businesses, and communities in understanding how a steel and mining company is adding triple-bottom-line value to its business role.

In line with Principle 5, partnerships ("We will interact with managers of business corporations to extend our knowledge of their challenges in meeting social and environmental responsibilities and to explore jointly effective approaches to meeting these challenges"), the project provides a collaborative research platform for students to understand the practical challenges that businesses face to solve environmental challenges while meeting community expectations. University of Delhi students traveled to remote areas in the country to gain firsthand experience of mining landscapes and work out strategies for their remediation.

Dialogue and debate aligns closely with Principle 6, dialogue ("We will facilitate and support dialogue and debate among educators, students, business, government, consumers, media, civil society organisations and other interested groups and stakeholders on critical issues related to global social responsibility and sustainability"). The project brought several sectors together to explore these pressing issues.

The project efforts have been appreciated at various national and international events. Particularly important was the invitation to present the first reports of the Ecosystem Restoration Program to audiences at the UNGC seminar held in New Delhi (Kakkar, 2012). Local mining companies, government agencies, forest-department officials, media, engineering students from universities, and business-school students are flocking to the site to see for themselves the transformation.

The Way Forward

The project provided local stakeholders an opportunity to mobilize their strengths in consonance with nature. Their desire to participate added a social dimension to the ecosystem restoration and was crucial to the success of the program. There are about 500 households in the vicinity of the mines. A large number of self-help groups, particularly those that are women-led, are now operational in the area and are active in collection of forest tree seeds, collection and rearing of saplings in nurseries, sericulture, apiary, and plantation work at site. More and more communities are coming forward to provide synergy to the Ecosystem Restoration Program.

These restored ecosystems truly have potential to serve multiple purposes:

(i)   Models to be replicated for restoration of mined-out areas

(ii) Demonstration field sites for training probationers and practitioners in ecology and environment

(iii) Long-term ecological observatory for monitoring responses to climate change

(iv) A general site to experiment with establishing links to local communities and assisting local skill and livelihood development, particularly in areas where mines are abandoned and/or closed. This will also ensure goodwill and changing perception among local communities.

Based on the project's experience on working with degraded ecosystems in India and visits to best-practice sites globally, there is a feeling that these restored ecosystems can serve as world-class models for ecological restoration of mined-out landscapes to fully functional and productive natural ecosystems that provide livelihoods to local communities.

A large number of ongoing community-driven ecological services programmes are being delivered to the locals of Purnapani mined-out areas after ecological restoration. Programs for lac culture, mushroom collection, tussah silkworm-rearing, apiary, and medicinal plant collection are becoming popular especially among the womenfolk who have formed self-help groups and cooperatives to take this forward (Kar, 2016). The local village market or Haat is today a vibrant place to sample the local produce from the forests and water reservoirs in the restored site.

These unique restored ecosystems are now being monitored for long-term changes in biodiversity values and ecosystem services and goods, and CO_2 sequestration under a five-year flagship maintenance project funded by SAIL. A dynamic team of university researchers and the Purnapani officials are monitoring the ecologically restored sites with the following objectives:

(i)   Track changes in the community composition

(ii) Evaluate the ecological services generated by the restored ecosystems

(iii) Monitor the introduction of additional native underwood species

(iv) Assess CO_2 sequestration by restored ecosystems

(v)   Create fire lines to prevent fire hazards

(vi) Ensure sustainability of restored ecosystems while providing ecological services and goods to local communities

Conclusion

The Purnapani program demonstrates the successful collaboration of multiple sectors working to bridge the gap between the discipline of ecosystem restoration and community development. The program provides a base of practical knowledge, scientific understanding, and technical expertise to mine managers, communities, researchers and non-professionals on the basic tenets of ecological restoration and restore ecosystem health of degraded landscapes. It also provides them with the tools and strategies needed to fund, plan, staff, implement, and monitor effective restoration projects. The project is now being replicated with much success at other mining locations of SAIL such as the Bolani and Barsua-Kalta iron ore mines. This model has also been replicated in various coal mines in coal belts in India.

Reclamation efforts may suffer from a lack of consideration of the needs of local communities. This case study serves not only as a model for successful reclamation, but as an example of how engagement with local stakeholders can be the turning point for long-term success. As such, it offers insights into how academia-business partnerships can foster successful models for ecological restoration of mine-damaged landscapes to fully functional and productive ecosystems that can support livelihoods of local communities.

The Ecosystem Restoration Program was conceptualized and coordinated by Meenakshi Kakkar, senior resource associate at Sustainability Resources Ltd (Calgary, Alberta) and former general manager of SAIL, New Delhi. The authors gratefully acknowledge the management of SAIL, the academic team led by C.R. Babu at the University of Delhi, and the Department of Biotechnology for the tremendous support toward the success of the project. Thanks are also due to Vivek Choudhary, an avid researcher at the CMPDE, University of Delhi who enthusiastically provided technical inputs and some images of the Ecosystem Restoration Program.

References

Dalei, N.N., and Gupt, Y. (2014) Livelihood sustainability of forest dependent communities in a mine-spoiled area. *International Journal of Ecological Economics and Statistics*, 35, 30-47.

Kakkar, M. (2012). Purnapani - An Ecosystem Restoration Study. UNGC Conference, Corporate perspective on sustainable development: RIO+20 and beyond. 7th National Convention, UNGC Network India, New Delhi.

Kar, P.K., Choudhary, V.K., Babu, C.R., &Sahay, A. (2016). Conservation of Tasar silkworm *Antheraea mylitta* in a recreated forest at degraded land of dolomite mines in Odisha. *Frontiers in Life Sciences, New Delhi*, 2016, 325-331.

Pradesh, A. (2011). Livelihoods, issues, and concerns in the Bauxite mining area. In R.K. Mishra & J. Raveendran (Eds.), *Millenium Development Goals and India: Cases Assessing Performance, Prospects and Challenges* (pp. 13-19). New Dehli: Allied Publishers PvT. Ltd.

Meenakshi Kakkar, Ph.D, M.Phil is an Environment Specialist and Senior Resource Associate with Sustainability Resources Ltd., Calgary. During her tenure with Steel Authority of India Ltd. as General Manager (Sustainability), she conceptualized and coordinated this ten-year flagship Purnapani Ecosystem Restoration Program.

meenakshi_kakkar@yahoo.com

Lisa Maria Fox is a Senior Policy Analyst and Executive Director of Sustainability Resources Ltd. She has exceptional knowledge of environmental policy and regulatory development processes and has contributed to the evolution of policies and regulations for air, land, and water management across Canada's diverse jurisdictional landscapes.

lisafox@sustainabilitycircle.ca

Section 4
Accelerating the Pace of Change

13

The UN Global Compact and the Governance of Situated Firms

David Williamson
Staffordshire University, UK

Gary Lynch-Wood
University of Manchester, UK

Introduction

The United Nations Global Compact (UNGC) is a membership-based, collective-action institution, which, like other such institutions (e.g., Ethical Trading Initiative), is designed to foster corporate citizenship (Bremer, 2008). It urges firms to align "strategies and operations with universal principles on human rights, labour, environment and anti-corruption, and take action to advance societal goals".[1] The ten specific principles referred to derive from other international initiatives, such as the Universal Declaration of Human Rights and the Rio Declaration of the UN Conference on Environment and Development (Kell and Ruggie, 1999). Since its establishment in 2000, the UNGC has attracted extensive debate, as well as support and criticism.

This chapter considers how the UNGC functions as an instrument of regulation and governance of firms. It explores the concept of "situated firms" and how differences across organizations shape responses to regulation. Linked to this, the chapter considers how regulation functions on the basis of regulatee conditions and suggests that the absence of these conditions will undermine the effectiveness

1 See https://www.unglobalcompact.org/what-is-gc (accessed April 13, 2016).

of particular initiatives. This provides the basis for understanding how and why the UNGC will or will not work, and indicates ways to enhance it.

Regulatory Mixes

The UNGC can be considered a regulatory instrument if we recognize that regulation is an increasingly pluralistic concept: an intentional and problem-solving process that both includes and extends beyond the activities of states (Havinga, 2006; Hutter and Jones, 2007). Regulation, as now often defined, encapsulates less direct instruments (e.g., market-based and disclosure mechanisms) and alternative forms of governance, social control, and influence (Baldwin *et al.*, 2012; Braithwaite *et al.*, 2007), and it includes those influences derived from alternative sources and institutions (e.g., consumers, supply chains, nongovernmental organizations). As such, voluntary initiatives and frameworks (e.g., ISO14001), codes, self-regulatory agreements (e.g., Responsible Care), and other self-governance frameworks like the UNGC, are regarded as important regulatory tools. Indeed, as part of the mix, the UNGC provides the UN with a scheme for attending to some of the criticisms of the social impacts of globalization without engaging in the arduous task of enacting legally binding regulations (Vogel, 2010). The framework is open to many forms of organization (e.g., NGOs, universities), with some exceptions.[2]

To appreciate its value as a regulatory framework, it is worth briefly outlining two issues: how firms "comply" and how they are currently performing.

First, as a voluntary initiative, the UNGC is on the softer side of the regulatory spectrum. The compliance mechanism is a modest one, with three key processes. A firm prepares a letter of commitment which is signed by the chief executive expressing commitment to the UNGC and its principles. Then, the firm should take action to support these principles. Lastly, it must submit annually a Communication on Progress (COP). The COP policy sets out key information including certain minimum requirements (i.e., a statement by the chief executive expressing continued support, a description of practical actions, and a measurement of outcomes). Thought to be central to participants' commitments, the COP is based on concepts of accountability, transparency, and continuous improvement. Apart from providing an opportunity for firms to gather data and to reflect on its practices, the COP is a public-disclosure tool that provides valuable information to stakeholders (investors, consumers, NGOs). There is an official process for addressing noncompliance by signatories. Ultimately, a firm that fails to submit a COP for two consecutive years will be deemed not to have fulfilled its commitments and will face expulsion, with its name being published on the UNGC website.

---

2 Micro firms (i.e., firms with fewer than ten employees) cannot be entered onto the participant database but are encouraged to stay informed about all UNGC activities.

Second, despite it being a relatively high-profile and prominent framework that has existed on the world stage for more than 15 years, membership appears limited. Though membership has grown annually, in 2015 there were only 8,381 business participants, 3,863 of which were large firms and 4,518 of which were small- and medium-sized enterprises (UNGC, 2015a). It was reported that in 2012 just 2% of the world's 46,737 listed companies (those whose shares are traded on stock exchanges) participated (UNGC, 2015b). It is also interesting that in 2015 there were 5,988 COPs (by 71.4% of the members) submitted (UNGC, 2015a). Perhaps more worrisome is the high number of expulsions. In 2015, there were 1,218 reported expulsions for failure to communicate on progress, of which 89% were smaller firms. Overall, more than 6,000 participants have been expelled. These levels of participation and expulsion suggest there is a regulatory problem, and that the cause of the problem has to be understood for it to be effectively addressed.

Situated Firms

A core part of the argument is the claim that rule-following is learned in the act of living our lives. Bourdieu (1984), for example, argues that "knowledge" is a practical ability embodied in skillful behavior. Social codes are therefore acquired as part of a taken-for-granted background to everyday life. Regularities of behavior as manifested in gang crime or religious devotion, for instance, can be explained in terms of their respective codes of masculinity and deliverance. This behavior is generally implicit since it is acquired in practice, and is a practical ability since it is learned through familiarization or "habituation". Bourdieu thus refers to the learning context as a "habitus" and uses it to explain, among others, judgments on taste and educational success. A habitus can thus be considered a system of dispositions acquired through practice. The world is made up of many different types of habitus, and these produce different practices, which are the basis for the drawing of distinctions, whether on taste, or, for current purposes, firms' interpretations of, and relationships with, regulatory frameworks. The firm is thus the setting where skillful behavior is learned, and where, by inference, distinctions on responses of regulation materialize themselves.

These differences in behaviour, which can constitute deep-seated and unconscious beliefs, operate in a structured domain of activity that Bourdieu calls a "field" (e.g., economy, family, education, law). And since they are relatively autonomous, the fields have distinct views on what constitutes legitimate opinion and what are appropriate power relations – they have, so to speak, their own logic. The habitus, in other words, provides the practical skills to navigate a field. For example, a university lecturer would presumably have the practical skills to navigate the field of higher education, and because of this his or her view on higher education may likely be different than, say, a plumber's. And since the lecturer may share and agree this with other lecturers, the habitus of the field that is higher education will constitute those shared beliefs and practices.

The rules and resources relating to the reproduction of learned practices are diverse. Giddens (1984) argues that rules range from those that are intensive/ shallow, tacit/discursive, informal/formalized, and weakly sanctioned/strongly sanctioned. Resources have to do with power and legitimation, about control over goods and materials, and the capacity to have command over individuals. Situated human agents operate within and determine these structural factors, and for this reason any investigation of social systems – and as argued here, the UNGC – has to accommodate both structure and system dimensions. Structure, in this context, refers to those varied arrangements of social institutions (e.g., politics and religion) which influence the choices that limit behavior, while system refers to how those institutions are configured to provide for stable arrangements, and thus for how individuals and firms collectively interact with one another. And since structure and system dimensions vary, we can see why UNGC practice will differ; it is because differences that accrue from social origin and power relations have their origin and basis in the control of physical and human resources. This has implications for how regulation is carried out, with the immediate and overarching implication being that, if it is to be effective in changing behaviors, regulation should be aligned with rule-following practices. In other words, you do not want to hinder beyond compliance behavior, just as you would not want to encourage noncompliance by applying the wrong regulatory fix.

These points converge to suggest that responses to regulation can only properly be understood by examining the practices of regulated entities. Likewise, the appropriateness of regulation can only be properly understood by looking at the practice produced by that regulation, since different settings will produce different practices. Indeed, one should expect that different settings will embody different constraints and empowerments (e.g., willingness to engage with human rights) as a result of different types of habitus and fields. One would also expect many of these learned practices to be difficult to change since a learned consciousness develops over time and can be difficult to undo (e.g., Aoki, 2007; Greif, 2006). Regulators and rule-makers have to, therefore, recognize a feature they may have always known: it is difficult to change a learned practice since the regulation is having to overcome the constraints that result from differences in class, power, function, and so forth. The immediate implication from this is that the UNGC will underperform unless it can address the constraints, and leverage the empowerments, across different types of firms. This is achievable, but only, as it will be subsequently argued, if the UNGC enables the application of equivalent minimum requirements across firms, and that this is enforced through the requirement that all firms report upon the meeting of those equivalent minimum requirements. These prerequisites need to be applied to firms that have signed up to the UNGC, and, more importantly, to all targeted firms if there is a wish to extend its reach and intent.

One of the reasons the UNGC may have underperformed is that it assumes a common form of regulatory response, which, given differences in rule-following behavior within and across jurisdictions across the globe and over time, is improbable. These differences, when looking at firms, are evident in many areas. They are reflected in the way firms are likely to belong to industries with different technologies and logistic chains, and how this then affects their views and behavior toward technology and logistics. These firms will also likely vary in size, and this will have a bearing on how they view and tailor their provision to suit the different types of customers they service. Some firms will also be more entrepreneurial than others, with their behaviours similarly being affected by factors such as ownership structure (e.g., family-run, shareholder-led businesses), geographic scope (e.g., global, local) and rates of change (e.g., static, dynamic).

Alongside differences highlighted, firms will try to differentiate themselves from their competitors, with the basis of that distinction again affecting and embodying behavior. This can follow on from competition on internal dimensions (e.g., supply-chain expertise, ability to develop brands, use of information technology) and through aspects that are market-based and internal to the firm: e.g., a firm in a market that is homogeneous and low-cost, where it has to compete on cost, will have little choice but to leverage factors that are internal to the firm if it is to maintain its position with, or outperform, other players in the sector (Porter, 1985). It also makes sense for firms that have a competitive advantage to seek to protect that benefit by making the resources that underpin the advantage difficult to copy. This can be generalized to the form that firms are competitively distinctive due to firms being unequal in their ability to acquire and utilise resources (e.g., Peteraf, 1993).

The situated behavior-regulation link is also affected by the structure of the firm. As Chandler (1962) observed, as firms grow they develop different organizational structures. These structures are associated with different behaviors (see Mintzberg, 1979). Indeed, they affect the tone of the strategy-making processes, and hence the preferences of the firm. It corresponds with the view that firms have bounded rationalities and cultures and these guide their decision-making (Prahalad and Bettis, 1986). This means firms do not always act in a rationally optimum way due to the constraints on their decision-making (e.g., they do not have the time or resources to gather all the information they need to make an optimal decision), with them instead simplifying their world by choosing the first alternative that is satisfactory (Simon, 1982). It corresponds with firms sticking with what has worked for them in the past (other explanations include reinforcement-expectancy learning, the efficiency of maintaining proven competences over developing new ones, performance exceeding aspirations, and difficult-to-change organizational structures). The history of the firm therefore matters, with the conditions that give rise to self-reinforcing feedback (to help maintain existing structures) being attributed to the historically embedded nature of cognitive selections, sunk costs making it difficult to switch to alternatives, complex interrelatedness (social, institutional, and technical), and increasing returns when using a common method (David, 1985; Arthur, 1989).

A further factor affecting the behavior of firms, by virtue of the way that it shapes the allocation and use of resources across firms, is the institutional environment. This is because institutions provide the rules of the game, and these guide and restrain the behavior of the firm (North, 1990; 2005). Rules can be formal or informal (e.g., norms, routines, political processes, contracts, incentives, authority, laws), and the weight given to these vary by firm. The institutional environment therefore helps to produce and sustain different behaviors. It influences the acquisition of organizational knowledge, and hence the building blocks of organizational behaviour (see Granovetter, 1985).

These examples support the case that persistent differences in behavior are inevitable. Indeed, the wider literature shows that the factors behind divergence in firm behavior comes from many sources and provides a compelling case for different forms of firm-level knowledge. On that basis, there is a need to consider how these differences are matched in regulatory practices and approaches. Specifically, there is a need to investigate how these differences are constituted in the "conditions" upon which any regulatory framework must operate. The consequent question therefore is: what conditions are required for a regulatory mechanism, like the UNGC, to be effective, and how do differences across firms affect these conditions? This will make it possible to see what equivalent UNGC minimum requirements might look like or how it can be configured so it is more amenable to different situated contexts.

Regulation Conditions

A feature of the argument is that, to be effective, a regulatory approach requires the existence of conditions; conditions relating to firms' characteristics and behaviors. Since an instrument relies on the existence of different conditions, then the instrument will be more effective if the conditions it assumes are – or need to be – present do in fact exist, or closely fit the social and economic conditions that shape regulated entities themselves. If those conditions are absent or poorly aligned, there will be a regulation deficit and the instrument will not achieve its full potential.

Here, a condition refers to a situation, state of affairs, or factor that must be present before something else is possible, permissible, or likely to occur. It could be declared, for example, that condition "X" must be present or in place before thing "Y" can take place, or thing "Y" will occur only if condition "X" exists. So how does this inform our views on regulation and how it functions in practice? It is posited that firms (e.g., their features, capacities, interactions with market and social contexts) provide some of those necessary conditions. That is, the characteristics of regulatees provide the conditions that determine whether regulations perform or fall short. Taking the firm as the unit of analysis, key questions are: "What *are* the conditions on the part of the regulatee that mean a particular instrument will perform, or that mean it is less or not likely to perform?," "What is it about firms' resources, behaviors, institutional settings, and circumstances that provide the conditions for successful regulatory implementation?," and "Are those institutional and organizational conditions in place, in relation to given instruments or approaches?" So far as it could be argued here, the idea of regulatee conditions has not been discussed in any explicit sense. It is recognized partly by Baldwin and Black's (2007) model of "really responsive regulation," which acknowledges the importance of taking account of the attitudinal settings of firms, their operative and cognitive frameworks, and their institutional frameworks. Yet the chapter takes this further by trying to identify those conditions that enable regulation to deliver its outcomes.

Moreover, it considers a broad spectrum of research to identify three broad conditions that determine whether and how firms will respond. These are (a) their understanding of the regulated situation, (b) their capacities to respond, and (c) their willingness or acceptance of a need to act. These conditions are referred to as follows: the *knowledge condition*, the *substantive compliance resources condition*, and the *agreement condition*. Firms, for example, have different levels of resources that can affect their ability to act, which is evidenced by the general observation that a critical factor affecting the compliance behavior of smaller firms is their limited competence level and capacity to adopt approaches of environmentally sustainable industrial development (OECD, 2007). In other words, resources affect compliance positions. There is also evidence of a corporate "attitude" toward compliance (Gray and Deily, 1996), suggesting that the way firms view the principles of a regulatory regime will be an important feature of the compliance process. Each condition has variability (e.g., different levels of knowledge), the implications of which are itemized for the UNGC in Table 13.1.

Table 13.1 **Regulation Conditions**

Condition	Meaning	Explanation	Implications
Knowledge	Understanding that the regulation exists and of what its demands are.	The regulatee must have a measure of regulatory knowledge and understanding. The regulatee needs to be aware of the existence of a regulatory measure and requires a reasonable and working knowledge of its requirements.	· Are all firms aware of its existence? · Is it promoted to all firms? · Are all firms part of the UNGC setting? · Are the knowledge demands of the UNGC aligned to the knowledge capacities of all firms?
Substantive compliance resources	Capacity and capability (resources to meet the demands and requirements of regulation).	Regulation requires firms to have the necessary resources that enable them to achieve actual or substantive compliance. That is, the effectiveness of regulation is dependent on regulatees having the necessary resources to know what the regulations require and to then put that knowledge into practical activities.	· Are the regulatory requirements of the UNGC aligned to the resource capacities of all firms? · Are the timeframes for compliance with the UNGC aligned to the resource capacities of all firms?

→

Condition	Meaning	Explanation	Implications
Agreement	Willingness, desire, or pressure to meet the demands and requirements of regulation.	There is a need for commitment to the regulatory cause – or a level of agreement or consensus on the part of the regulatee. Specifically, the regulatee needs to "agree" to compliance, or to acquiesce to the compliance process, and then respond in the right way. The term "agree" is used broadly, in that agreement to comply can be "voluntary," "desired," or "preferred," as well as "forced" through appropriate enforcement or pressurized through appropriate social pressure or norms.	· What is the setting that promotes engagement? · Are the pressures to engage with, and to comply with, the UNGC, the same for all firms?

It is suggested that these are the essential conditions that apply to all forms of regulation, and that the way they interact will determine how different regulations perform. Importantly, it is only when all three conditions are present that there will be no regulation deficit (see Figure 13.1).

Figure 13.1 **Regulation Conditions**

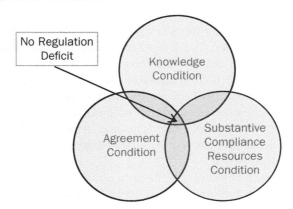

By looking at regulation and its relationship with regulatee conditions, it is possible to get a more sophisticated view of how measures such as the UNGC may work in practice and why such instruments may underperform. For example, what knowledge deficits need to be addressed? Are these deficits likely to be greater for smaller firms than their larger counterparts? Thus, having introduced what conditions mean for our understanding of regulation, a brief look at differences and conditions in the context of the UNGC can be taken. It requires, given the differences across firms, that: there is equivalent knowledge requirements on firms; there is equivalent resource requirements on firms; and there is an equivalent level of pressure on firms to engage and comply.

Final Comments

The ideas outlined have important implications for schemes such the UNGC. Showing that firms differ, and that differences manifest themselves as variable conditions that determine the effectiveness of particular regulatory instruments, has implications for how regulation is perceived and what can be done to improve it. It enables an understanding of why there may be regulation deficits, and how such deficits may be reduced.

As a voluntary initiative, with a modest compliance mechanism, the UNGC has a set of standard and basic procedures. Firms make a commitment, take actions, and make public disclosures. The COP should reaffirm commitment, specify practical actions, and measure outcomes. Given these requirements, which are implicitly taken to be proportionate in their demands on firms, and given that there are vast numbers of firms across jurisdictions, the fact that so few firms have "complied" with the UNGC after more than 15 years suggests a problem exists. To move beyond easy-to-reach firms (i.e., progressive and socially responsible firms that one would expect to be first movers), the full nature of why firms are not engaging with the UNGC needs to be appreciated. While this would no doubt benefit from a more substantial empirical analysis, it is nevertheless possible to suggest some tentative ways forward.

If it is accepted that poor compliance has much to do with differences across organizations, and that these differences produce multifarious firm-level regulatory practices and approaches, then it must also be accepted that these differences constitute a set of real-life and variable "conditions" upon which any regulatory framework must operate. It is then arguable that regulatory deficits are avoided only when regulatory frameworks accommodate the conditions produced by firm-level differences. By inference, the demands of the UNGC appear poorly aligned to conditions created by the different rule-following behaviors among firms. Only a limited number of firms have the requisite knowledge, resources, and willingness to comply with the framework.

The solution has to focus on both the regulation itself (i.e., the requirements of the UNGC) and the enforcement of, or pressure to accept, those requirements among firms. A useful starting point might be to consider how and why the current signatories differ from non-signatory firms and those who have been expelled. Beyond this, an assessment has to be made on the specificity of the UNGC requirements and the implications that arise from this. For instance, it may be the case that the requirements are not aligned to the specific requirements of different sectors and industries. If this is remedied by tailoring the requirements of the UNGC then it is important, in turn, to be aware of the diminishing return that will accompany this remedy (i.e., the costs of the regulatory effort will increase as ever more specific knowledge, resource, and agreement conditions are accommodated; and as new tailored solutions are implemented there will arise new and more specific knowledge, resource, and agreement deficits). Because of this, the solution may need to be more radical and deep-rooted, by acknowledging the need to make the requirements of the UNGC more open textured so that it can accommodate the variability in conditions that exists across firms, and to likewise accept that this will lead to variable levels of success until the context within which firms learn to follow rules is addressed. The view here is that a principles-based approach would seem sensible, although it could be advocated that this needs to accommodate specific minimum requirements to help minimize undesired behavior. General minimum requirements – whether mandatory or the existing voluntary approach – are important because of the need to "oblige" compliance as a consequence of the compliance constraints that invariably accrue from the difficulty in firms' profiles matching the requirements of the three conditions (i.e., the aim is to minimize the compliance constraints imposed by the three conditions). The use of minimum requirements within a voluntary setting, however, is likely to require a focus on ways to greatly increase the agreement condition since this can be considered to be independent of, although it is affected by, the knowledge and resource conditions.

Altogether, the intention is to facilitate a reduction of the hurdle that the knowledge, agreement, and resource conditions represent, since it is essential that the constraints created by these conditions are recognized and acted upon. When it comes to enforcement and implementation, careful thought has to be given to how the knowledge, agreement, and resources could be increased (while noting that this helps minimize those conditions). The use of minimum standards also provides a proper standard against which all firms must comply while allowing, and preferably rewarding, behavior that goes beyond minimum requirements. The details around this reconstituted regulation and enforcement regime are clearly far beyond the scope of this overview, but progress will be hampered until this is done. Yet it is also an area that provides opportunities for a joint effort on the part of the UNGC and the Principles for Responsible Management Education (PRME). While having unique research, educational and community-service capabilities of its members and collectively, the PRME movement itself is a membership and collective action institution that is facing similar regulatory and governance challenges. It is therefore incumbent on the PRME to better understand these challenges and to diligently seek to address and resolve them.

References

Aoki, M. (2007). Endogenizing institutions and institutional changes. *Journal of Institutional Economics*, 3(1), 1-31.

Arthur, B. (1989). Competing technologies, increasing returns, and lock-in by historical events. *Economic Journal*, 99,116-131.

Bourdieu, P. (1984). *Distinction: A Social Critique of the Judgement of Taste*. Cambridge, Mass: Harvard University Press.

Braithwaite, J., Coglianese, C., & Levi-Faur, D. (2008).Can regulation and governance make a difference? *Regulation & Governance*, 1(1), 1-7.

Baldwin, R. & Black, J. (2007). Really responsive regulation. *Modern Law* Review, 71(1), 59-94.

Baldwin, R., Cave, M., & Lodge, M. (2012).*Understanding Regulation*. Oxford: Oxford University Press.

Bremer, J. (2008). How global is the Global Compact? *Business Ethics: A European Review*, 17(3), 227-244.

Chandler, A.D. Jr. (1962). *Strategy and Structure: Chapters in the History of the American Industrial Enterprise.* Boston: MIT (1969 paperback edition).

David, P.A. (1985). Clio and the economics of Qwerty. *American Economic Review*, 75, 332-337.

Giddens, A. (1984). *The Constitution of Society*. Cambridge: Polity Press.

Granovetter, M. (1985). Economic action and social structure: the problem of embeddedness. *American Journal of Sociology*, 91, 481-510.

Gray, W. & Deily, M. (1996). Compliance and enforcement: air pollution regulation in the U.S. steel industry. *Journal of Environmental Economics and Management*, 31, 96-111.

Greif, A. (2006). *Institutions and the Path to the Modern Economy*. Cambridge: Cambridge University Press.

Havinga, T. (2006). Private regulation of food safety by supermarkets. *Law & Policy*, 28(4), 515-533.

Hutter, B. & Jones, C. (2007). From government to governance: external influences on business risk management. *Regulation & Governance*, 1(1), 27-45.

Kell, G. & Ruggie J. (1999) Global markets and social legitimacy: the case for the "Global Compact," *Transnational Corporations*, 8(3), 101-120.

Mintzberg, H. (1979). *The Structuring of Organisations*. Englewood Cliffs, NJ: Prentice Hall.

North, D.C. (1990). *Institutions, Institutional Change and Economic Performance*. Cambridge: Cambridge University Press.

North, D.C. (2005). *Understanding the Process of Economic Change*. Princeton, NJ: Princeton University Press.

OECD. (2007). Small Businesses and Environmental Compliance: Review and Possible Application of International Experience in Georgia.

Peteraf, M.A. (1993). The cornerstones of competitive advantage: A resource-based view. *Strategic Management Journal*, 14, 179-191.

Porter, M.E. (1985). *Competitive Advantage: Creating and Sustaining Superior Performance.* New York: The Free Press.

Prahalad, C.K. & Bettis, R.A. (1986). The dominant logic: A new linkage between diversity and performance. *Strategic Management Journal*, 7,(6), 485-501.

Simon, H.A. (1982). *Models of Bounded Rationality* (2 vols.). Cambridge, MA: MIT Press.

United Nations Global Compact (UNGC). (2015a). Communication on Progress: 2015 Key Facts.

United Nations Global Compact (UNGC). (2015b). Impact: Transforming Business, Changing the World.

Vogel D. (2010). The private regulation of global corporate conduct: Achievements and limitations. *Business and Society*, 49(1), 68-87.

14

Integrating Social Responsibility into Public Institutions, Organizations, and Administration

Athanasios Chymis
Centre of Planning and Economic Research (KEPE), Greece

Paolo D'Anselmi
University of Rome, Italy

Christos Triantopoulos
Centre of Planning and Economic Research (KEPE), Greece

UNGC Principles and the Public Sector[1]

In order to better address global issues such as poverty, gender equality, and corruption, there is a need to take a broader look at organizations and include in our research and teaching agenda not only private business but also public organizations. The public sector makes up 30%, 40%, or even, in some cases, 50% of a country's gross domestic product (GDP) (Di Bitetto *et al.*, 2015). More importantly, public-sector organizations worldwide are responsible for the physical and social infrastructures as well as the legal environment in which business operates. Governments, public administrations, and public organizations in general define the quality of such infrastructures and the institutional framework (i.e., the rules of

---

1 The authors would like to thank the editors of this book for their comments and suggestions, which helped improve the chapter considerably.

the game) for every business activity. It is very important that a country's institutional environment operate effectively and efficiently in order to promote businesses' social responsibility and facilitate their role in acting in a sustainable way. An important aspect of public organizations' social responsibility is the effective and efficient use of public money.

The purpose of this chapter is to argue that a new generation of leaders is necessary not only for business but also for public organizations such as public administration as a whole as well as state-owned enterprises, nonprofits, and the like. The role of the new generation of leaders is to reshape public institutions in such a way that they create appropriate incentives scheme that can be conducive to the implementation of the UN Global Compact (UNGC), eradicating corruption and poverty, as well as for advancing the Sustainable Development Goals (SDGs) in general. The chapter's goals are to:

(a)   Identify the need for explicitly including public organizations in the responsible management education agenda in order to extend the integration of the UNGC and PRME (Principles for Responsible Management Education) not only by private business but also by public organizations;

(b)   Explain why this is important; and

(c)   Offer suggestions on how this can be done and how responsible management education can have an impact in making public organizations more responsible (i.e., more effective and efficient in terms of the use of taxpayers' money, as well as more transparent and accountable)

Public Institutions and Organizations

An important observation in the call for contributors for this book sparked the idea of this chapter: "All too often, the social safeguards provided by *public institutions* and the responses of the affected communities have not kept pace with the impact of business practices" (p. 2, emphasis added). This chapter argues that responsible business management requires responsible public institutions, which, in turn, are mostly the outcome of responsible public organizations (governments, public administrations, public enterprises, etc).

According to the New Institutional Economics (NIE), firms (businesses in general) do not operate in a vacuum (North, 2005). They operate within a more or less developed institutional environment. This environment is, to a significant degree, the responsibility of many organizations such as governments (federal, national and local, as well as supranational in the case of countries that are members of international organizations/associations), and public authorities (licensing, tax, regulatory, and judicial.) All of these organizations fall under the general rubric of public administration. Moreover, all of these organizations have their own management, and their degree of success is dependent on the quality of the institutional and legal framework in which they operate, as well as the quality of their leaders, managers, and employees. As many scholars argue, the development of effective and efficient institutions and public administration is a catalyst for the sustainable development of the whole society (Acemoglu and Robinson, 2012; Buchanan and Tullock 1962; Olson, 2008).

This chapter makes a distinction between institutions and organizations following North's definition of institutions: "Institutions are the humanly devised constraints that structure political, economic and social interaction. They consist of both informal constraints (sanctions, taboos, customs, traditions, and codes of conduct), and formal rules (constitutions, laws, property rights)" (North, 1991, p. 97). Consequently, organizations include groups of people whereas institutions do not.

Public organizations refer to every organization that is not private. Public administration covers most public organizations. The term public administration is preferred over the term government because the latter has the meaning of public administration mostly in the Unites States, while in other countries government has a more limited sense of the ministerial cabinet. State-owned enterprises (SOEs) are also considered public organizations as they are under some control of the public sector.

Institutions have been recognized to play significant roles in the way a country is organized and an economy is run (North, 1991, 2005; Williamson, 2000). These reflect the wellbeing of a country's people (Olson, 2008). Williamson (2000) describes several levels of institutions and how they permeate the socioeconomic reality of every society. Cultural institutions such as informal rules, religions, norms, customs, and traditions indirectly affect economic development, but they change very slowly. Formal rules such as constitutions, laws and property rights are also called the rules of the game, where "game" is the human socioeconomic activity. Institutions of governance and contractual relations such as the legal and the enforcement system are necessary for the game to be played. This is where public organizations play a significant role. Organizations responsible for high-quality formal rules as well as good governance of contractual relations include "the executive, legislative, judicial and other bureaucratic functions of government" (Williamson, 2000, p. 598). Once the institutional framework has been set, the last level of analysis refers to purely economic conditions such as resource allocation and employment. This last level of social analysis deals with the economic bottom line.

This chapter goes beyond the bottom line in the sense that it calls attention to public organizations, which are mostly responsible for the creation of healthy institutions, which lay the groundwork for the private sector to pursue the bottom line in a socially responsible way.

The Crucial Role of Public Institutions and Organizations

International organizations such as the International Institute for Management Development (IMD), Organization of Economic Cooperation and Development (OECD), Transparency International (TI), United Nations (UN), World Bank (WB), and the World Economic Forum (WEF) increasingly focus on the public sector, in general, and on the quality of public-organizations management, in particular. The OECD in 2005 published a report on *Modernizing Government*, recognizing the need for making the public sector more effective and efficient (one could argue that long-run efficiency and effectiveness come close to the concept of social responsibility) regarding spending constituents' resources.

Especially after the 2008 Eurozone and U.S. financial crisis, which evolved into a deep recession in many countries, international organizations have been trying to help countries to improve public-sector management, increase effectiveness and efficiency of the state and thus reduce deficits and unsustainable levels of debt. It is worth noting that while in most countries (e.g., the United States, Iceland, and Ireland) the banking sector went bankrupt, in other countries (e.g., Greece) it was the heavily indebted public sector that caused the economic crisis (Mitsopoulos and Pelagidis, 2011). Moreover, according to the European Commission 2015 report of public finances, 17 out of the 28 European Union member-states and 14 out of the 19 Eurozone members have a public-debt level above the Maastricht ceiling of 60% of GDP. Six member-states have a public debt above 100% of GDP (European Commission, 2015).

The data and indicators published by the aforementioned international organizations reveal a clear correlation between public organizations' long-term effectiveness and efficiency on one hand, and economic performance, competitiveness, wellbeing, social indicators, and even ethical behavior of firms, on the other. Specifically, IMD ranks countries based on competitiveness. There are four major factors on which IMD measures competitiveness, namely, economic performance, government efficiency, business efficiency and infrastructure. Countries that rank high in economic performance, business efficiency or infrastructure also tend to rank high in government efficiency (IMD, 2015).

The World Bank's *Ease of Doing Business* report shows that countries with a "friendly" institutional environment toward business are those with higher levels of economic wellbeing. In the Doing Business (DB) report (2015), the quality and efficiency of regulatory authorities are linked to the level of economic, social, and environmental performance of business and the national economy as a whole. The DB report uses a new global database named Citizen Engagement in Rule-making. This index measures the degree of government's publication and communication to its citizens of proposed regulations as well as an invitation to citizens to actively take part in developing these regulations as an effort to engage a wide range of stakeholders. It is shown that the greater the transparency and citizens' participation in the rule-making process, the higher the quality and efficiency of the rules and regulations (DB, 2015). It is interesting that the DB report calls for a wider effort regarding measuring quality of public organizations. Specifically, the report states that "we need a comprehensive index on quality of the public sector. The United Nations could support such an initiative" (DB, 2015, p. 2).

WEF publishes, annually, the Global Competitiveness Index (GCI). This is one of the most comprehensive indices since it contains more than 100 subindices and thus captures a great part of the socioeconomic life of a country. More importantly, it clearly distinguishes between public and private institutions and facilitates research on the relation between quality and efficiency of public institutions on one hand, and a series of indicators regarding economic performance on the other. What makes the GCI dataset unique is that it captures specific public institutions that directly reflect the quality of public-organizations management. GCI uses institutions as a basic requirement of a country's development. It breaks institutions down to several categories such as property-rights protection, public-sector ethics and corruption, public-sector undue influence, and public-sector performance (WEF, 2015).

Simple regressions and correlation analysis show that public-organizations performance as measured by a series of public-sector outcomes such as regulatory efficiency and quality, level of ethics, corruption and undue influence, and so forth are closely related to income levels. For example, countries that score high in regulatory quality and efficiency also score high in other indices reflecting public organization management and outcome[2] (WEF, 2015).

Similarly, TI's Corruption Perception Index (CPI) shows a strong correlation between high levels of ethics (i.e., low corruption) and high income levels (i.e., low poverty) (TI, 2015). A simple correlation does not suffice to establish causality (McCloskey, 1994). A theory is needed. Many studies have demonstrated the relation between corruption and poverty (Chetwynd *et al.*, 2003; Gupta *et al.*, 2002; Rose-Ackerman and Palifka, 2016), as well as income inequality (Gupta *et al.*, 2002) and growth (Chetwynd *et al.*, 2003; Mauro, 1995; Mo, 2001; Rose-Ackerman, 1999). They find strong evidence that corruption increases poverty and income inequality while it decreases growth. Particularly, Chetwynd *et al.* (2003) find that corruption decreases governance capacity. As a result, political institutions get weaker, citizen participation decreases, and the overall quality of government services and infrastructure deteriorates. Moreover, these studies show that poor people are more vulnerable when public services are inadequate.

The role of public management and its outcomes such as quality of public institutions has also recently been the focus of the corporate social responsibility (CSR) literature. Recent CSR research focuses on cross-country comparisons with respect to social performance of firms (Ioannou and Serafeim, 2012; Jackson and Apostolakou, 2010; Gjølberg, 2009a, 2009b; Ringov and Zollo, 2007). In a first attempt

---

2 Such indices are, for example, on infrastructure quality, health and primary education, higher education and training, goods and labor market efficiency, and innovation.

to identify reasons why business in some countries demonstrates higher levels of social responsibility than in other countries, Chymis and Skouloudis (2014) found that public institutions play a significant role in corporate social performance (CSP), corroborating previous theoretical research (Campbell, 2007) that states that high-quality public institutions incentivize and facilitate private firms to be socially responsible.

The Role of Competition

Since the time of Adam Smith, if not earlier, economists and management scholars have praised the benefits of competition (Friedman, 1962; Porter, 2008). It has been argued that Friedman's famous 1970 *New York Times* magazine article regarding business' social responsibilities, was largely misunderstood (Chymis *et al.*, 2015a, 2015b). The article was one of the major milestones for the development of the whole CSR idea. The misunderstanding, which is the reason behind a generally unfriendly sentiment toward Friedman, is that CSR scholars mostly focused on the aphorism expressed in the title of Friedman's article, "The Social Responsibility of Business Is to Create Profits." What Friedman actually argues is that *if* competition is free and open, *then* businesses that pursue profit maximization also maximize social benefit (i.e., they are socially responsible) (Chymis *et al.*, 2015a, 2015b). In other words, Friedman urged for more competition. He also stresses the need for firms to abide by the law and ethical custom of the society (Friedman, 1970).

Competition offers the incentives to improve. Some recent theoretical and empirical work on CSR predicts and has also provided evidence of a curvilinear relationship between CSP and competition within a country and across industries (Berman *et al.*, 2005; Campbell, 2007; Chymis, 2007). Chymis *et al.* (2015a), based on WEF data, find a positive relationship between ethical behavior of firms and competitive market conditions, across countries.

A common characteristic of public organizations is that by their nature they are prone to monopolistic conditions (Niskanen, 1968; D'Anselmi, 2011). While businesses face competition, public administration is often beyond the litmus test of competition (excluding periodic political elections, of course). There is one government (typically unique in each country); each bureau of public administration is also typically unique, and citizens generally do not have the choice of another public administration in a given country. This gives rise to monopolistic conditions and increases monopolistic power of public administration. As D'Anselmi *et al.* (2017) illustrate, competition increases as we move from government to big corporations, to large firms to, finally, myriads of small and medium enterprises (SMEs).

The literature of new public management (Lane, 2000; Osborne and Gaebler, 1993) which followed the public choice literature (Buchanan and Tullock, 1962;

Niskanen, 1968) particularly stresses the need for improving competitive conditions within public-goods providers. According to this literature, public organizations need to become more entrepreneurial, to operate more like a competitive private firm. Traditional public organizations are mostly driven by rules and bureaucracy, whereas they should be driven by their mission (high-quality service to citizens) (Osborne and Gaebler, 1993). Traditional public organizations serve mostly the bureaucracy, which tries to increase its funding regardless the results. They even get more funding when they fail (Osborne and Gaebler, 1993). What is needed is a change in the incentives scheme.

Monopolistic conditions for many public-goods providers should be eliminated by allowing for the creation of many providers (Lane, 2000; Osborne and Gaebler, 1993). The citizens should have the freedom to choose (Friedman, 1962). Rotation within public administration (i.e., not the same official in the same area or bureau for too long), avoiding consolidation (have different bureaus competing instead of one monopolistic type), and allowing for multiplicity of bureaus all increase competition and offer citizens the power of choice. (Frederickson and Rohr, 2015; Osborne and Gaebler, 1993).

Increasing accountability can help shift the power from the bureaucrats to the people they serve. Becoming results-oriented and customer-driven also empowers citizens, families, and local communities (Osborne and Gaebler, 1993). Decentralization and community ownership can incentivize local communities to solve their own problems (Lane, 2000; Osborne and Gaebler, 1993). Putting mission first, becoming customer-oriented and results-oriented, public organizations can improve their incentive systems and allow their employees and managers to be free to pursue these high goals under healthy competitive conditions. Osborne and Gaebler (1993) say it is a paradox that while we praise the blessings of competition for the private sector, at the same time we embrace monopolies in the public sector.

International comparisons based on international organization indicators that measure public-sector performance could also help increase competition given that the information is disseminated to citizens. Information is a catalyst for citizen engagement and participation. Many of the poverty- and corruption-ridden countries suffer from lack of information diffusion to their citizens (Dreze and Sen, 2002).

Beyond the Bottom Line: Implications for Management Educators

This section proposes possible ways of how to go about meeting the need for public organizations to work toward integrating UN and PRME principles, as well as the need to increase competition within the public sector. At the same time it relates the propositions to the PRMEs.

A Broader View

The title of this book, *Beyond the Bottom Line: Integrating the UNGC into Management Education*, offers a timely opportunity for management educators to take a broader look at organizations and include in their research and teaching agenda public organizations, most of which are not-for-profit organizations. Public administration, for example, is a nonprofit and by its nature lies beyond the economic bottom line. However, it manages taxpayers' money and has the responsibility to use this resource effectively and efficiently. Each dollar (used/saved by an effective and efficient public administration) can make a difference for the poor and the socially excluded. *Beyond the Bottom Line* calls for nonprofit public organizations to integrate the UNGC and responsible management principles, while also calling on management education to support this through incorporating the six PRME into research and teaching. A first suggestion – related to PRME 3, method – is that responsible management education could extend beyond business schools to reach students of public-administration schools, schools of public policy and management as well as the national schools of public administration. All countries need responsible public officials and accountable public organizations.

Changing the Public Sector

Business-school students may go to work in the public sector, which actually makes up almost half (in some cases) the size of the national economy. Management educators, very much in line with PRMEs 1 and 2 – purpose and values – have an important role to play in changing the public sector in such a way that it produces an institutional environment that promotes competition; accountability; and citizens' information, awareness, and involvement. The new, healthy public institutional environment will be a major weapon against corruption, poverty, and inequality. Management educators in business schools most probably do a fine job in creating the future leaders and managers of public as well as private organizations. However, this may not be enough to combat corruption. The new leaders, no matter how enlightened, are human and thus not incorruptible. Management educators cannot change the human nature of their students, the future managers. What they can do, though, is to help them realize that institutions shape incentives and govern human behavior. While business schools teach these principles and demonstrate their application in the (private) world of corporations and firms, it seems that public corporations, organizations, and administrations remain mostly under the radar of the responsible-management academic community.

Asking the Right Questions

Management educators play a critical role in accomplishing the goals of "reinventing government" (Osborne and Gaebler, 1993), "modernizing government" (OECD, 2005) and making the public sector more socially responsible (D'Anselmi *et al.*, 2017). Business managers, management academics, educators, students, and practitioners may be particularly interested in asking questions such as "What can be done to ensure public organizations behave with integrity and public leaders remain incorruptible?" Relating to Principle 4 (research), it is suggested that case studies, theoretical and empirical research can be useful tools for management educators in researching and teaching how more competition in public administration can be successfully infused. As Allen *et al.* (2015) demonstrated, introducing competition between officials is more effective than trying to ban corruption by law.

CSR literature has a long experience dealing with the concept of "beyond the bottom line." Similarly, international organizations such as the UN urge businesses to go beyond the bottom line and address major social issues such as poverty, gender equality, and anticorruption. If we take the example of bribery, CSR mostly looks at the problem from the side of business. However, it is often the case that a bribe is offered by a private executive or even a simple citizen to a public official. Moreover, in many cases public officials solicit a bribe (Allen *et al.*, 2015). Management educators could address the causes of institutional weaknesses of public administrations around the world asking the question, "What institutions do we need to change in order to shape incentives and make public organizations transparent, accountable, and responsible?" As already mentioned, a theory-building is needed to address the interrelationship between the issues addressed by the UNGC (e.g., corruption and poverty).

Partnership and Dialogue

TI (2015) data reveal public administration officials' corruption is rampant in many countries surveyed. This means that public organizations also need to integrate the UNGC and PRME. The UNGC and PRME can significantly contribute to this purpose if they both explicitly include public organizations in their principles. For example, each of the UNGC principles begins with "businesses should." This chapter proposes this be changed to "organizations should." This will be more inclusive of all organizations, both public and private. All UNGC principles refer to humans and human actions. Human rights, labor, environment, and anticorruption involve employees and leaders in all organizations, both from the private sector and public administration. Moreover, in quite a few countries, the public sector is responsible for business ventures and social enterprise, for example, the military undertakes construction projects, the state owns and runs a variety of for-profit (e.g., electricity, telecommunications) as well as not-for-profit organizations such as charities.

Comparative studies could identify best practices in some countries that could be used as exemplars to amend poor public institutions in other countries. Moreover, international organizations such as the UN as well as scholars' networks and movements such as PRME could diffuse information regarding public-organization performance (such as judiciaries, municipalities, licensing authorities, tax authorities, public education, and public health organizations as well as the police) to citizens. The call to the UN, mentioned earlier, from the World Bank's *Doing Business* report regarding the need for a comprehensive index on quality of the public sector is timely and complements this chapter's suggestion of international organizations' infusion of competition among public administrations through comparison. Partnership and dialogue (Principles 5 and 6) between PRME and the UN, on one hand, and other international organizations, public administrations, citizens, and stakeholders groups on the other, is very important for the successful implementation of all the above principles.

Final Thoughts

Following the recommendations in this chapter, responsible-management scholars should help public organizations improve transparency, accountability, effectiveness, and efficiency which, in turn, will likely produce an institutional environment that enhances ethical business practices. Not only that, but it may also directly decrease levels of poverty and corruption by increasing citizens' engagement, participation, and positive feelings that public administration can really change for the better (Osborne and Gaebler, 1993). This is very important given that, unfortunately, in many countries people often lose hope for possible improvement of the public sector's status quo.

Business students – as well as many people in society – may think of public administration as a necessary evil. They may think they cannot do anything about it (D'Anselmi, 2011). They may think of public-sector employment as marginal and more like as a "social shock absorber," having only a minor impact on the overall economy. However, this chapter demonstrates that public administration has a key role in creating the institutional environment where business can operate and contribute to society. Moreover, the better the institutional environment, the better the climate for business to contribute to society, maximize social welfare, and minimize (and – why not? – eliminate) corruption and poverty.

The planet is in need of not only enlightened business leaders but also a new generation of public-organization leaders who will: a) craft such institutions that could shape incentive schemes in public organizations that will be conducive to anticorruption; b) infuse competition among public officials, bureaus, and public service providers so that they boost effectiveness and efficiency and, thus, make the most out of each tax dollar; c) strive for more transparency in rule-making, policy-making, and other key functions in public administration; and d) conduct international comparisons and communicate the necessary information to citizens and stakeholders who in turn could spark a virtuous circle, increasing demand for socially responsible behavior in both private- and public-sector organizations.

References

Acemoglu, D. & Robinson, J.A. (2012). *Why Nations Fail: the Origins of Power, Prosperity, and Poverty*. New York: Crown Publishers.

Allen, F., Qian, J., & Shen, L. (2015). Corruption and Competition. Available at SSRN 2685219.

Berman, S.L., Phillips, R.A., & Wicks, A.C. (2005). Resource dependence, managerial discretion and stakeholder performance. Paper presented at the Academy of Management meetings, Honolulu, Hawaii, August 5–10, 2005.

Buchanan, J.M. & Tullock, G. (1962). *The Calculus of Consent*. Ann Arbor: University of Michigan Press.

Campbell, J.L. (2007). Why would corporations behave in socially responsible ways? An institutional theory of corporate social responsibility. *Academy of Management Review*, 32, 946-967.

Chetwynd, E., Chetwynd, F., & Spector, B. (2003). Corruption and poverty: a review of recent literature. Final Report. Washington, D.C.: Management Systems International, Inc.

Chymis, A. (2007). Using Friedman to understand the relationship between market competition and corporate social performance. PhD dissertation, University of Missouri-Columbia. Retrieved from https://mospace.umsystem.edu/xmlui/handle/10355/4841.

Chymis, A. & Skouloudis, A. (2014). National CSR and institutional conditions: An exploratory study. Paper presented at the European Economic Financial Society (EEFS) 13th annual conference, Thessaloniki, Greece, June 12–15, 2014.

Chymis, A., Di Bitetto, M., & D'Anselmi, P. (2015a). Corporate social performance needs more competition not less: An idea for a paradigm shift. In A. Stachowicz-Stanusch (Ed.), *Corporate Social Performance: Paradoxes, Pitfalls and Pathways to the Better World* (pp. 37-56). Charlotte, NC, USA: Information Age Publishing.

Chymis, A., Di Bitetto, M., D'Anselmi, P., & Skouloudis, A. (2015b). The importance of responsible public management for addressing the challenge of poverty. In M. Gudić, C. Parkes & A. Rosenbloom (Eds.), *Responsible Management Education and the Challenge of Poverty: A Teaching Perspective* (pp. 222-235). Sheffield, UK: Greenleaf Publishing/PRME.

D'Anselmi, P. (2011). *Values and Stakeholders in an Era of Social Responsibility: Cut-Throat Competition?* London: Palgrave Macmillan.

D'Anselmi, P., Chymis, A., & Di Bitetto, M. (2017). *Unknown Values and Stakeholders: The Pro-Business Outcome and the Role of Competition*. London: Palgrave Macmillan.

Di Bitetto, M., Chymis, A. & D'Anselmi, P. (Eds.). (2015). *Public Management as Corporate Social Responsibility. The Economic Bottom Line of Government*. Heidelberg: Springer International Publishing.

Dreze, J. & Sen, A. (2002). *Participatory Growth and Poverty Reduction*. New Delhi: Oxford University Press.

European Commission (2015). Report on Public Finances in EMU. Institutional paper 014. Retrieved from http://ec.europa.eu/economy_finance/publications/eeip/pdf/ip014_en.pdf.

Frederickson, H.G. & Rohr, J.A. (2015). *Ethics and Public Administration*. New York: Routledge.

Friedman, M. (2002). *Capitalism and Freedom.* Chicago: University of Chicago Press. (Original work published 1962).

Friedman, M. (1970, September 13). The social responsibility of business is to create profits. *New York Times Magazine*, pp. 32-33, 122-126.

Gjølberg, M. (2009a). Measuring the immeasurable? Constructing an index of CSR practices and performance in 20 countries. *Scandinavian Journal of Management*, 25, 10-22.

Gjølberg, M. (2009b). The origin of corporate social responsibility: global forces or national legacies? *Socio-Economic Review*, 7, 605-637.

Gupta, S., Davoodi, H., & Alonso-Terme, R. (2002). Does corruption affect income inequality and poverty? *Economics of governance*, 3(1), 23-45.

International Institute for Management Development (IMD). (2015). World Competitiveness. Retrieved from https://worldcompetitiveness.imd.org.

Ioannou, I. & Serafeim, G. (2012). What drives corporate social performance? The role of nation-level institutions. *Journal of International Business Studies* 43, 834-864.

Jackson, G. & Apostolakou, A. (2010). Corporate social responsibility in Western Europe: an institutional mirror or substitute? *Journal of Business Ethics*, 94(3), 371-394.

Lane, J.E. (2000). *New Public Management.* New York: Routledge.

Mauro, P. (1995). Corruption and growth. *The Quarterly Journal of Economics* CX, 681-712.

McCloskey, D. (1994). Other things equal: Why economists don't believe empirical findings. *Eastern Economic Journal*, 20(3), 357-360.

Mitsopoulos, M. & Pelagidis, T. (2011). Understanding the Greek Crisis: Unlocking the puzzle of Greek banks' deteriorating performance. *World Economics*, 12(1), 177-192.

Mo, P.H. (2001). Corruption and economic growth. *Journal of Comparative Economics*, 29(1), 66-79.

Niskanen, W.A. (1968). The peculiar economics of bureaucracy. *The American Economic Review*, 58(2), 293-305.

North, D.C. (2005). *Understanding the Process of Institutional Change.* Princeton, NJ: Princeton University Press.

North, D.C. (1991). Institutions. *The Journal of Economic Perspectives*, 5(1), 97-112.

Olson, M. (2008). *The rise and decline of nations: Economic growth, stagflation, and social rigidities.* New Heaven, CT: Yale University Press.

Osborne, D. & Gaebler, T. (1993). *Reinventing government: How the entrepreneurial spirit is transforming government.* New York: Plume.

Organization for Economic Co-operation and Developement (OECD). (2005). Modernizing Government: The Way Forward. Retrieved from http://www.oecd-ilibrary.org/governance/modernising-government_9789264010505-en.

Porter, M.E. (2008). *On competition.* Cambridge, MA: Harvard Business Press.

Ringov, D. & Zollo, M. (2007). The impact of national culture on corporate social performance. *Corporate Governance*, 7(4), 476-485.

Rose-Ackerman, S. & Palifka, B.J. (2016). *Corruption and government: Causes, consequences, and reform.* Cambridge: Cambridge University Press.

TI (Transparency International). (2015). Corruption Perception Index 2015. Retrieved from https://www.transparency.org/cpi2015.

Williamson, O.E. (2000). The new institutional economics: taking stock, looking ahead. *Journal of Economic Literature*, 38, 595-613.

World Bank. (2015). Doing Business Report 2016. Retrieved from http://www.doingbusiness.org/~/media/GIAWB/Doing%20Business/Documents/Annual-Reports/English/DB16-Full-Report.pdf.

World Economic Forum. (2015). Global Competitiveness Report 2015-2016. Retrieved from http://www3.weforum.org/docs/gcr/2015-2016/Global_Competitiveness_Report_2015-2016.pdf.

Athanasios Chymis is a Senior Research Fellow at the Centre of Planning and Economic Research (KEPE) in Athens, Greece. He holds a PhD from the University of Missouri-Columbia in Agricultural Economics. He is interested in the connection between ethics and economics, and, currently, his research is focused on how social responsibility could be infused in public administration as well as in all organizations both of the private and the public sector.

athxymes@yahoo.com

Paolo D'Anselmi is a practitioner of management consultancy and policy analysis. He teaches Corporate Social Responsibility at the University of Rome Tor Vergata, Italy. He is a graduate in engineering (Sapienza, Rome) and in public policy (Harvard). He is currently working on extending corporate social responsibility to public administration.

paolodanselmi@gmail.com

Christos Triantopoulos is a Research Fellow at the Centre of Planning and Economic Research (KEPE) in Athens, Greece. He holds a PhD from Athens University of Economics and Business in Political Economy of Financial Structures and Supervision. During the same period he was a Visiting Research Fellow at the University of Sussex. He has also worked as a consultant at the General Accounting Office of the Ministry of Finance. His research interests focus on financial supervision, banking market, institutions and economy, and public finances.

ctrianto@gmail.com

Concluding Remarks and Looking Ahead

Milenko Gudić, Tay Keong Tan and Patricia M. Flynn

This book presents a wide spectrum of challenges that businesses and organizations worldwide have been facing in their increasing efforts to go beyond the bottom line and provide value not only for their shareholders but also to protect the interests and needs of other stakeholders in the community and the wider world.

More importantly, the book provides a number of solutions and indicates new avenues and opportunities related to how organizations can effectively contribute to a better world through the integration of the Ten Principles of the United Nations Global Compact (UNGC) in the issue domains of human rights, labor, environmental protection, and ethical business practices.

These concluding remarks summarize some of the key lessons that stem from the creative solutions described and new opportunities identified in the chapters. These lessons are relevant for managers, executives, and leaders who are aspiring to manage and lead their organizations in an economically sound, socially responsible, and environmentally friendly way. They may also speak to the other stakeholders, such as the public sector and international organizations and networks, including the UNGC itself.

Last but not least, these lessons provide a source of inspiration for business schools and management-development institutions, including the PRME community, that are aspiring to support business to go beyond the bottom line, through responsible-management education for today's leaders and managers, as well as the development of a new generation working for a more sustainable world.

Embracing UNGC Principles and Spirit

The book showcases solutions based on two different streams of approaches in integrating the UNGC principles into management and business practices. The first stream comes from companies whose approaches are characterized by predominantly individual business initiatives for sustainability through new products, services, and business models. The second stream offers solutions from companies taking an inclusive approach based on a broader collaboration, networking and partnerships, and creativity contributing to a new global architecture of practices on sustainability.

Companies with these approaches come from both highly industrialized countries as well as from emerging economies. Among them are the UNGC signatories and founding members – including an advanced group of sustainable companies, called the UNGC LEAD, that are taking an active part in projects that go beyond the UNGC and that support the 17 Sustainable Development Goals (SDGs) – as well as non-signatories. Whether large or small in size, they all have in common approaches stemming from their mission statements, while employing diverse organizational policies and strategies, implementation mechanisms and systems, and practices relating to supply chains and other stakeholders.

Addressing Issues

Solutions described in the book show that the integration of the UNGC's spirit and values into management and business practices could be achieved if companies focused their attention and activities on addressing specific issues, either those that are covered by the UNGC principles or those that are related to the spirit and values of the UNGC.

These issues could range from specific local/regional contexts to those that are global and systemic in nature. The book includes inspirational examples of addressing the issues specifically covered by the UNGC but also those related to the UN's SDG Issues addressed in the chapters include, for instance, poverty alleviation, health and globally spread diseases, discrimination, gender and diversity, sanitation, ecological restoration, material recycling, institutional voids, the lack of infrastructure, access to technology, finance, and education, the role of leadership, governance and the public sector.

The book provides evidence and actual cases to show that it is possible to create an impact either by focusing on individual issues, or by integrating the UNGC and SDG principles into the organizational philosophy and practices as a comprehensive platform.

Business Models and Strategies

In order to be effective in addressing the challenges and issues related to the Ten Principles of the UNGC, companies need to develop creative and inclusive business models and strategies. Inclusive business models, such as those emerging out of African countries, provide significant benefits for addressing the multidimensional limitations of poverty and inequality. These benefits include value for the business in terms of driving innovation, building markets, ensuring employee commitment, and strengthening supply chains, as well as for the poor in the form of increased access to essential goods and services, sustainable earnings, empowerment, and higher productivity.

Implementing the UNGC principles in managing workplace issues offers many opportunities to create multiple forms of value, such as human, social, environmental, and economic, particularly when an individual company's approach is supplemented by similar approaches and practices in the supply chain (Chapter 6).

The book also demonstrates that new business models can play a pivotal role as economic powerhouses to advance sustainable development and the evolution of socially responsible enterprises. In this context, sanitation is an area of significant need and could provide a business opportunity for a broad segment of stakeholders, including the public sector and rural poor (Chapter 10). Another equally significant area is energy. Off-grid solar lighting could be a business opportunity in the promising area of green, renewable energy. However, as Chapter 4 shows, businesses entering these spaces need to do so thoughtfully, and be prepared to establish creative and adaptive business practices. By working closely with communities, building local capacity, forging new partnerships, and filling institutional voids in developing markets, enterprises can successfully bridge the gap between opportunity (or demand) and their own organizations (or supply), for the benefit of individuals, their communities, and the environment.

Recognizing the potential of gender diversity for the success of their respective businesses on all three dimensions of corporate sustainability (economic outcomes, social responsiveness, and environmental quality), some companies have developed human-resources policies and leadership development strategies that include concrete gender diversity targets and associated compliance mechanisms (Chapter 8). The book also showcases an investment company whose mission statement and unique business model serve a very specific and under-recognized market niche – companies led by gender-diverse teams (Chapter 7).

Engaging Internally and the Role of Leaders

To be effective in delivering on their mission statement and the respective business approaches and strategies for addressing the principles of the UNGC, companies need to engage their employees, staff, and managerial teams at different levels. This requires not only communicating the organization's mission statement but also engaging people in the process of articulating, adopting, and implementing the values and philosophy for which the company stands (Chapter 2). These processes also help in formalizing expectations and delivery mechanisms, including breaking the functional silos and developing internal dialogue with the employees, unions, and other internal partners (Chapter 6).

Engaging everyone in the organization to act responsibly and nurture a culture of CSR and sustainable development requires two-way communication in which individual values are acknowledged and integrated into the shaping of overall principles and values at the workplace. In this respect, mission-driven enterprises, including those from the not-for-profit sector, could be a source of inspiration for rethinking the role of business in society, sustainable development, and responsible leadership (Chapter 2).

While listening and engaging are two pillars of responsible leadership and the foundation for building legitimacy and authority in organizations (Chapter 2), the personal qualities and values of leaders are equally important factors for creating responsible and sustainable organizations. On strategic approaches and good practices, the book suggests that prosocial leaders are well-suited to embrace and fulfill the UNGC principles. Prosocial (others-directed) leadership provides a perspective that helps leaders to balance profits and sustainability and ultimately act as global stewards who take responsibility for the world's economic and social issues (Chapter 1).

Engaging Externally and Establishing Partnerships

Engaging external partners and stakeholders is essential for creating a broad impact on CSR and, as demonstrated in the chapters, could take place in various forms. These partnerships are consistent with the findings of a longitudinal survey of the UNGC signatories' CEOs regarding the challenges in the implementation of the UNGC principles, which also call for more extensive collaboration and increased national regulation (Chapter 5).

Engaging partners in the supply chain proves to be powerful since it can provide for multiplier effects, and a wider and deeper impact downstream. The consistency and power of this approach can be further strengthened if it involves third-party audits regarding compliance with the values for which a company stands or international standards to which it adheres. External partnerships can be effective and are essentially needed for pursuing the idea of inclusive development and dealing with complex issues such as those related to public health, sanitation, access to energy, and information technology. This book suggests that public-private partnerships, either at local, national, or international levels, can play an important role in bringing together businesses and other external stakeholders, including the public sector, to collaborate on advancing the agenda.

The same applies to environmental issues, where the ecological restoration case from India provides important lessons and a model for possible replication in other contexts. In addition to the external sources of scientific and technical knowledge and expertise involved, the local community and the public sector are important partners in the ecological-restauration project (Chapter 6).

This and other examples of partnerships described in the book also provide lessons for critically evaluating and rethinking how public-private and other partnerships are governed in order to promote collaborative approaches to CSR and sustainable development and deliver on the expected purpose and effects.

In this respect, the lessons from the case of Sustainable Sanitation Alliance – SuSanA (Chapter 10), on one end of the spectrum, and the UN Global Alliance for Information and Communication Technologies and Development (GAID) on the other (Chapter 3), deserve to be further explored. Established in 2007 with a single purpose of bringing together organizations and individuals to advise the UN prior to its Year of Sanitation in 2008, SusanA self-ignited once it established a 12-member working-group structure, which helped to gather 6,500 members and develop new activities. In contrast, GAID, which was established in 2006 under the auspices of the UN to create public-private partnerships, has faced problems in keeping the pace and building on the great initial interest and momentum created in its formative years.

Some of these lessons might also be of interest to the UNGC itself. Although it has a modest compliance mechanism, this voluntary initiative is still facing problems in the enforcement and implementation of its principles and values. The issue here is how the knowledge, stakeholder consensus, and resources needed for the adoption and implementation of the principles, could be increased, while maintaining minimum standards on compliance.

This is also an area that provides opportunities for a joint effort on the part of the UNGC and the PRME. While having unique research, educational, and community-service capabilities of its members and collectively, the PRME movement itself is a membership and collective action-institution that faces similar regulatory and governance challenges. It is, therefore, incumbent on the PRME to better understand these challenges and to diligently seek to address and resolve them (Chapter 13).

The role of the public sector is essential, and the recent national regulation introduced in Denmark provides interesting lessons (Chapter 5). Equally important are suggestions on the role of public administration and the need for this sector to be critically evaluated regarding its own effectiveness, efficiency, and responsibility in creating and managing institutions, which would promote sustainable development in their respective communities and countries, while being themselves (as organizations in their own right) led in accordance with the principles that resonate with the UNGC spirit and values (Chapter 14).

While providing evidence of how the lack of proper leadership and governance can result in disastrous human-rights abuse and tragic consequences, the case of the Chibok girls (Chapter 13) underscores how the issues covered by the UNGC principles are interrelated and should be dealt with in tandem. The message of the chapter is also that there is a need to shift the prevailing attention and action from the symptoms and manifestation of the problems to their real causes and roots, including the systemic ones. That is also one of the main tasks and challenges for responsible-management education.

Implications for Responsible-Management Education

To the extent to which creative solutions and best business practices described in the book reflect fresh managerial and leadership approaches, they call for and indicate new directions in the development of new managerial and leadership capabilities. Business schools and other management-development institutions can learn from these practices and instill the respective lessons into their efforts to integrate the principles and spirit of the UNGC through the development of capabilities needed for the new role of business in society, sustainable development, and responsible leadership (PRME 1, purpose, and PRME 2, values).

The book chapters offer interesting and inspirational material that either fits into existing materials, processes, and environments that enable effective learning experiences for responsible leadership or that could be the impetus for development of new educational frameworks (PRME 3, method). The list of the management-education areas (not only in business education, but also in public management and other fields) that could benefit from the book is quite comprehensive and goes from the functional managerial disciplines to those that are integrative in nature – leadership, in particular.

The chapters provide evidence on the importance of various partnerships and a wider and deeper dialogue with different stakeholders, in addressing social and environmental challenges related to the issues covered by the UNGC principles. They also are good examples of how management educators, business practitioners, and not-for-profit leaders – all of whom have contributed to this volume – could provide their own contributions to the collaboration and exchange of ideas (PRME 5, partnerships, and PRME 6, dialogue).

The special value of this contribution is that it emerged from the hard work and enthusiastic research efforts, both conceptual and empirical, of the chapter authors who contributed to the advancement of our understanding about the role, dynamics, and impact of organizations and about the creation of sustainable social, environmental, and economic values (PRME 4, research).

It is encouraging that this research goes beyond the individual UNGC principles and addresses their complex relationships, including perspectives of the more recently initiated UN SDGs . We look forward to further research on the successes, struggles, and champions in the advancement of these SDGs.

If business "needs to redefine customer as society," as suggested in Chapter 10 and supported by best practices described in the book, management education should support and encourage change with new educational frameworks and concepts that will help management and businesses to "redefine success," in business as well as among not-for-profit organizations, including the public sector, and in management education.

Redefining Success: Integrating Sustainability into Management Education, the second in this two-book series, focuses on how management education can support and encourage such change. It provides another volume of best practices and inspirational stories on creating a better world.

About the Editors

Milenko Gudić is Founding Director of Refoment Consulting and Coaching, Belgrade, Serbia, and visiting lecturer at University Donja Gorica, Montenegro. He has worked as a consultant, researcher, and lecturer at the Economics Institute, Belgrade, as a visiting lecturer in several countries, and as a speaker in over 30 countries. He has been engaged as a consultant to OECD, UNDP, UNIDO, etc., on various entrepreneurship, regional, rural, and public management-development projects. Milenko was Founding and Managing Director (2000–2014) of the International Management Teachers Academy (IMTA), while also leading CEEMAN's major international research and educational leadership capacity building projects. He was Program Chair of EURAM 2008. Since 2008 he has been co-coordinating the UN Global Compact PRME Working Group on Poverty, a Challenge for Management Education. milenko.gudic@gmail.com

Tay Keong Tan is Director of International Studies and Leadership Studies, and an associate professor in the Department of Political Science at Radford University, USA. His research interest is on integrity systems and global sustainability. He has headed public and nonprofit organizations in Singapore, Israel, and the United States, and for more than a decade worked in development projects on governance and anticorruption in more than 20 countries. He is a member of the PRME Working Groups on Sustainability and AntiCorruption. ttan2@radford.edu

Patricia M. Flynn, PhD, is Trustee Professor of Economics and Management at Bentley University, USA, where she served as Dean of the McCallum Graduate School of Business for ten years. Her research and publications focus on corporate governance, women in business, and technology-based economic development. She has served on numerous corporate, mutual fund, and nonprofit boards, and testified before Congress on the impacts of technological change on jobs and workers. In 2016, she became the inaugural recipient of the Distinguished Women Leader in Business Education Award given by the Women Administrators in Management Education at AACSB-International; the award now bears her name. pflynn@bentley.edu